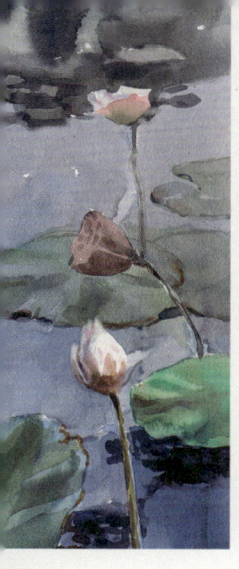
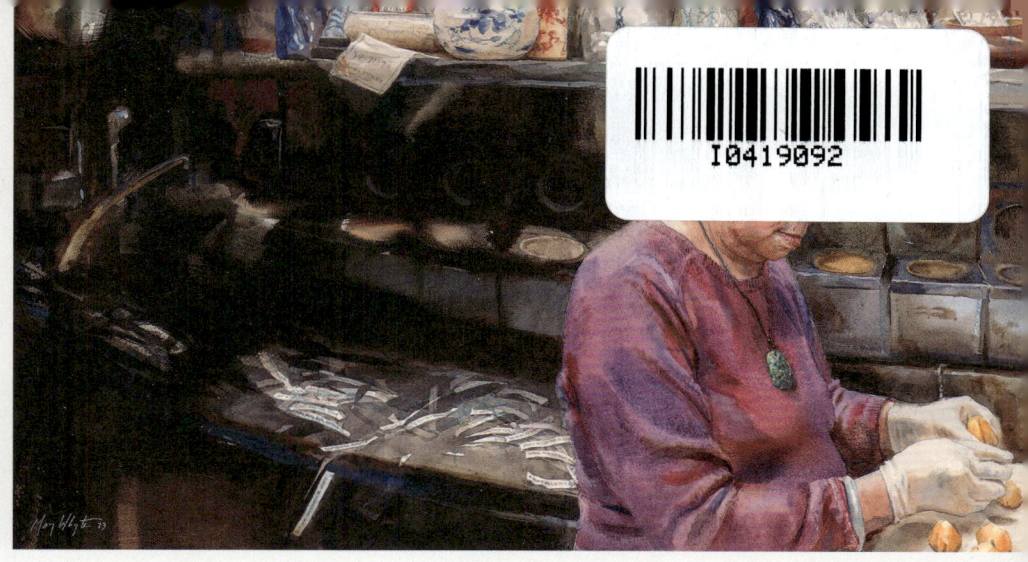
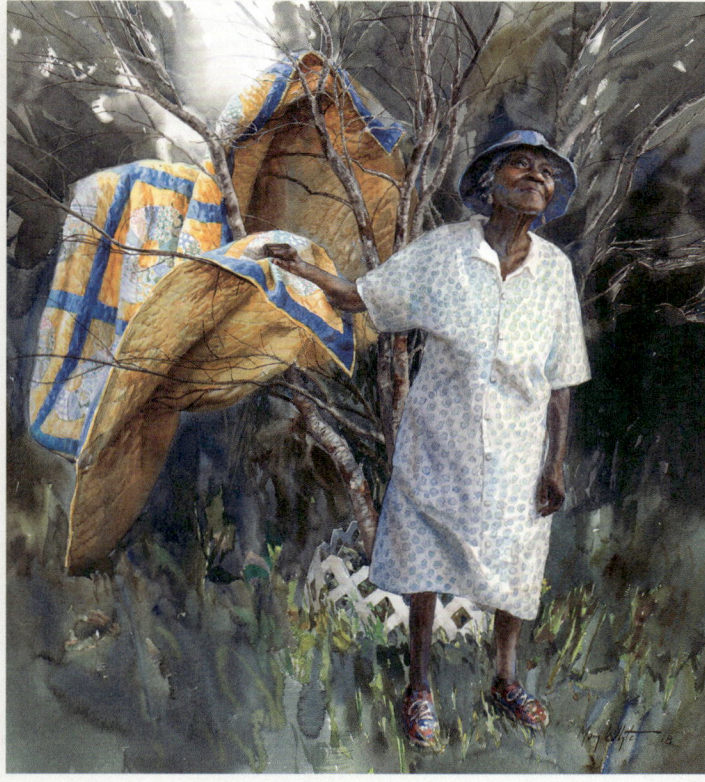
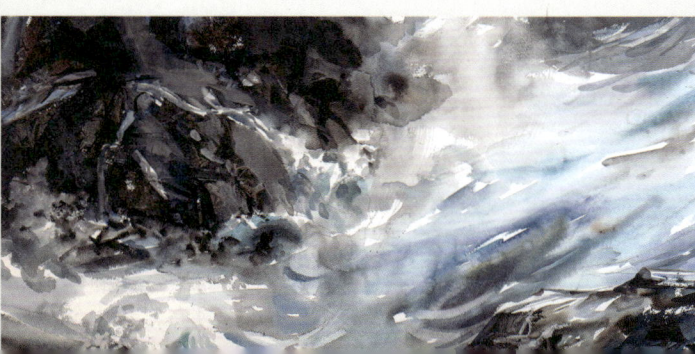
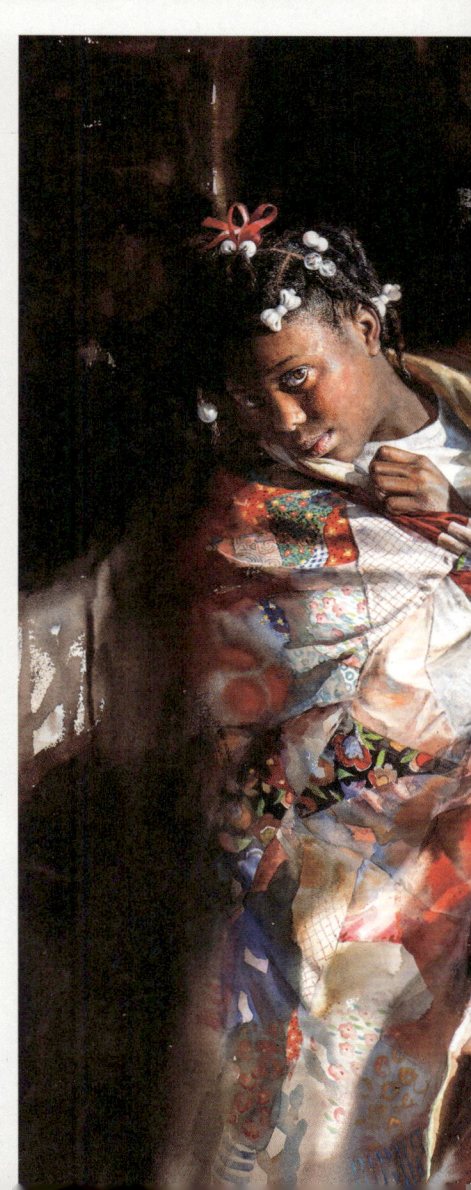

An
Artist's
Life

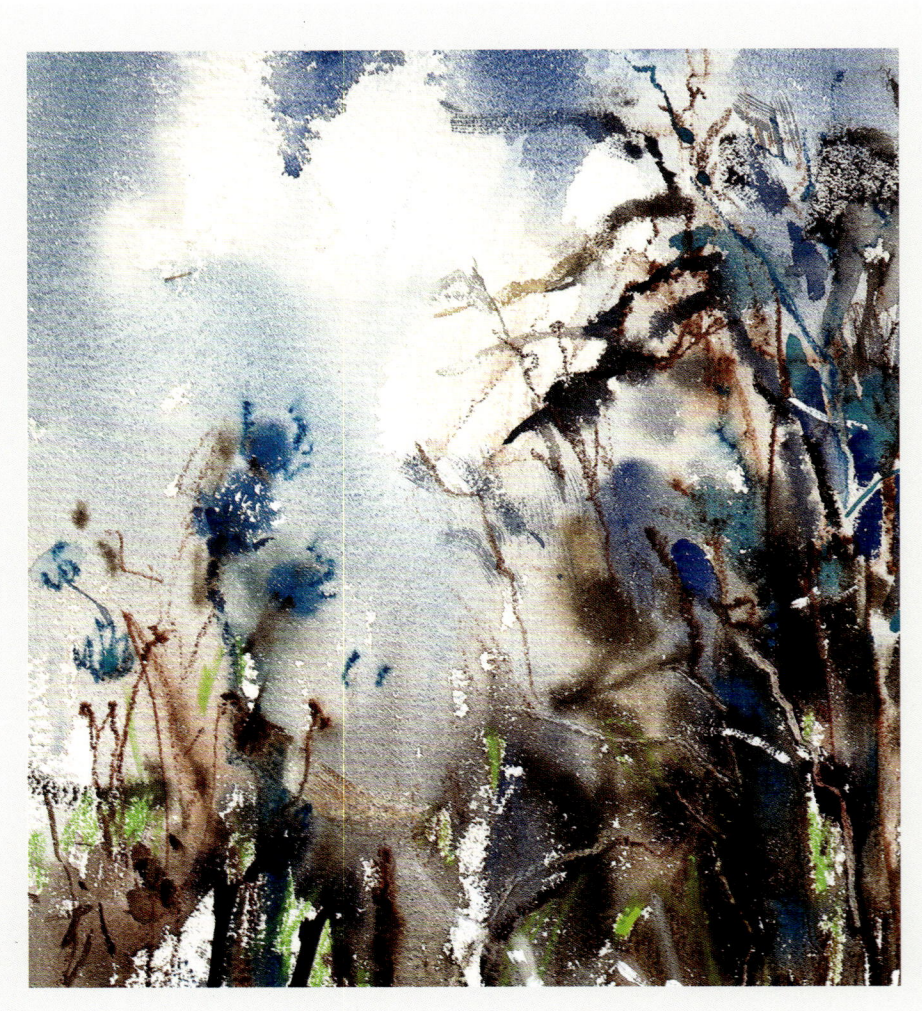

An Artist's Life

UNLOCKING CREATIVE EXPRESSION

Mary Whyte

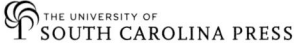

THE UNIVERSITY OF
SOUTH CAROLINA PRESS

Published by the University of South Carolina Press
Columbia, South Carolina 29208

uscpress.com

Printed in China

Library of Congress Cataloging-in-Publication Data can be found at http://catalog.loc.gov/.

ISBN: 978-1-64336-540-4 (hardcover)
ISBN: 978-1-64336-603-6 (ebook)

FOR ARNIE

Life is either a daring adventure, or nothing.
—HELEN KELLER

CONTENTS

LIST OF ILLUSTRATIONS

INTRODUCTION

In my fifty years of teaching art, I have never had a student ask how to nurture creative expression. I've been asked how to paint an eye, clouds, or steam; how to be famous; how to make a painting that wins an award; and how to get a child to sit still for a portrait, but never have I been asked how to access and foster the deepest part of one's most creative self.

Making art is about so much more than fabricating things to fill space. Being an artist is a joyful way of moving through the world and transcribing our experience for others to see and feel. Knowing what is essential to one's soul and finding one's true artistic voice is the catalyst and gateway to producing one's most meaningful works of art.

Living a life filled with artistic expression has multiple benefits. There is ample evidence that creativity can improve brain function, lessen stress, and improve one's chances of staying healthy longer. Creative thinkers are natural problem solvers, nimble at considering new information and possibilities. Those who think innovatively often have more understanding, discernment, and empathy, allowing them to see others and different points of view in new ways. For these reasons alone, the world could use a few more artists.

In my workshops I teach students of all levels, including ones who are squeezing paint onto the palette for the first time. Invariably, the beginners report back to me after the class that they are now seeing everything differently. The landscape has more atmosphere, the shadows have more nuance and softer edges, the flowers have more colors, and every face is a story waiting to be told. They are becoming artists.

Moving up the learning curve as an artist takes persistence, tenacity, and courage. There are many challenging lessons to be learned along the way, several of which I gained an understanding of first-hand. In the pages that follow, I share these insights as well as stories behind some of my paintings. In the very back of this book is a QR code linked to an online supplement with suggested reading and exercises readers might use to continue their artistic growth.

My hope is that, whether you are an artist or art lover or you simply want to explore your creativity, this book will help guide you on your way to a more meaningful, healthy, and rewarding life overflowing with the beauty of the everyday.

Mary Whyte
CHARLESTON, SOUTH CAROLINA

Spring

CREATING A LIFE OF DISCOVERY

Every child is an artist.
The problem is how to remain
an artist once we grow up.

—PABLO PICASSO

It was the chartreuse crayon. The intense yellow green that stood apart from the others in the box of vibrant colors, ready for my six-year-old imagination. The set of crayons had been a gift from my father one evening. I remember him towering in the doorway in his heavy, black winter coat, stomping the snow from his rubber boots, then hoisting me up, wriggling and protesting, onto his shoulders. He handed me the box of crayons. The next few days were pure heaven. Sitting on the floor by myself in the den, with dozens of scrawled drawings strewn around me, and my small army of colors lined up at attention, ready to be picked. A black and white I Love Lucy came on the TV promptly at 10:30, followed at noon by my mother's peanut butter and jelly sandwich sliding across a thin paper plate. It was an artist's perfect world, a self-contained haven of fantasy and invention,

with the mesmerizing chartreuse crayon the first to be worn down to a pea-sized nub. That became the magical place of being I have strived to maintain ever since.

To this day the imaginings of my six-year-old self remain with me in my studio, that chartreuse echoed in the lime green leather chairs that sit by the eastern window and on my palette, in swirls and puddles, mixing with other pigments. At various times during my life that intense color has disappeared, replaced by my fickleness for a different hue. Regardless, chartreuse holds firm as my favorite color of spring, marked by emerald tree frogs, the forest's unfurling fiddlehead ferns, and the yellow green pollen that blankets the gnarled oak trees along Bohicket Road. The original chartreuse, held in a much smaller hand, still marks the resolution of the seasons and the pacing of the ensuing years. ▪

EDEN   *2023, watercolor on paper, 32.5 × 28.25 inches*

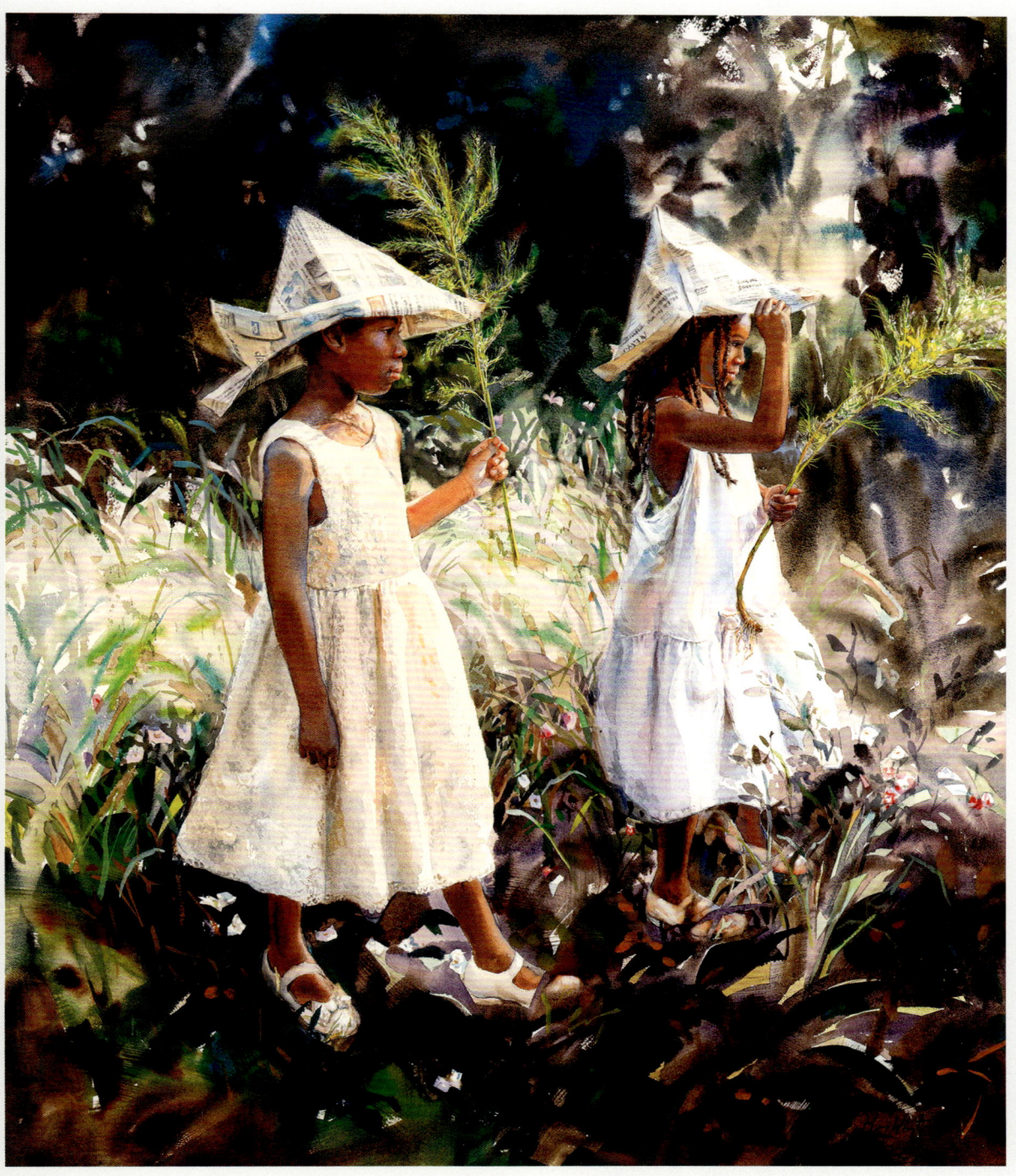

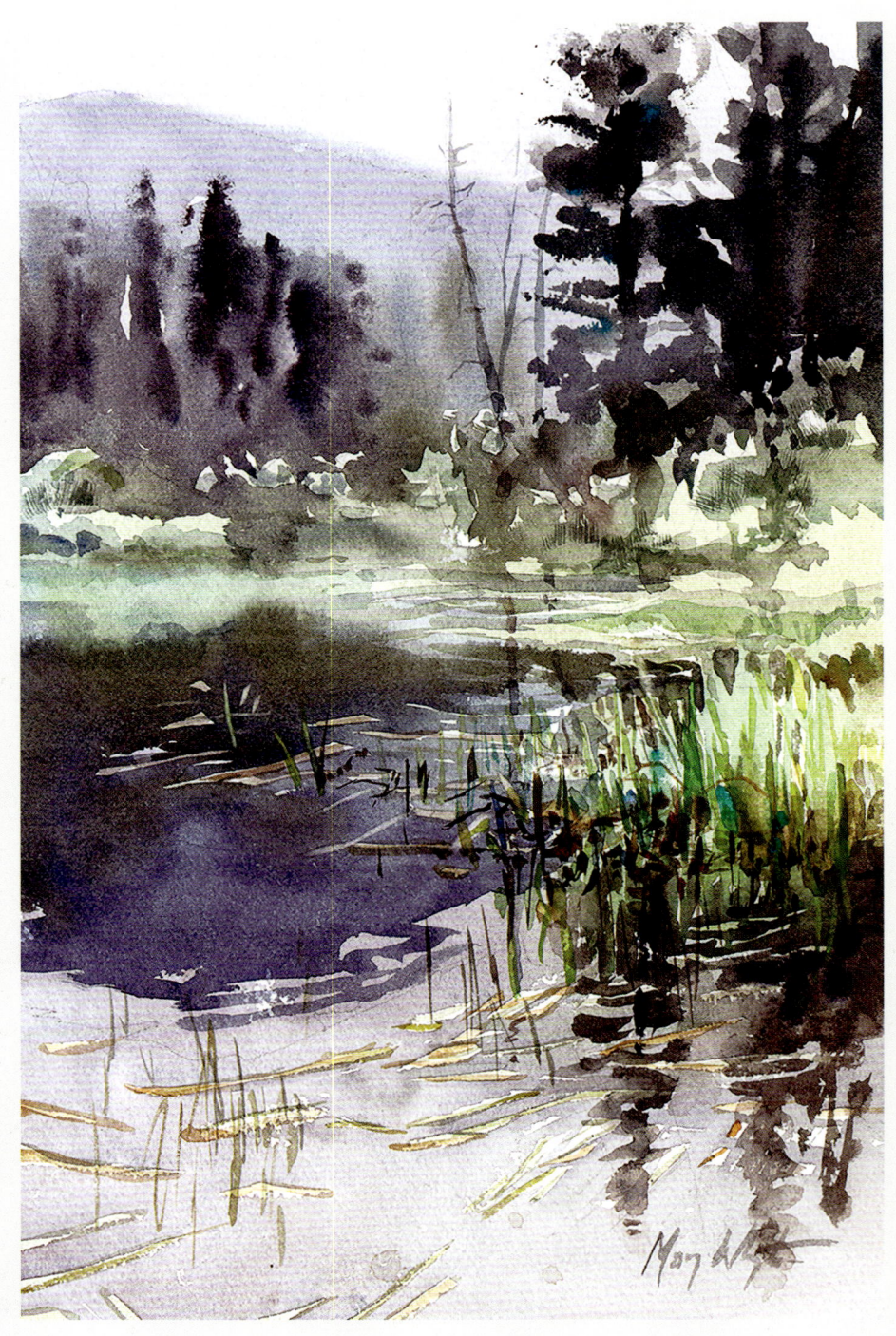

My desire to be a professional artist developed the summer before I started eighth grade. I had been visiting my aunt and cousins in New Jersey and was sitting on the front steps of their home, doing a pen and ink drawing of the bar and restaurant on the other side of the street. My aunt came out onto the porch and, bending down to take a closer look, commented that the owner of the establishment might be interested in buying the drawing to reproduce on his menus or cocktail napkins. I offered up the paper, which she carried across the street to the restaurant. Several minutes later she came back and placed a twenty-dollar bill in my hand.

That was the day I turned pro.

After that I spent all of my summer days and most evenings painting in my bedroom. I sat on a pink stool with my drawing board propped between my lap and the side of the bed, my brushes, palette, and spent rags strewn across the paint-spattered bedspread. My models were often my brother and close friends who posed for me, smoking cigarettes by the open window. I started offering pencil portraits (for twenty dollars each) and selling small oil paintings in a gift shop in town. When I was eighteen, I had my first official one-person show in the lobby of the local playhouse. My life as a professional artist had begun.

It was how I'd always imagined my life would be: creating paintings and showing them. I would make it happen and, regardless of how much money I might or might not make, I was determined to live my life as an artist.▪

MEADOW POND, LAKE TAHOE   *2023, watercolor on paper, 13 × 9 inches*

My very first studio was actually a small closet with a window. With my arms outstretched I could touch both walls. Into the cramped, dimly lit space I managed to squeeze a wobbly drawing table, lamp, and stool. Drawings were taped haphazardly to the wall and ceiling.

My second studio was quite the opposite. Located on the third floor of an old cigar factory, it was a cavernous, drafty space with a single light bulb dangling from the center of the room. During the day the high ceilings and tall windows offered an abundance of northern light. At lunchtime and the end of the workday the two other artists in the building provided camaraderie. There was no air conditioning or heat to speak of, so in winter I painted at my easel, standing next to a kerosene heater. I wore a heavy jacket, boots, knit hat, and thick mittens with holes cut so my fingers could hold a paintbrush. Although the working conditions were modest, my excitement and determination to press forward in my art only grew.

Eventually I had a studio in my home. Located on Seabrook Island, just south of Charleston, my first South Carolina studio was a cozy room over the garage. I added three northern skylights, which not only brought in much needed light, but also opened up views to the tops of the oak trees and the squadron of squirrels that chased after each other from branch to branch. When I opened the windows wide, I could hear the muffled sound of the ocean in the distance and the exquisite conversation of the owls calling to each other across the marsh.

The Seabrook studio became my daily refuge, a place of quiet pondering, where unfinished sketches and paintings lay waiting to

VIEW FROM THE STUDIO   2021, *watercolor on paper, 17. 5 × 15.5 inches*

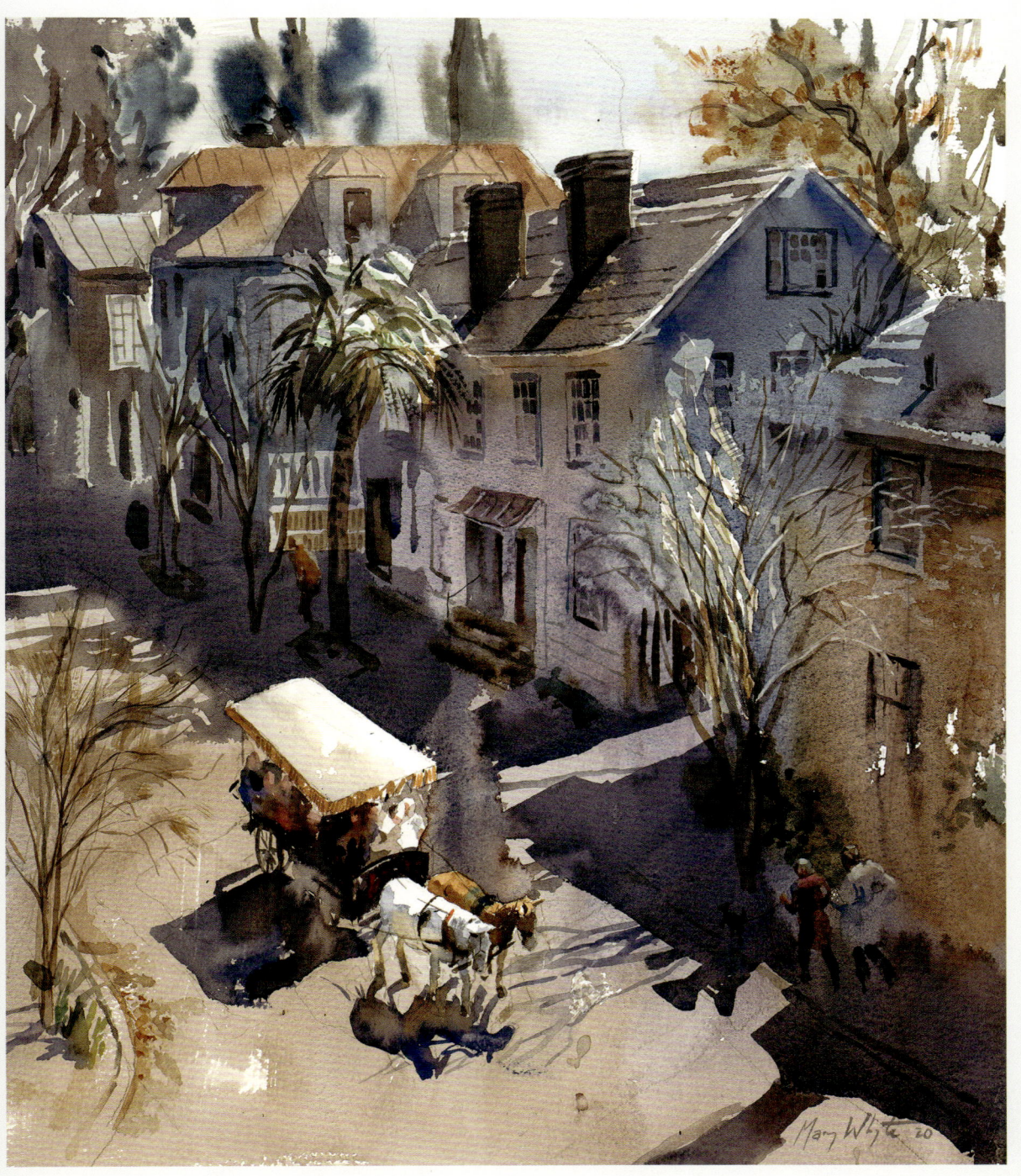

*"Going up the steps each morning I passed over my mantras,
the very things I needed in order to do my work: Forza, Coraggio,
Fantasia, Perseveranza, Ispirazione, Visione, and Fede."*

be completed. Art books were jumbled onto shelves and stacked hip high on the floor. A rarely polished silver tea set, given to me by my grandmother, was put to the task of holding brushes. Leading up to the studio from the kitchen were seven steps. As an homage to the year I spent as an art student in Rome, I painted words in Italian on the face of each step. Going up the steps each morning I passed over my mantras, the very things I needed in order to do my work: Forza, Coraggio, Fantasia, Perseveranza, Ispirazione, Visione, and Fede. Translation: Strength, Courage, Imagination, Perseverance, Inspiration, Vision, and Faith. I often paused for a moment on the step marked Faith.

I worked from the marsh studio for almost thirty years, producing countless paintings, drawings, and manuscripts. It was there that I painted most of my watercolors of the Gullah women of Johns Island, as well as the grittier blue-collar workers of the South. For many of those years I was accompanied by a large golden retriever, sprawled at my feet, snoring and twitching in his sleep, legs stretched out long, as if caught running midair. If I left the room, Boomer would lift his head, shaking his ears and collar hard, and dutifully follow closely behind me, bumping into the back of my legs if I stopped. When it was time to quit for dinner or for bedtime, I never needed to check the clock, because there he was, now sitting at attention at the bottom of the steps, eyes locked on me.

These days my studio is in the center of Charleston, the region where I have lived and worked for more than half my life. The restored space has exposed 1800s brick walls, high ceilings, and abundant light. Outside my second-story windows the scene is a mix of young women in billowing dresses, slick cars pulsing with hip hop music, and the slow, steady clopping of horses pulling carriages filled with tourists more interested in looking at their cell phones than the historic buildings around them. It is a parade of subject matter and ideas, ripe for my sketchbook. The studio's proximity to the art museum, restaurants, and galleries instills a feeling of being in the center of intellectual and creative motion. Although I largely do my work in solitude, I am surrounded by the inspiration of the people around me.

When I teach, I encourage my students to find a place solely for the purpose of making art—a sanctuary that allows them the freedom to explore ideas with little distraction. That private haven can be a spare bedroom, the back porch, or an out of the way corner of the kitchen. Without the need for clearing away art supplies after every session, there is less interruption of flow, allowing one to quickly recapture a paused tangent of thought. Most important, designating a place just to create art announces to your family and the world that this is your walled kingdom. You now have a place to call your very own where you can nurture and grow your art freely.

I have always felt that a studio should be one's most favorite place, an inner sanctum to be entered with reverence and high expectation. I go to my studio five days a week. For me a perfect day means painting for most of it, followed by writing. Emails and professional correspondence are left until late in the afternoon when the light has dimmed. It is a constant battle to guard my work from the outside onslaught of daily distractions.

The pull of social media, as well as balancing business and family commitments, is an ongoing juggling act. As artists we must plan for and protect our studio time with steadfast determination.

Even though I love going to new places to paint the landscape and its people, my studio will always be my center of gravity, the familiar touchpoint where ideas can be prodded into possibility and swirls of paint can be shaped into something recognizable. Every morning my studio beckons. It has become as necessary to my feeling of well-being as getting exercise and sleep. It is the place where the world yields and the heart prevails. ∎

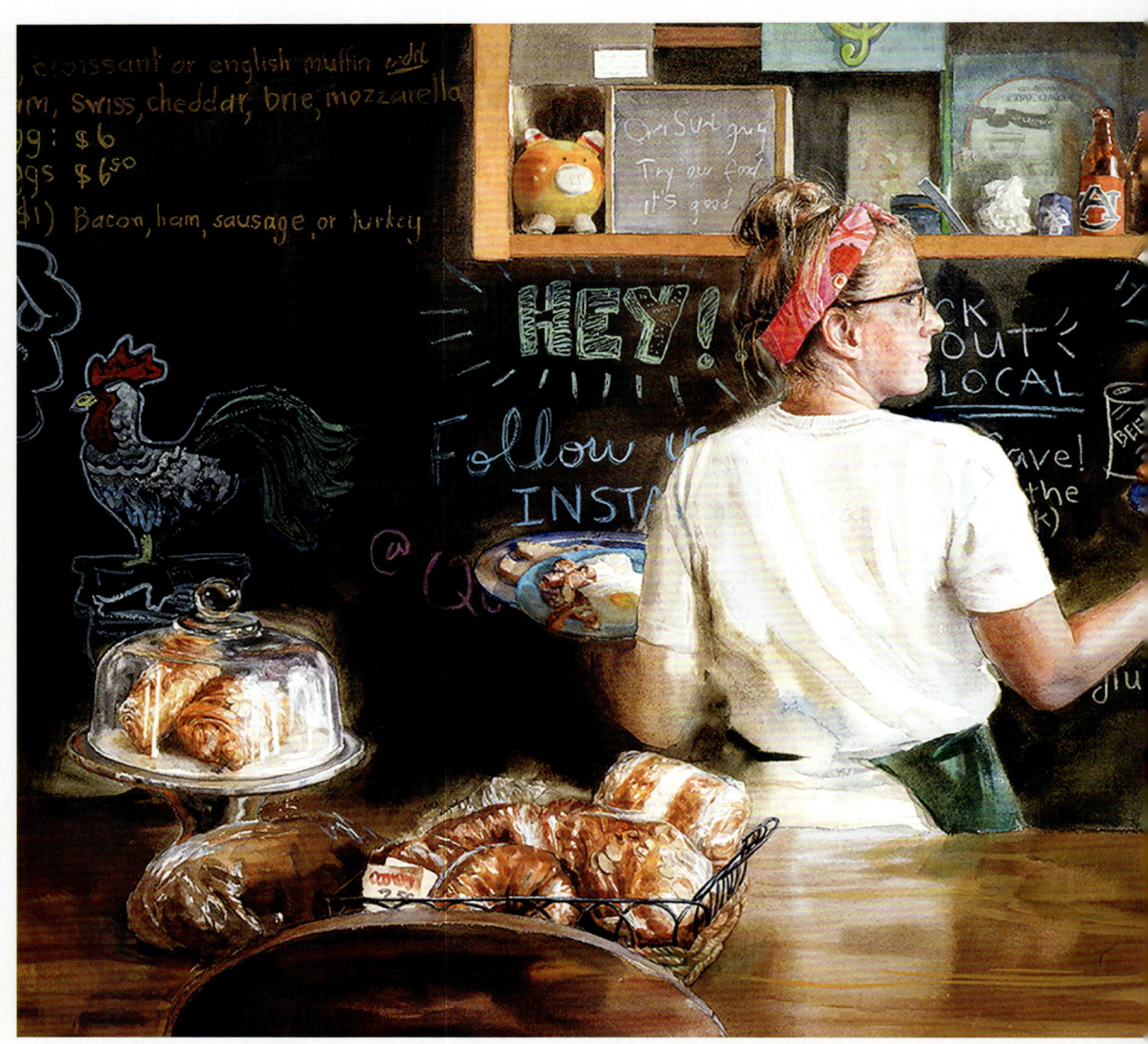

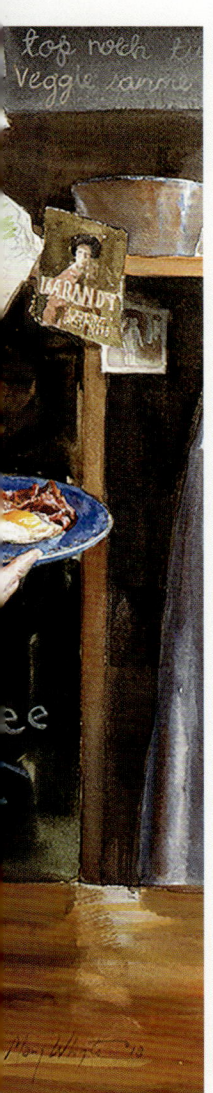

My first formal instruction in watercolor occurred when I enrolled in an adult art class near my home in Chagrin Falls, Ohio. I was the only teenager in the group and was mesmerized by what I perceived as the dazzling abilities of the adult students. And, oh, the colors that teacher mixed! Who knew that Ultramarine Blue and Burnt Sienna could create such beautiful neutral hues of both warm and cool nuances. His beguiling combination of blue and brown I use to this day. It was an eye-opening experience, and a far cry from using the inferior materials we struggled with in my public high school. Here I discovered the heavenly textural quality of handmade paper with its slight irregularities and deckled edges, the sensuous jewel colors squeezed from small tubes marked with exotic names such as Cerulean and New Gamboge, and the total wizardry of a brush that snapped to a perfect point and could dance across the paper in a wide stroke or an imperceptibly delicate line.

BLUE PLATE SPECIAL   *2018, watercolor on paper, 23 × 33 inches*

The instructor noted my enthusiasm and invited me back for another semester at no charge. From that point on I painted every hour I could, copying the work of artists from books that had been given to me and going out on my own to paint the landscape. Long before I ever heard the words "plein air" (the term for painting outdoors directly from life), I was sitting by the side of a dirt road, doing paintings of wildflowers, clouds, and insects. When I was old enough to drive, I often took my mother's car, driving miles away into the rolling Amish countryside to paint the barns and buggies, as well as the children skating on the frozen patches of ice in winter. The landscape all around my Ohio home was fodder for endless paintings: our long-neglected apple orchard, the busy bird feeders outside the kitchen window, and the clear, fast streams on our wooded property. At times I would take my supplies to the center of town and sit on the sidewalk to paint the bright storefronts and the band gazebo.

To earn extra money, I worked after school at a restaurant, serving up sandwiches, hamburgers, salads, and hot fudge sundaes. It was there I learned how to make salad dressing for a hundred people, how to flip hamburgers using both hands at once, how to wait on the pickiest diners, and how to calculate a 15 percent tip in my head twice as fast as it takes to figure it out on paper. On Saturdays I worked for the local newspaper laying out ads for car dealers, dress shops, and grocery stores, coming up with headlines and catchy phrases. Both experiences taught me communication, sales, and business

skills; I learned to think on my feet and to show up on time and ready for work. I made more mistakes than anyone would want to admit but rapidly discovered that a friendly smile and polite effort go a long way. Years later, my friend Alfreda would echo my early education by saying, "Manners will take you places money never will."

When I was eighteen, I entered art school in Philadelphia. The portfolio of paintings that I had done mostly in my bedroom passed the scrutiny for acceptance, and my trunk of clothes and art supplies were shipped to my assigned dorm room. My previous experience of dominating the world from the confines of my rural Ohio bedroom was now upended by more worldly pupils who had created their portfolios while studying at such prestigious locations as the Art Students League in New York or in European ateliers. Before I entered art school I had never heard of such exotic terms as *croquis, conte, sanguine,* or *tromp l'oeil,* which the other students bandied about freely in conversation. I had never heard of the artists Cimabue, Caravaggio, or Cellini and was laughed at when I said I admired Norman Rockwell.

The four years passed quickly, with the highlight coming my junior year when I was able to study in Rome. I had just turned twenty and found myself totally immersed in the history of Renaissance artists, learning the language and customs of the locals, and reveling in the regional food and wine. Never had I seen such opulence in art and architecture, and I spent many afternoons sketching in the parks along the Tiber River.

> *"A good teacher opens the door, and as students we are left to our own devices to find our way through it."*

My roommates Marcy and Raymond were my frequent companions, willing to join me in exploring the trattorias, night clubs, piazzas, and flea markets in the city and beyond.

Though my time in art school in Philadelphia and Rome gave me a solid background in art history, it did little to further my knowledge of classical techniques or how to pursue a career after graduation. In class we were taught to emulate the ideology of the artists who were showing in New York but were given little clue how to grow our own work, much less make a living at it.

For years I begrudged not having had a true classical education. But after many decades as a teacher myself, I am beginning to think differently. A good teacher opens the door, and as students we are left to our own devices to find our way through it. If art is to come from the heart, it must be given full reign and not be hampered by the imposing philosophies of others. Through exploration and perseverance, we must contemplate the world and things as they are and see them without inherited bias. We must educate ourselves one painting at a time. ▪

Not long after I finished art school, I was offered a job at a garden center. My responsibilities would be to handle retail sales, the weekly newspaper advertising, and to design and construct the seasonal displays. Although the thought of a steady paycheck was especially appealing to me, spending forty hours a week doing something I wasn't passionate about felt like a hand around my throat. Forfeiting my creativity for a nicer apartment wasn't a bargain I was willing to make, so I turned down the offer. Although I knew it was a gamble, I would take my best shot at being an artist.

I knew that being an artist isn't a job in itself. Being an artist is a calling. It is a mission expressed in the way we live and view the world around us. Pursuing this amazing, uncharted, and often haphazard adventure is in itself a lifelong class in wonderment and exploration. Having an artist's nature is about seeking and nurturing our unique place of being in the world and then giving expression to what we have discovered.

Creativity isn't just about making art. What you create doesn't have to be worthy of a frame, hang over a mantle, earn a blue ribbon, or have a price tag. Through our natural being we are already creators in the deepest sense, inventing our own perception of the world and navigating our own course through life. We view the world, each through our own lens, producing our own response. We curate our likes, our preferences, and our dreams in a world of our own creation.

Being an artist is one of the very few vocations where age is an asset. Many of my students are well into their sixties, seventies, and even eighties, proving that making meaningful art can happen at any age. The older you are, the more experience you bring to developing the content of your narrative, while gaining a deeper well of life-earned wisdom and an ever-widening picture of yourself. You are your own amazing work of art.■

GLORY   *2015, watercolor on paper, 28.5 × 20 inches*

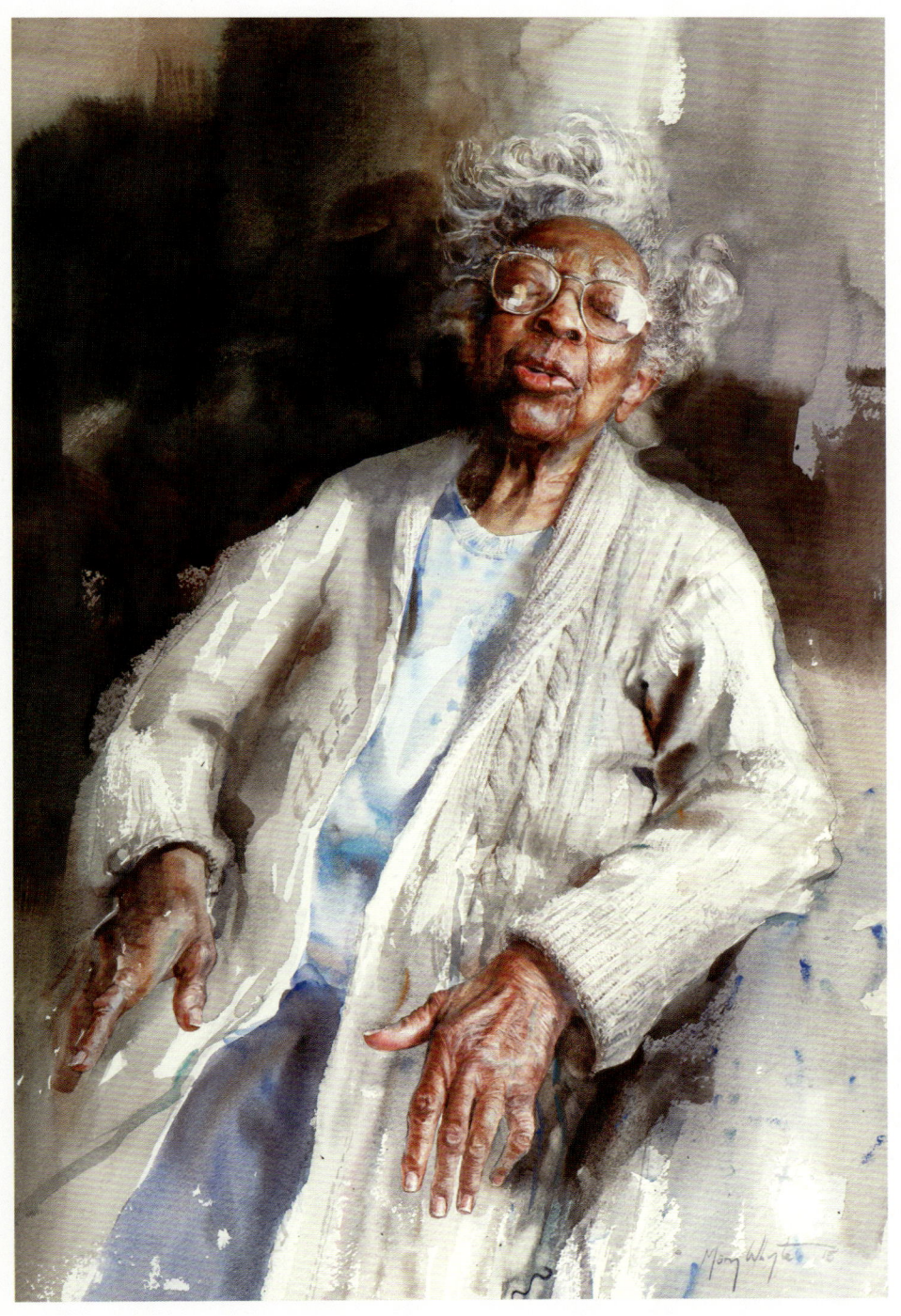

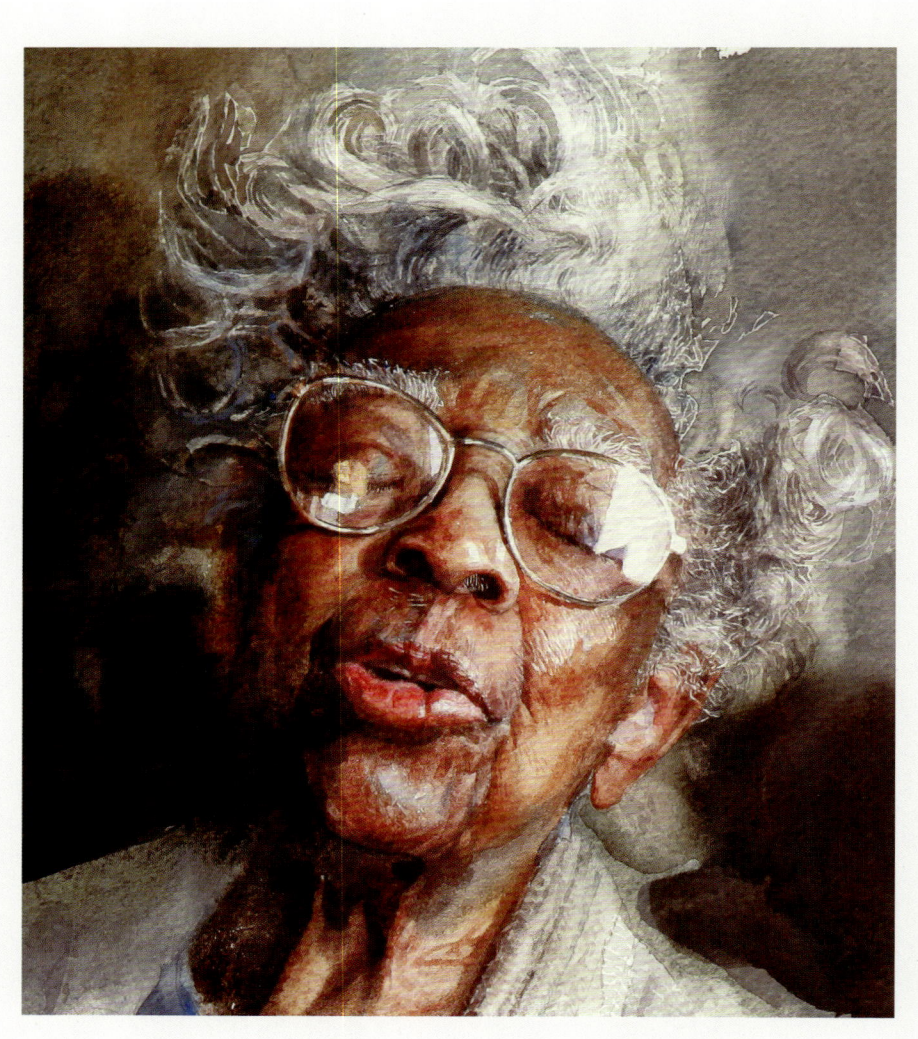

"Having an artist's nature is about seeking and nurturing our unique place of being in the world and then giving expression to what we have discovered."

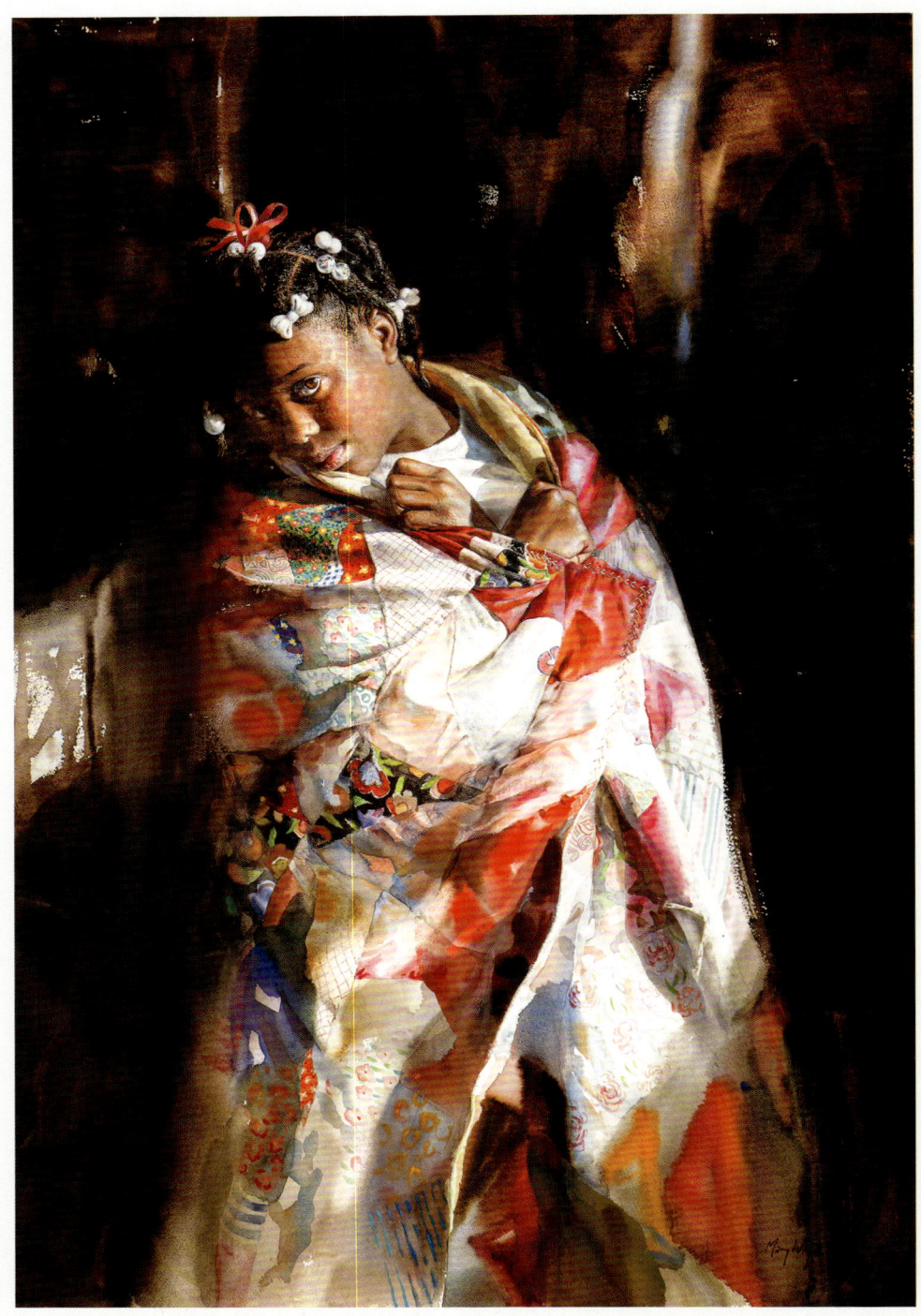

Creativity is seeing what
others see and thinking what
no one else ever thought.

—ALBERT EINSTEIN

Each of us is born with imagination and the ability to be creative. How to invent that which has never before existed can't be learned, ordered online, or willed into being. Creativity is something that is let loose.

Being an artist doesn't mean your eyesight is different, or that you are more emotionally sensitive, or that you have mystical clairvoyance. Being an artist simply means that you see with your heart. As artists we notice details others miss. We pay attention. We look and feel deeply, seeing past the mundane to what otherwise might be invisible. We are on the lookout for beauty that surprises and sensations that are unexpected. We become the ambassadors of amazement.

Most people only note beauty that is rare or fleeting, such as a butterfly or a rainbow. When a full eclipse of the sun occurred several years ago, the phenomenon excited millions of people, many of whom made expensive travel plans to be in the perfect place just to observe and photograph the moment. All of that expectation for two minutes of wow and then it was over and everyone went home to ordinary lives. Just imagine what would happen if you could go about every day knowing you would likely witness something as miraculous as an eclipse.

Welcome to the world of an artist.∎

PERSIMMON   *2012, watercolor on paper, 40.75 × 28.75 inches*

> Painting is easy when
> you don't know how, but
> very difficult if you do.
>
> —EDGAR DEGAS

Early on in my painting career there were several established artists I admired for their creative and commercial success. I tracked their exhibitions, read their interviews, and studied their lives as much as I could, thinking there had to be a formula to their impressive outcomes. Surely, there had to be a set procedure, starting with which brush and paper to use, the exact colors to have on the palette, and what coffee to drink. When I finally had the opportunity to ask one artist how he had risen to such a level of accomplishment, his answer was, "There's no secret. You just do the work."

As I was to learn over and over again, there is no recipe for success in painting or in life. At best there are only examples of what has worked for others. The most direct route to creativity and self-fulfillment will be the one in which there are no arrows, road maps, or fellow travelers. Creating work that is similar to that of others, or made to please someone else, means it can never be truly original. To make work that is unique, we must forge our own path.

The good news is that in the quest to make authentic work, each of us is the commander-in-chief. As artists, we get to decide the vision, the destination, and exactly how we want to get there. We are the ones who decide what subject to paint, which colors to use, what coffee to drink, and how our work will look. Producing art that is unlike anyone else's won't guarantee critical acclaim and financial success. However, time spent creatively can be far more satisfying than anything money can buy or accolades from others can bring. ■

TAMALES   *2023, watercolor, acrylic, and charcoal on paper, 41 × 29 inches*

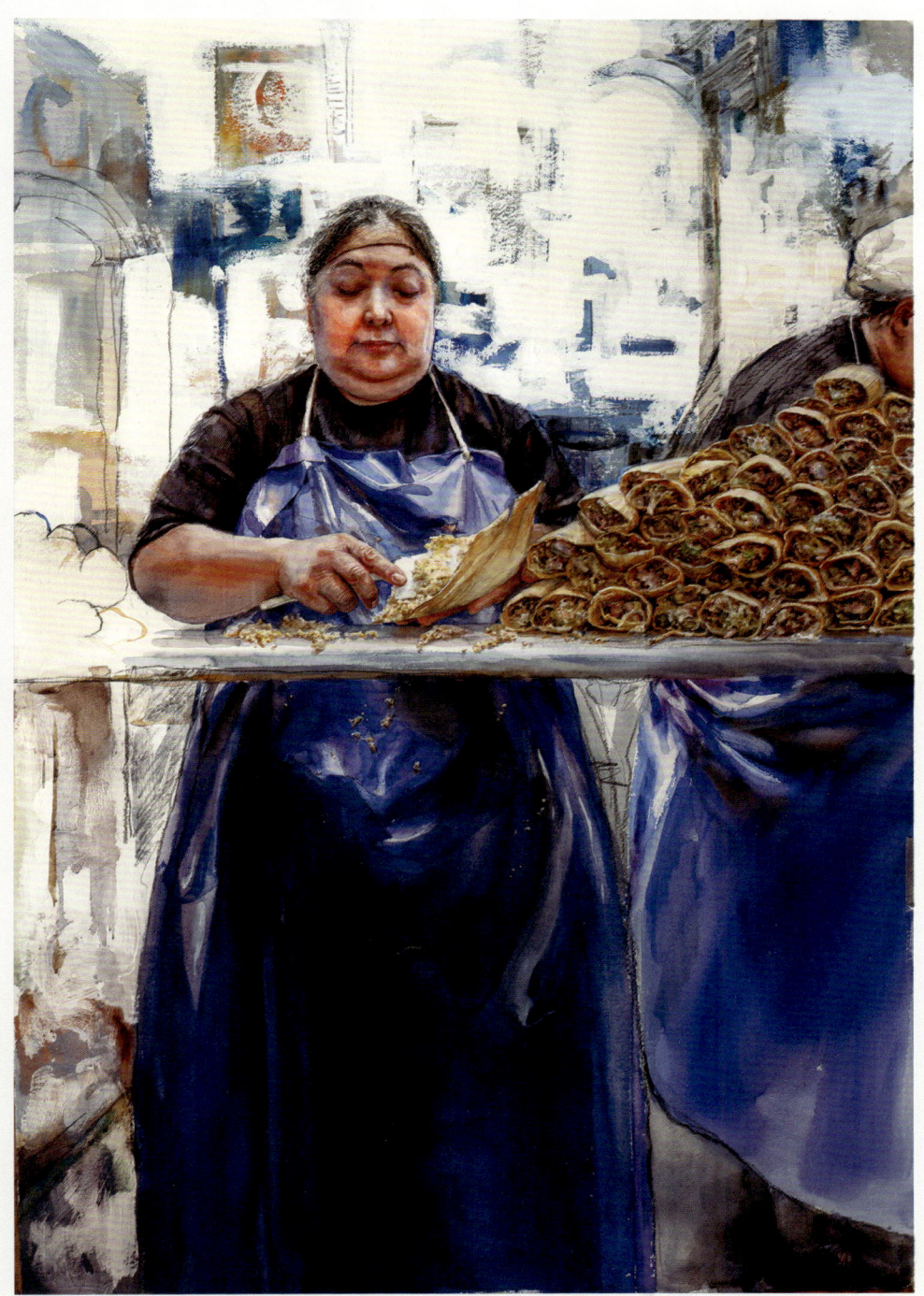

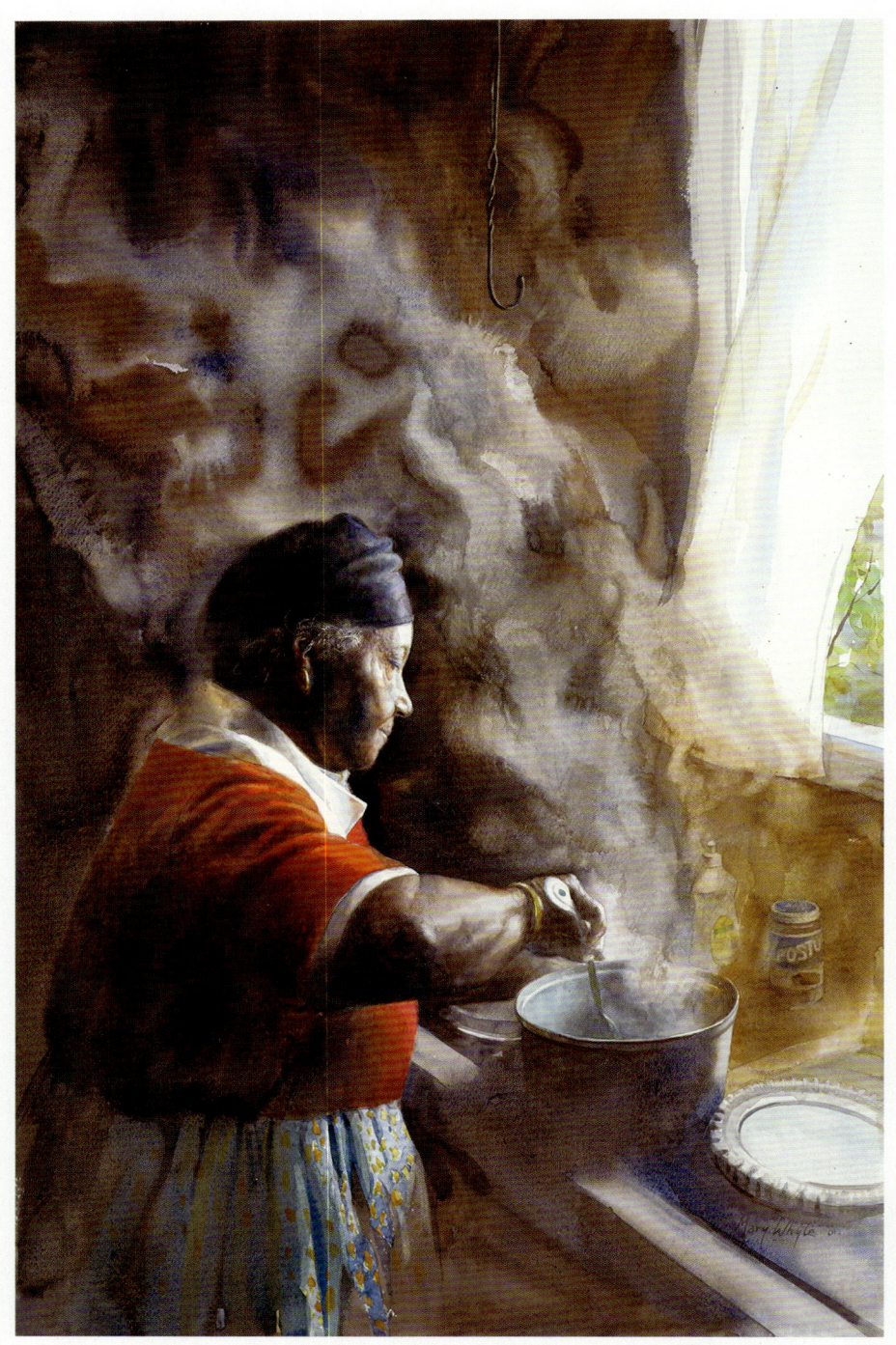

There are times in an artist's life when one painting completely alters the course of their work. It happens when a singular piece—totally unexpected, surprising in its making, and determined in its force—veers the artist in a completely new direction. The result can be a body of work that is startling and original, giving the artist a newly discovered purpose and fervor.

My work swerved unexpectedly into new terrain when I moved to the South in my mid-thirties. Previously, my life and paintings had been centered around the Northeast, with its umber stone barns and the plain-spoken Mennonite and Amish people of Pennsylvania. Many of my oils and watercolors depicted local landscapes, with fields of fall pumpkins and rusted buckets hanging on weathered doors. Such themes were big sellers in the gallery but empty of the kind of authenticity that only comes with firsthand experience. What I longed for in my work, but didn't know how to get, was the kind of passion that comes from the near-blinding desire to tell one's story.

And then I moved to South Carolina and met the women of Johns Island.

Longtime descendants of enslaved Africans, the small communities of Gullah-speaking people live in pockets up and down the coasts and barrier islands of South Carolina and Georgia. It was on Johns Island that

---

SISTER HEYWARD   *2001, watercolor on paper, 27 × 18 inches*

I met the women of the Hebron St. Francis Senior Center making quilts in a small, dilapidated church on Bohicket Road.

When I wandered into the leaning church I was embraced by a sisterhood of hardscrabble seniors in homemade aprons and sequined hats. Bent over colorful quilts made from salvaged scraps of clothing, their Gullah voices swirled around me. Each spiritual the women sang merged strength, endurance, and survival bequeathed to them by their enslaved ancestors. Through the windows I could see the small cemetery. Beneath the brown tangle of brush and tree roots lay a scattering of unadorned headstones marked with few words, as if none were ever needed.

It was a Wednesday in February. The church was heated by three kerosene heaters and an enormous black oven that baked the chicken, sweet potatoes, and pungent cornbread I would come to love over the ensuing years. Thirty years later I still cannot explain how it happened—how a white Yankee girl managed to find herself sitting in the middle of a weekly gathering of Gullah women for Bible study and fellowship. They called me their Vanilla Sister.

The paintings began spilling out of me. The very first watercolor was of Mariah, then in her nineties, sewing a quilt that cascaded over her lap like a royal robe. When I took the painting to the gallery, the director was surprised I would even consider submitting such a thing. "Who is going to buy it?" she asked. I was undaunted. The practicality of making sales no longer mattered to me, as I had discovered a passion in my work I had never known before. In the women of Johns Island I had found a remarkable story that needed to be told. With a newfound ferocity of brushstrokes and nuance of color, I would spend the next twenty-five years telling their story.

Many of the paintings I did were of Alfreda, a woman thirteen years older than I, who lived a few miles from me, in a cinderblock home painted bright turquoise. I also painted Georgeanna, who lived most of her life in a tiny house next to the Episcopal church. Whenever I had an idea for a painting, I would call Georgeanna and ask if I could come over. No matter what time of day it was, the septuagenarian never once said no. When I arrived, she was always waiting at the door, wearing what she imagined would make a really fine painting. More than once I arrived to find her wearing a flannel bathrobe, adorned with a necklace she had fashioned out of yarn and plastic beads, and her best Sunday hat.

Most of the time I sat with Georgeanna in her warm kitchen, with the screen door open, sketching and photographing her as she cooked large pots of collard greens or shrimp. Steam would encircle her head like a wreath, leaving droplets of violet moisture on her forehead as she peered into the dented pot, stirring. As she cooked she often sang or quoted short verses from the Bible. Some phrases were all her own. "Knock and the door shall open." Or "The family that prays together stays together." My favorite was "God didn't have to do it but he did." I was never quite sure what she meant by this one but figured that if it was good enough for Georgeanna, it was good enough for me. ▪

"What I longed for in my work, but didn't know how to get, was the kind of passion that comes from the near-blinding desire to tell one's story."

After my first visit to the senior center, I returned almost every Wednesday. In between the weekly gatherings, I went to the women's homes, to paint them in their kitchens cooking, sitting on their back steps snapping beans, or in their yards hanging heavy, wet laundry on lines propped up by poles or brooms.

From that experience I learned about the value of establishing an unbreakable trust with the model. The artist trusts that the model will be amenable. And the model trusts that whatever the artist does will be honorable.

Over many years, outsiders have taken advantage of the people of Johns Island. Properties were swindled out of them. Photographs of the locals were made into books or merchandise. These proud people received no recognition and certainly no compensation. I was determined not to treat them similarly and made sure the women I painted were paid appropriately. When my collection of works evolved into a book, I committed all the royalties to the Senior Center and did what I could to protect the community from the kind of public exposure that would bring in busloads of camera-toting tourists.

The women of the senior center saw my paintings and were proud that their lives were being affirmed. Many of them would sit beside me at book signings, signing pen in hand, proudly reciting to buyers the page number that featured their portrait. ▪

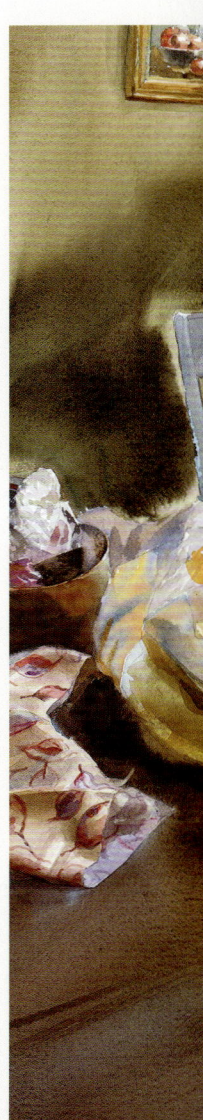

DOUBLE STITCH   *2016, watercolor on paper, 21 × 30 inches*

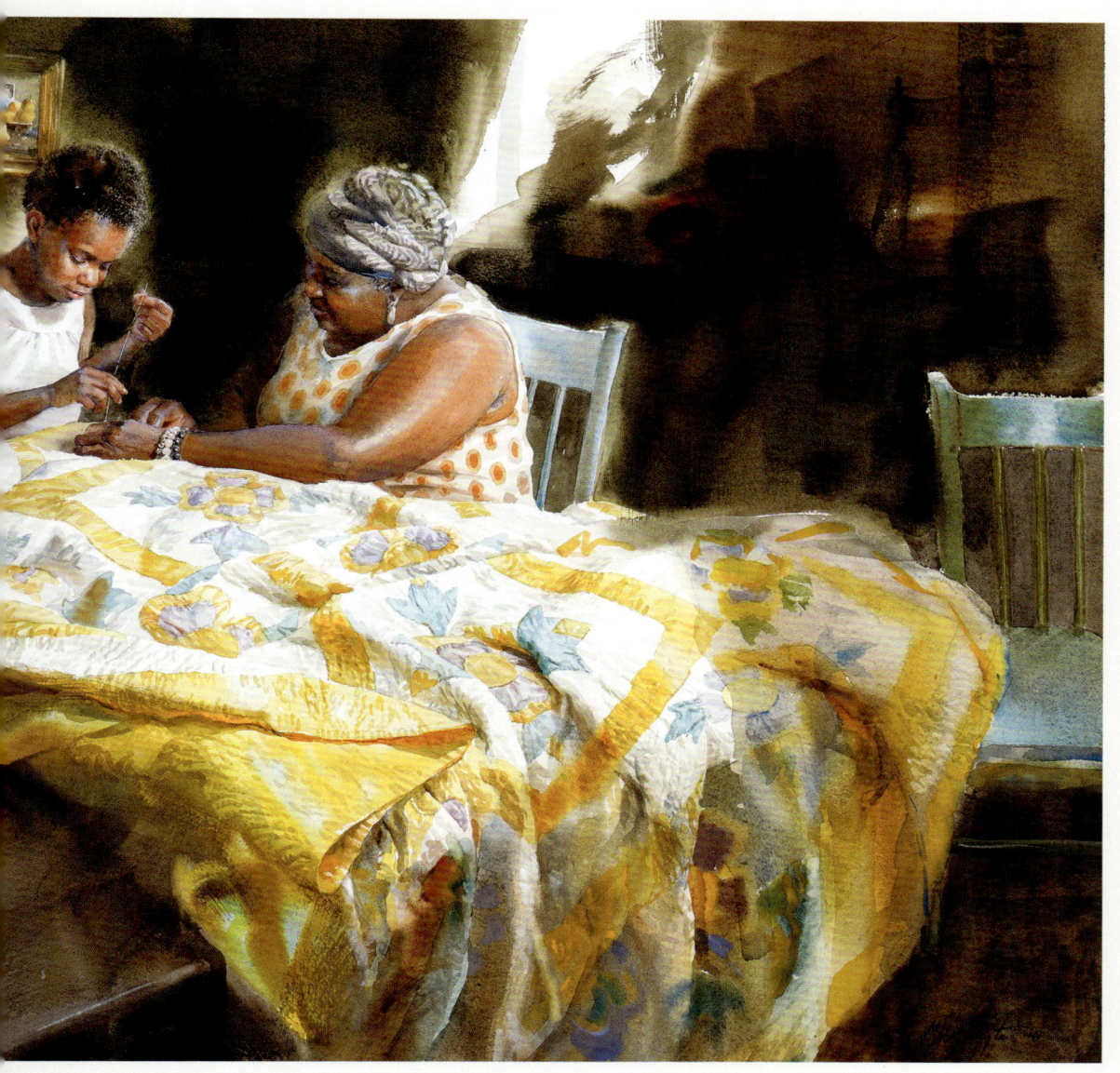

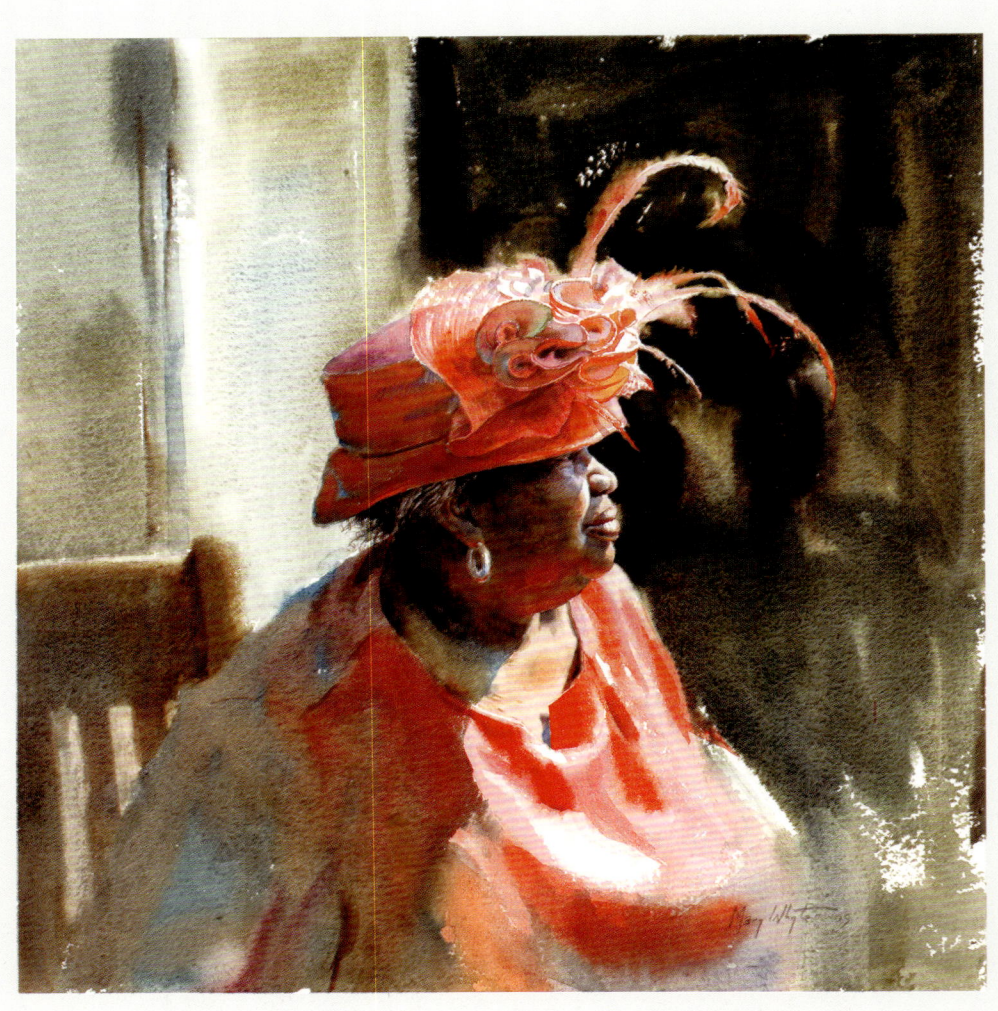

When an artist paints a portrait, two people are involved: one who forever changes the sitter, and one who forever changes the artist. Such was the case with my model Alfreda who, over the years, would become one of my closest friends and the subject of my book *Alfreda's World*. Almost every time I drove past her home on Bohicket Road, I would see her in the garden weeding between the rows of vegetables or hanging up a quilt on the roadside stand her husband Isaac had cobbled together out of lumber scraps and a reclaimed door. Freshly picked produce was displayed in tin pans and market baskets, with hand-scrawled signs notifying customers of the price. Her dog, Princess, was usually sleeping on the step by the kitchen door. I always tapped the horn when I drove by.

Alfreda invited me to her raucous family reunions, taught me how to make sweet potato pie, and patted my hand at funerals. She accompanied me to book signings and speaking engagements, frequently getting a standing ovation. Her message to the audience was always the same: "We have to stop all this fussin' and fightin' and get about the business of loving each other."

The daughter of sharecroppers, Alfreda lived on Bohicket Road, not far from the fields where she had picked cotton and potatoes as a child. She and I once visited the plantation where she grew up, a sandy lane leading to the long-abandoned shack where the entire family had once lived. Most of the trees the family had slept under on sweltering nights still stood, including one that was taller than the rest with limbs that reached across the road. It was the tree she once told me about, where several of the islanders had been lynched. She did not witness this herself, but her mother had. For this, too, she had pieced together a patchwork of love and forgiveness.

Alfreda, Georgeanna, Tesha, and all the women of Johns Island changed me in unexpected ways. Through them I learned not only the power of faith, but also the value of being frugal with money and extravagant with love. I was the witness to a unique and noteworthy way of life, one in which the compass pointed to plain and simple truth. Because of them, I wanted my work to reflect the same. ∎

RED   *2009, watercolor on paper, 18.5 × 18.5 inches*

I first met Tesha when she was taking art classes at Johns Island High School. A few years later I saw her again working as a server in a restaurant and asked her to model for me. The first time she posed, I depicted her lighting a carved pumpkin, with the golden candlelight washing over her face.

Tesha is now a grandmother. The passing years have been marked with watercolors of her sleeping in a small boat, picking flowers, hanging laundry, cooking for her family, and wading in the marsh creek with her young daughter. Many of the places where I once painted Tesha and the other women have since been paved over by encroaching development, and many of the seniors who I met that first afternoon in the little church on Bohicket Road have passed on. I am grateful I was there to witness their lives and commit this little-known community to paper.

As an artist I have made it my mission to paint, as honestly and as truthfully as I can, the people and places of our times. It is the only thing I really know. I never planned on making the paintings of Johns Island into a series or assembling the growing body of work into several books. Nor did I anticipate that I would find myself returning to the same Lowcountry barrier island again and again after so many years. As artists we follow our hearts, and sometimes the heart insists on staying in one place a little longer.▪

WAITING *2002, watercolor on paper, 40 × 27 inches*

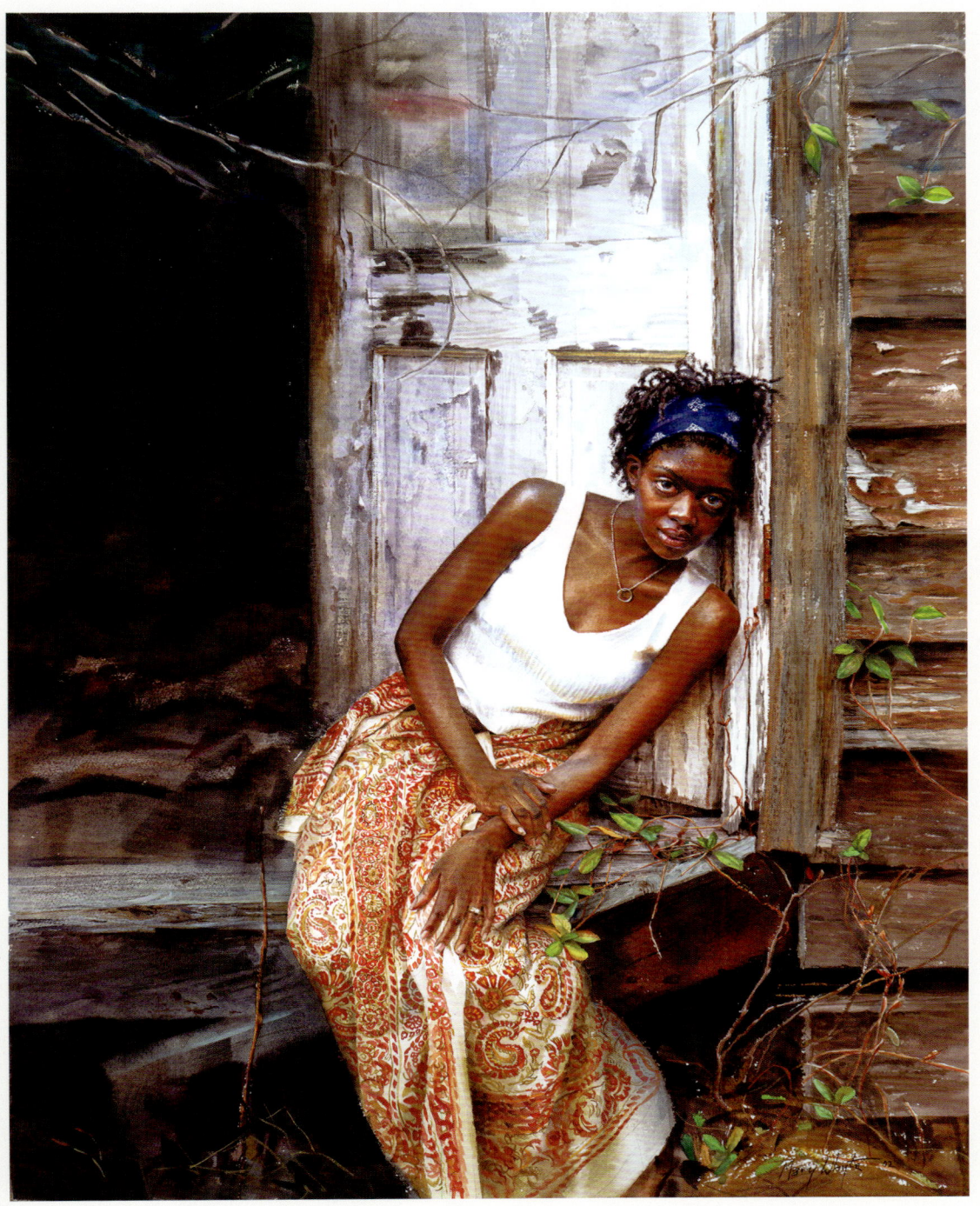

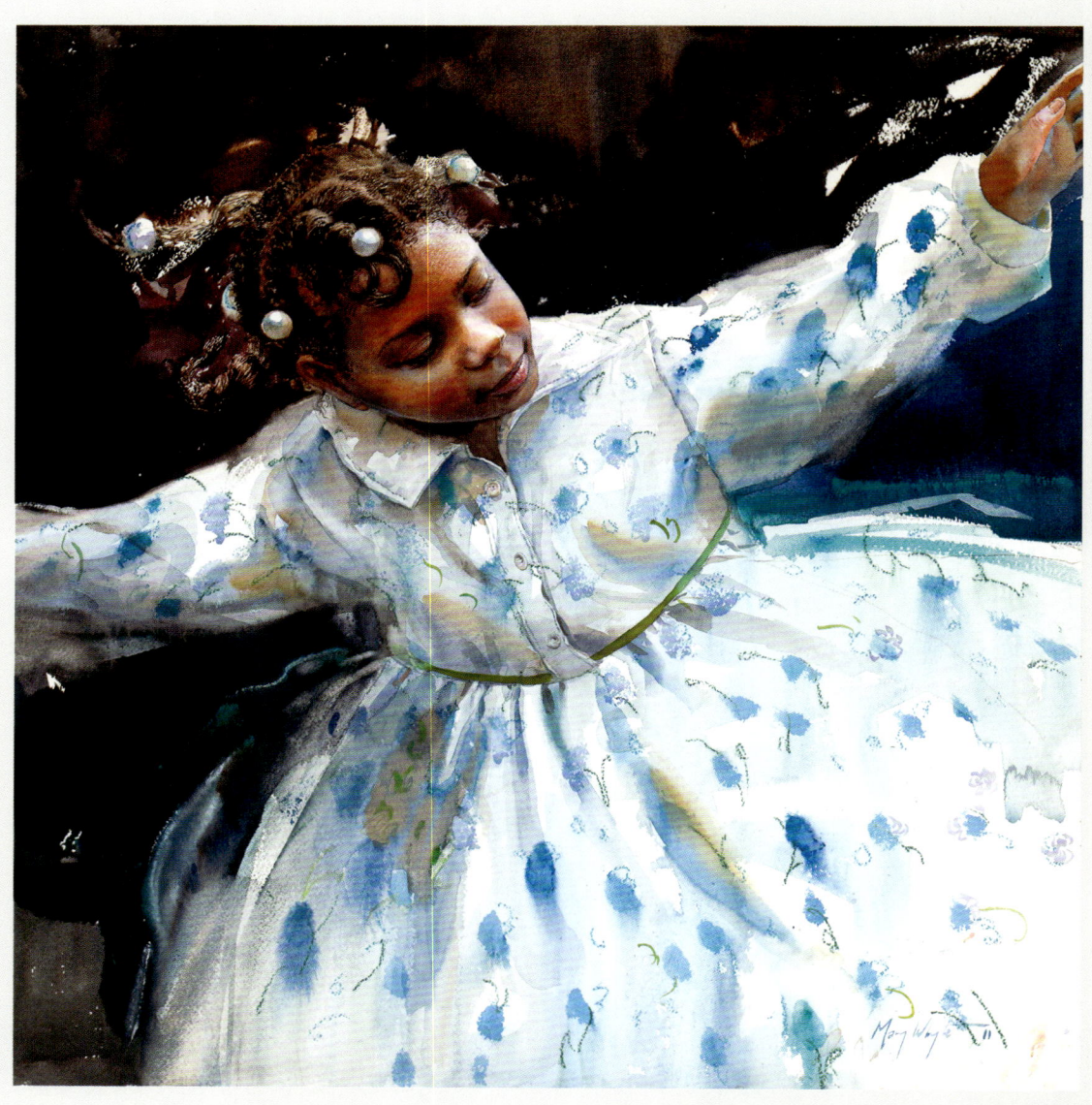

A creative life is an amplified
life. It's a bigger life, a happier
life, an expanded life, and a hell
of a lot more interesting life.

—ELIZABETH GILBERT

Our goal as artists is more than just making stuff. Our job is to create work that appeals to the senses, not just ours, but others' as well. We plant, nurture, and grow our corner of the garden and then share our bounty. Our great privilege is to show others the surprising and miraculous world in which we live.

Creativity is about being ever ready for the presence of magic and viewing the world around us as if through the eyes of a child. Unfortunately, by the time most of us are ten, fantasy and imagination have been squeezed out of us; the only thing we want is to conform and be just like everyone else. Looking or acting differently from others is likely to be met with ridicule and exclusion. It's safer to blend in.

To embrace the feeling of childlike wonder, it's helpful to remember that everything we have experienced in life had a first time: the first time we saw the Grand Canyon, tasted homemade ice cream, went on a roller coaster, or heard a live band. Each event was a remarkable and memorable experience. We recorded it firmly in our mind and heart

TWIRL   *2011, watercolor on paper, 18.5 × 18.5 inches*

because at the time, all of our senses were heightened, which is nature's way of helping us navigate unfamiliar terrain. As we become more accustomed to recurring experiences, such as seeing the ocean again and again, our intensity of sensory input decreases. But only if we let it.

Keeping watch with fresh eyes and all our senses engaged takes full-on awareness. Although we may never be able to get back our original childlike amazement, we can certainly be ready to witness the extraordinary hidden in the everyday. If we can turn on that unique switch in our brain for great expectation, and really *see*, then we are much more likely to experience the wonder around us.

Encountering the world with an innocent perspective can be freeing. There are no confines or parameters, just possibilities. While experience might teach us what has worked in the past, it can hamper the magical power of playfulness. The ability to value imagination and curiosity above all is one of the most powerful ways we can keep the avenues of creativity open.

When you view the world around you as if through the fresh and inexperienced eyes of a newcomer, you begin to realize how astonishing it all is—a tiny red ladybug, the glow of fireflies in the meadow, the sound of the train as it rumbles by. It's all there, waiting to be discovered, if not for the very first time, then once again. ∎

"Creativity is about being ever ready for the presence of magic and viewing the world around us as if through the eyes of a child."

What I remember most was the sound. Our Kenyan guide brought the jeep to a stop and switched off the engine, motioning with his hand for us to be still. Hidden low on my lap was my open sketchbook. I drew quickly, as the family of eight elephants moved toward us and then split into two lines around the vehicle. The sunbleached savannah grass made a soft swishing sound against their legs as their trunks gently probed the jeep, sweeping over our shoulders, taking in the scent of us.

That memorable day was one of several in Kenya when, instead of taking a camera on safari like most tourists, I took a sketchbook. From the jeep I was able to make many quick studies of sleeping lions, wading hippos, whimsical monkeys, and exotic birds. By the end of two weeks, my sketchbook was full, gifting me the best possible souvenir of a once-in-a lifetime trip.

My sketchbooks have become my personal journals. They are a visual diary, the recollection of the places and people I've known, a documentation of a singular life explored. A few sketchbooks have gone to institutions, others have been packed away. Many volumes are no more than a hodgepodge of scribbled ideas, to-do lists, studied observations about the work and practices of great masters, or strings of circles and doodles made during long phone calls.

Long ago I discovered that sketching is similar to making a grocery list. If the needed items are put in writing, we are more apt to remember everything on the shopping list without having to refer back to it. Drawing is like that. The more we draw, the more we remember the inventory of quintessential characteristics of what we have witnessed. ∎

ELEPHANTS   *2013, graphite on paper, 11 × 8 inches*

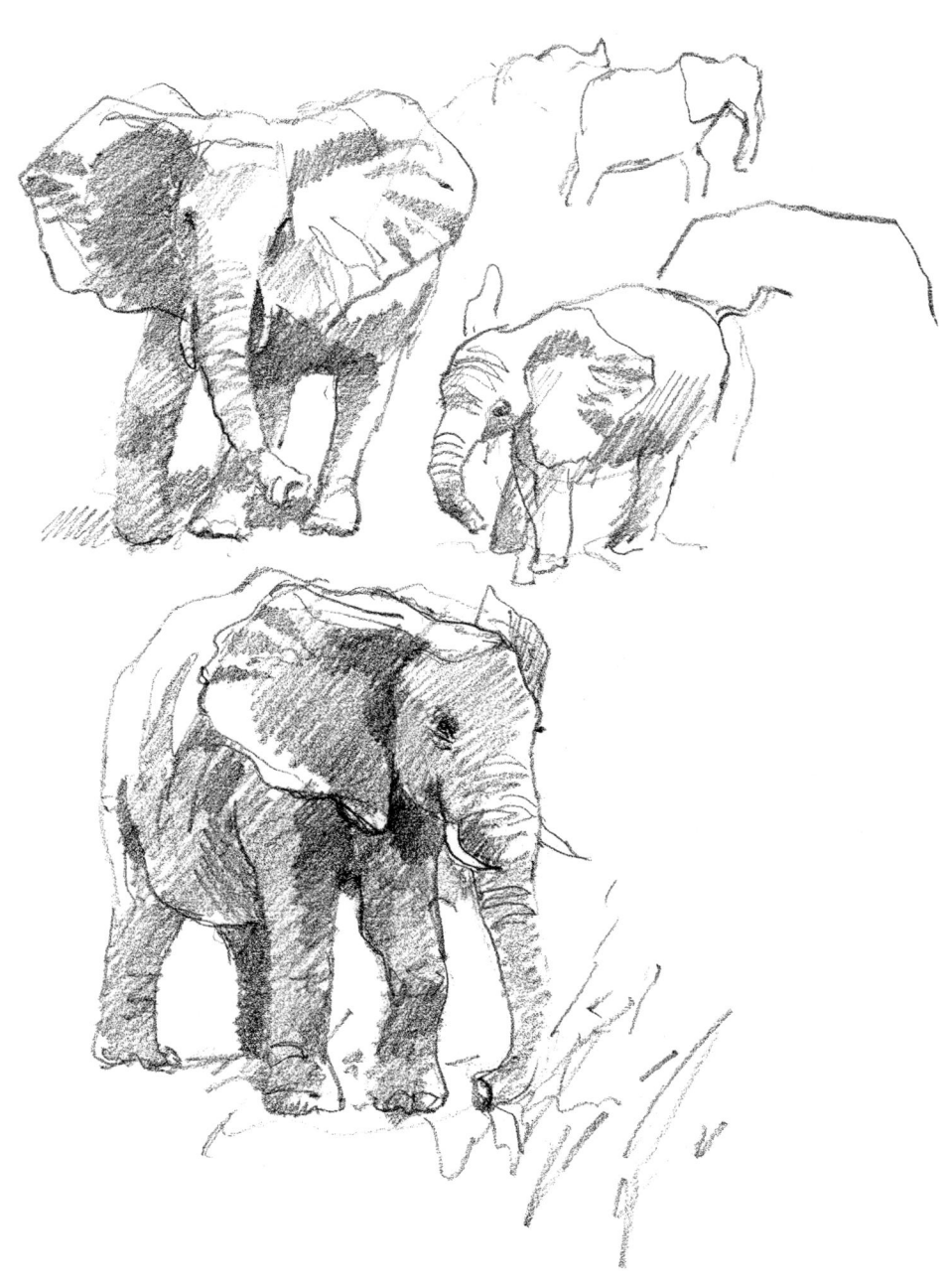

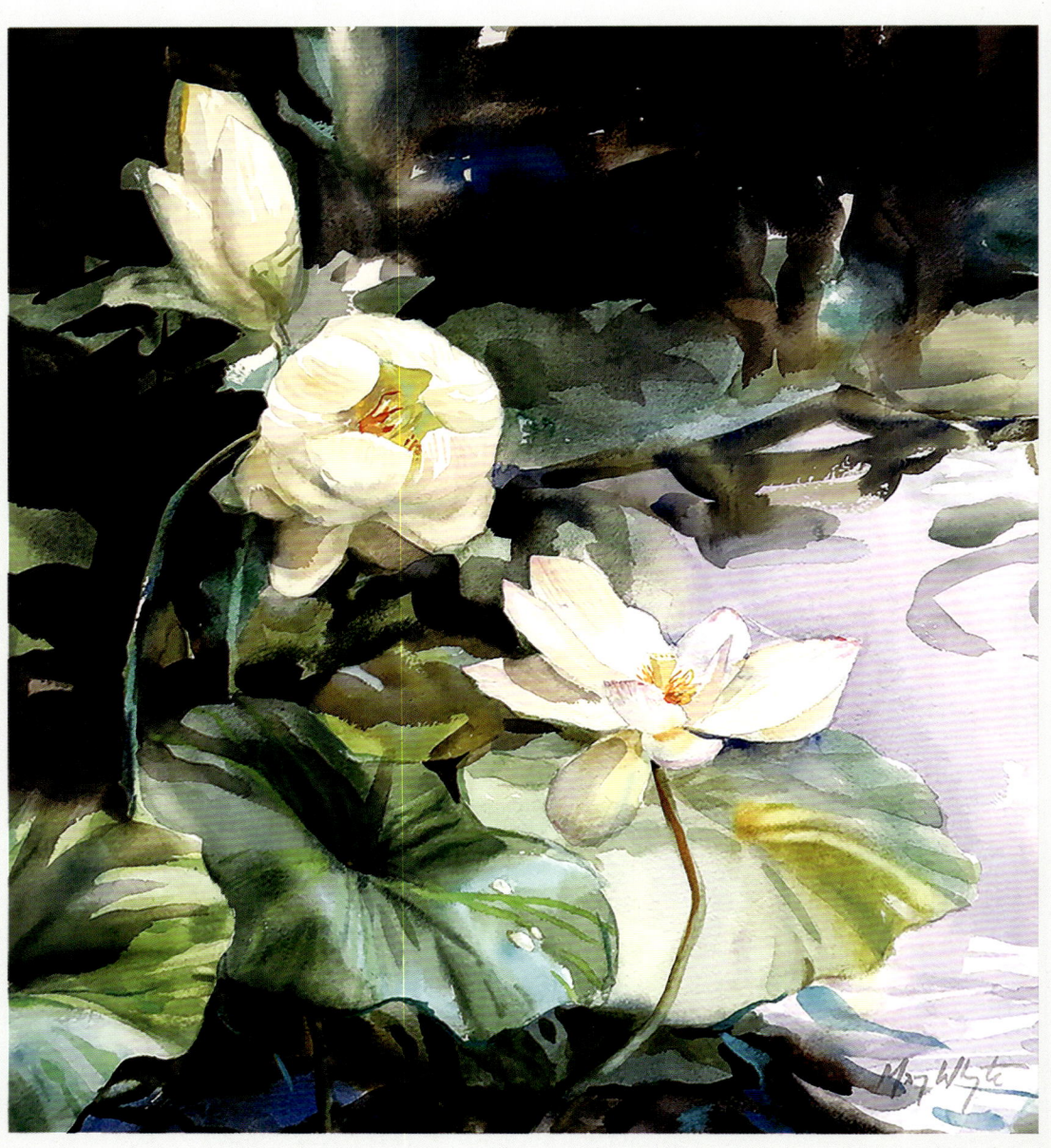

Being an artist isn't just about making things. Being an artist is a way of life. The difference was first made evident to me when I was in my early twenties. I was visiting the artist John Falter (1910–82) in his home near Philadelphia. One of the most prolific American illustrators of the twentieth century, Falter was known for producing more than 120 cover illustrations for the *Saturday Evening Post*. When I entered the artist's stately home, I was spellbound by its artfulness. Having been raised in a Midwest Ohio house furnished strictly for practicality, it had never occurred to me that a home could also be a work of art, or a place to surround oneself with beauty. Every room in the Falter house was a feast for the eyes: colorful rugs, richly woven textiles, oil paintings with ornate gilded frames, delicate orchid plants, and bronze sculptures were everywhere, even in the powder room. However, the real lesson for me was how Falter *lived* art. It was evident in the way he designed the garden and created costumes and theatre sets for his children, made frequent trips to New York to visit with writers and other artists, sketched in honky-tonk jazz clubs, and carefully selected just the right spot along a pristine creek to lay out a springtime picnic.

Falter taught me that being an artist isn't so much about the number of pieces we produce, but the number of ways in our life we express what we see and feel. Ours is a lifetime of pursuing beauty. As artists, our way of life becomes its own creation.∎

TRIO *2023, watercolor on paper, 19 × 18 inches*

Exhibiting your work for the world to see can be unnerving for most artists. It can make you feel vulnerable, as if you are letting strangers traipse into your house to read your diary and look inside your closets. Of course, for many artists the goal is to create work that others will actually want to pay money to possess. Achieving that goal takes time and commitment. Building a body of cohesive work, getting it framed, and submitting it to juried shows requires effort, perseverance, and money, with little guarantee of financial return. Once a body of work is built, there are the necessities of inaugurating a website, engaging in social media, and seeking gallery opportunities. Only after creating a body of work and promoting it can an artist begin to gain exposure and start to garner an income doing something they love.

Many artists start by joining a local art league, subscribing to art magazines, attending gallery openings, and participating with other artists in painting groups. The intricacies of accounting and marketing one's work are beyond the expertise of most artists, who would much rather be in the studio anyway. In my early years I bartered paintings for professional services, including advertising, landscaping, dog sitting, housekeeping, and dental care. I even offered to trade a portrait for golf lessons, until after the first session the instructor admitted neither one of us would survive it.

I encourage students to maintain a source of income until they have a reasonable following and enough resources to accommodate painting full time. Knowing that the bills are paid can allow breathing room to experiment and grow. More important, I tell them that whatever they think or believe they can do, they should start by taking the first step. One is rarely given a dream without also being given the ability to make it come true. ▪

FRONT ENTRANCE   *2019, watercolor on paper, 21.5 × 17 inches*

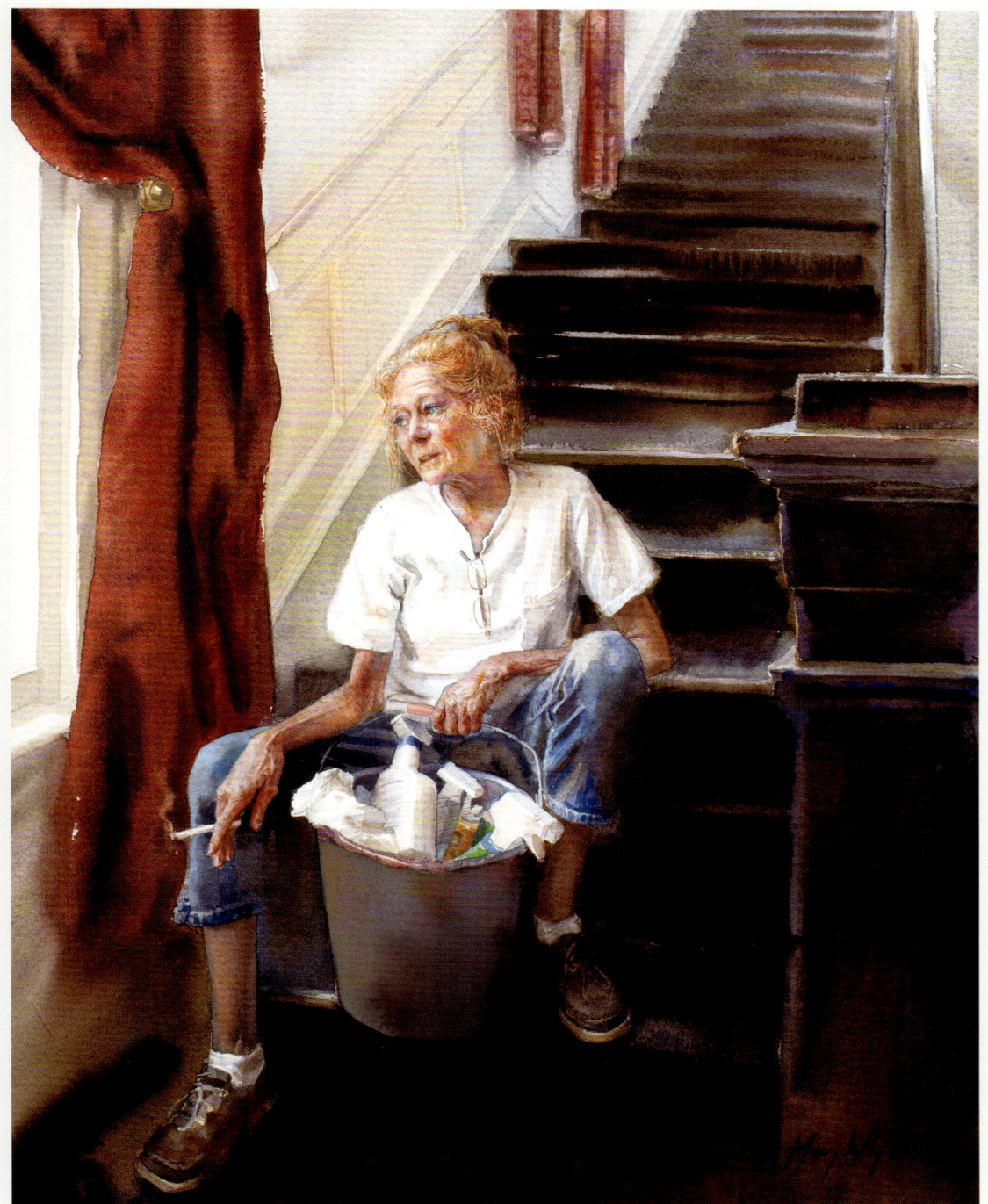

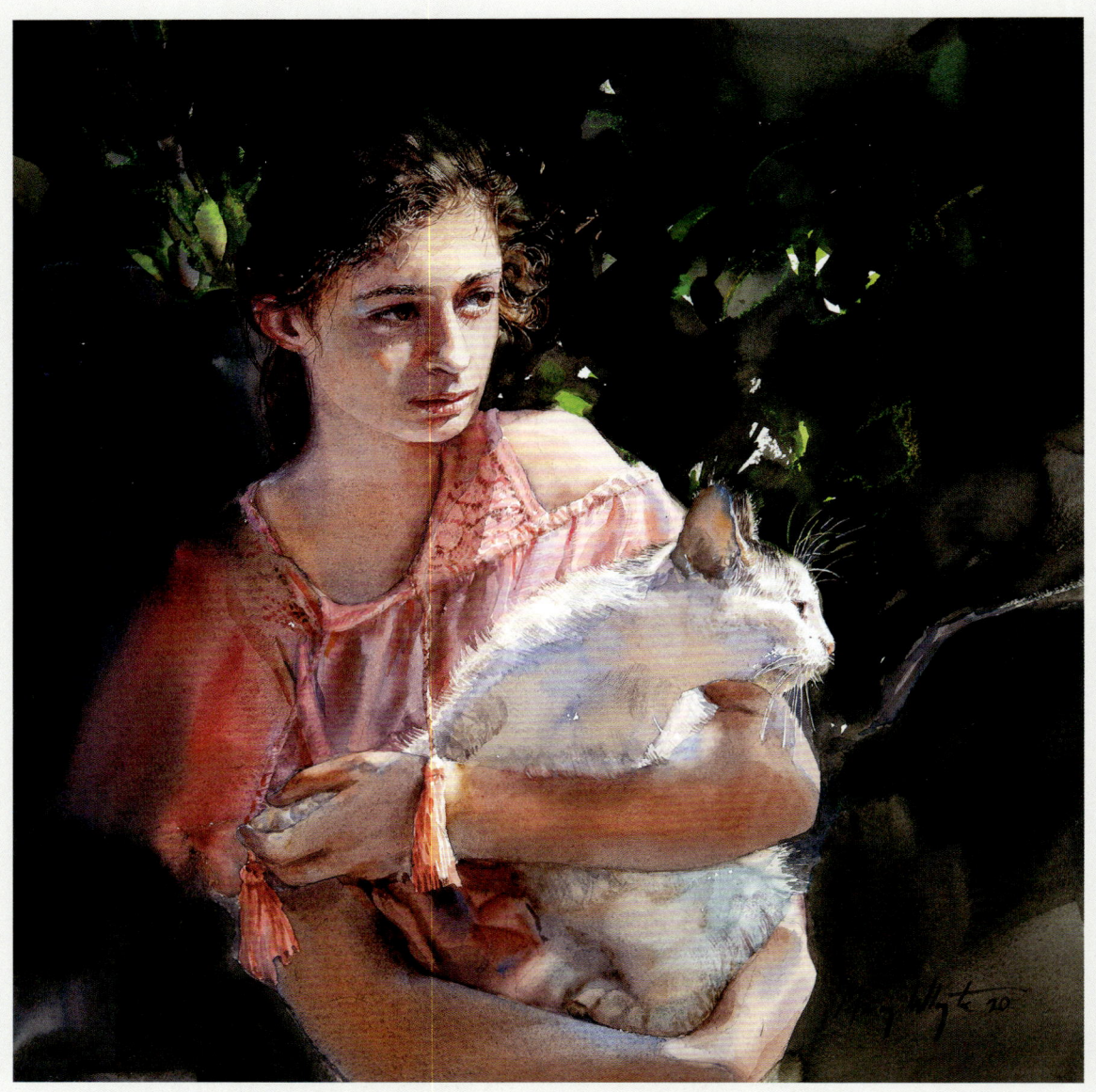

Imagination is the beginning
of creativity. You imagine
what you desire, you will what
you imagine, and at last, you
create what you will.

—GEORGE BERNARD SHAW

Being an artist requires more than having the right art materials and subject matter. It requires having something meaningful to say. Whether through music, poetry, photography, glass blowing, painting, or dance, our goal is to communicate our personal point of view with freedom, emotion, and earnestness. It's not enough to copy what already exists or what someone else has already done. We are here to tell our own story in our own way. As creators it is our task and privilege to bring into existence something as distinct, unique, and original as ourselves.

Simply having the desire to paint isn't enough to get the job done, any more than sitting a child in front of a piano and telling him to "Play Beethoven," will produce a musical prodigy. Giving full rise to self-expression to convey one's ideas requires study, practice, and a range of skills. In addition, we must also have a heart brave enough to forge ahead, past all obstacles or doubt.

Ultimately, being an artist requires that we have three things:

Something to say.

The ability to say it.

The courage to do it. ∎

ONE'S OWN   *2020, watercolor on paper, 17.25 × 17.75 inches*

Summer

THE PATH WITHIN

It's not the destination, it's the journey.

—RALPH WALDO EMERSON

I learned a long time ago that the act of painting isn't just about the finished picture.

It was summer, I was sixteen, and I had convinced my mother to let me have her car for the day. Driving the wooded back-roads of the Ohio countryside, I passed the familiar Amish barns, farm stands and endless rows of corn that were already knee high. A paintbox with my name lettered across the top in red marker and a crumpled McDonald's bag were on the back seat. In the rearview mirror dust and gravel spiraled behind me.

I was looking for the perfect place to paint. It had to be something I had pictured in my head. A barn, maybe some cows. A few flowers. Not too many, otherwise it might seem corny. I was down to my last few French fries. According to my new self-imposed rule, when the last fry was gone, that would mark my stopping place if I had

---

SUMMER FIELDS   *2024, watercolor on paper, 13.5 × 9.75 inches*

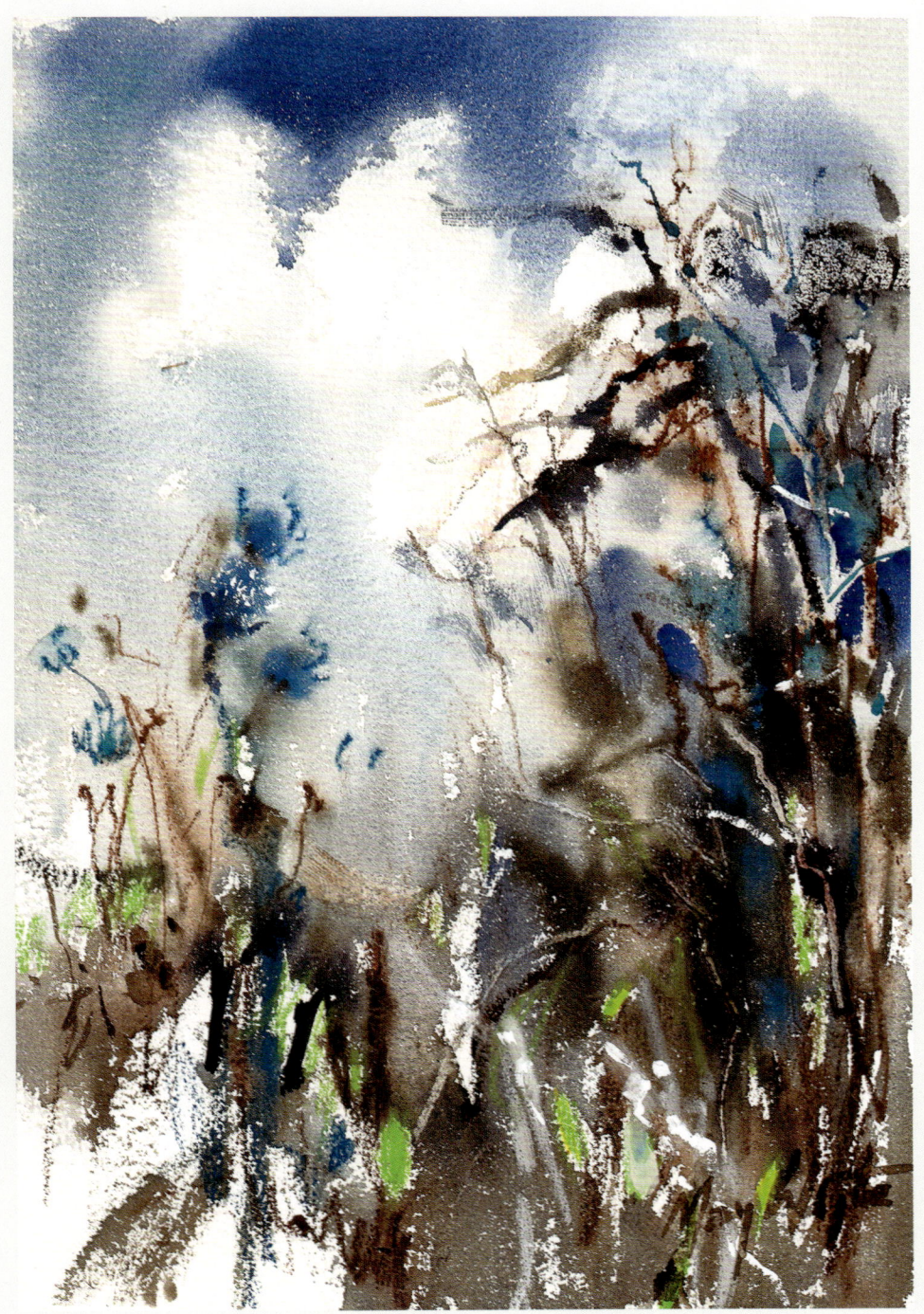

not already found a better one. With the last salty bite, I swept my hand across my jeans and pulled over.

I retrieved my gear from the back seat and stood on the side of the road, looking in both directions. There wasn't a house in sight, and no cars had passed me for quite some time. A chain of low-slung barns stood like boxcars on the horizon. I hadn't thought about bringing something to sit on, so I stepped a few feet off the gravel and plopped down on the ground with my supplies. The weeds were over my head.

I began laying out my palette, taking in the scene, then paused as I watched a bright green grasshopper flicking from stem to stem. When it was just a few inches from my hand, I reached out and watched it ping away. Nearby, the throaty song of red-winged blackbirds mixed with the high-pitched chord of crickets. The ground smelled of a summer in its fullness, the damp, pungent blend of decaying peat and renewing life. Overhead white clouds swelled and billowed, tipping a cascade of blue onto my palette. Sun and sky enveloped me, as I felt my brush moving across the paper.

That summer day, in an unmarked field, breath became color. Pollen, weeds, insects, and a celestial tide guided my hand. There was no wrestling with decisions, what color to mix, or where to put it. It was simply a call and answer of the Divine Creator at work. Painting became a oneness with all that was around me and in me.

Over the course of my career, I have heard artists talk about having felt as if they were in a trance while painting. Some describe the experience as the presence of wonder, the welcoming in of a wider mystery and dimension far beyond the scope of our understanding. It is a heightened sense of existence, of feeling fully alive, that transcends time and place. At that very moment, we become witness to the highest order and are the conduit of a joyful state of being that makes art inevitable.

I learned there is never a shortage of intoxicating beauty to be found outdoors. After that day I went out to paint as often as I could. Admittedly, part of the allure was the thrill of having the absolute freedom that only a teenager with a car can possess, if only for an afternoon. Most of the time I frequented the Amish farms where I loved sketching the horse-drawn buggies and pastel laundry strung aloft between the barns and houses. Other days I headed to our nearby town to paint watercolors of the Victorian houses. I distinctly remember one glorious afternoon lying by the Chagrin River, listening to its mighty engine and looking up at the clouds through the swaying treetops.

These many decades later I have given up the French fry rule, though never the desire to regain the experience I had that first time I painted outside. These days I still try to settle on a painting location within a set amount of time and without too much deliberation. Every destination, even one I have never been to before, will guarantee discovery and learning, if not always a successful painting.

I have enjoyed trips with my husband, Arnold Nemirow, to Italy, Mexico, Portugal, France, Norway, Netherlands, and Sweden more fully because I was able to do multiple small watercolors along the way. Whether I painted off the stern of a boat, from the bank of a river, in a museum garden, or overlooking a vineyard, each small snippet of an image filled my heart in a way no photograph can.

Tourists have no idea what they are missing while busy taking videos and selfies. While they are focusing on framing the camera and fixing their hair, they miss the experience. In contrast, when an artist is painting, all of their senses come into play: sight, sound, taste, touch, and smell. The artist disappears and self-expression steps forth. At that point a remarkable state of being engages, as miraculous and unexpected as the sound of blackbirds singing on a summer day. ■

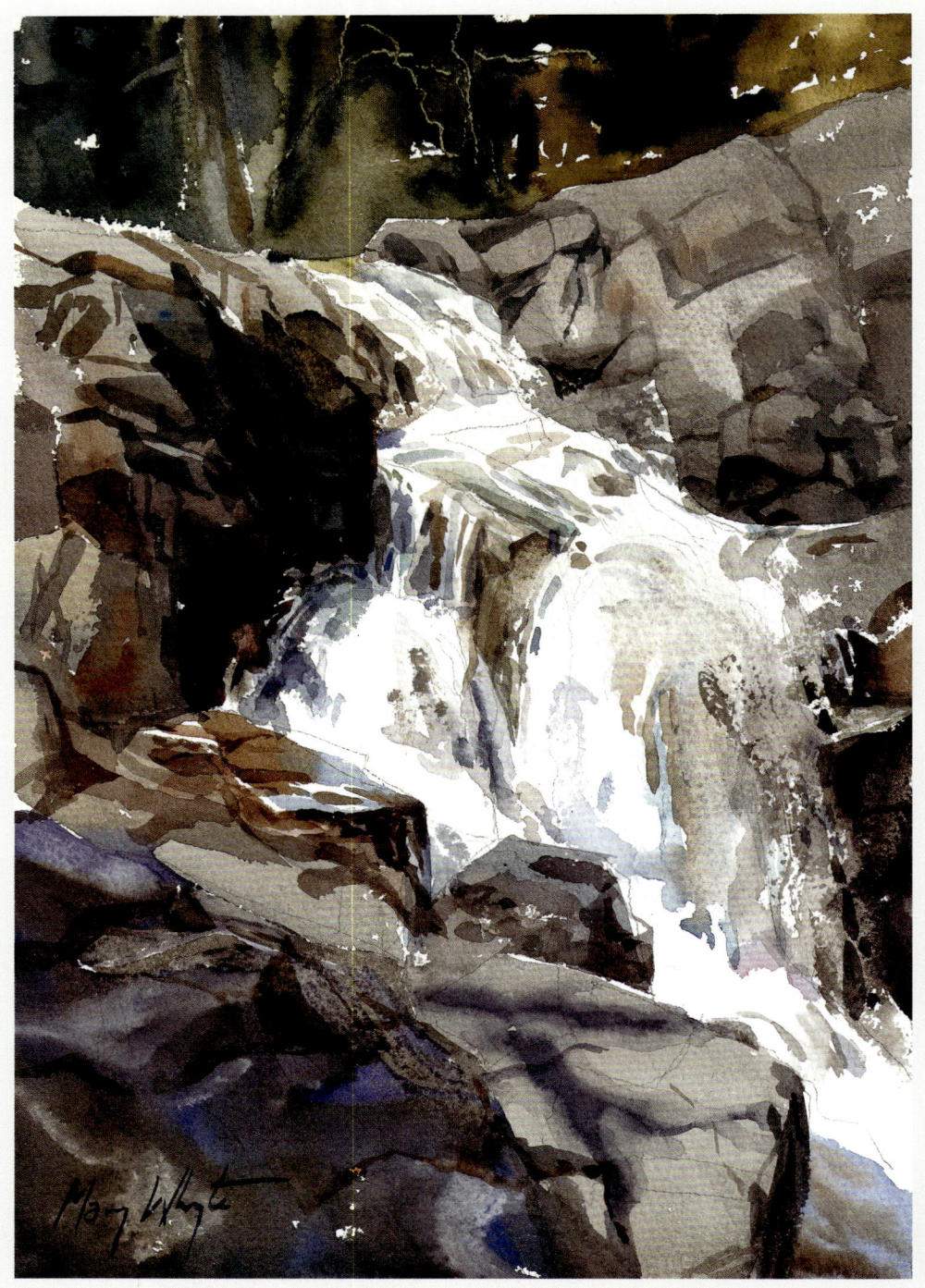

Historically, plein air landscape artists ventured out in the warmer months. American artists would pack up their gear and head to places such as Cape Cod, the Adirondacks, or the Rockies. The numerous studies done on location were generally accomplished in a few hours, capturing the natural light, shadow, and color before it changed with the movement of the sun. Over the long winter months back in the studio, the sketches would be turned into major works.

Many of my own plein air paintings have focused on the different qualities of water. Images of ponds, cascading waterfalls, and the frightening force of pounding waves have found their way onto my paper. Each location poses its own set of unique challenges: the fleeting nature of reflections, cast shadows, and water movement that then needs to be witnessed, understood, harnessed, and reinterpreted. However, what I often find most mesmerizing about a location is the *sound*. The deafening roar of a waterfall or the whisper of a muskrat skimming across a pond—each situation requires a different hue, brush, timing, and heartbeat. Even though what we might have heard in real life may be absent in the studio, through our art we can create the visual sensation of sound.

I have found that working outside with its inherent time constraints has taught me some of my most valuable lessons about painting, both in watercolor and oil. The essence of a work must be determined at the start. I have learned to be much more direct and concise in my decision making and application of brushstrokes. In watercolor there are few opportunities to fix mistakes, so one must be confident, if not downright fearless. As watercolor artists, we jump in with both feet and then spend the rest of the time getting out of our own way. ▪

FALLS, LAKE TAHOE   *2023, watercolor on paper, 13 × 9.25 inches*

When I travel, most of the space in my suitcase is devoted to painting supplies. Depending on the destination, I will take one of two different art tote bags that fit into my suitcase. The larger one holds a folding easel, standard palette, paper, and brushes. The optional smaller bag holds a wallet-sized palette and postcard-size paper. The goal is to make getting around as easy as possible.

When I go out to paint by myself, I look for a shady out of the way place where I won't attract an audience. I know many people are curious about watching a painter at work, including myself. However, I just don't want to be the one putting on the show. The optimal location for me is standing against a wall or tree, so no one can be looking over my shoulder, taking photos and crunching on potato chips.

For me it doesn't really matter where I paint. It can be watching the ferry in Stockholm or overlooking the street from my studio window. Every location and day offers something new, with different color, light, energy, and people. Each excursion is a new experiment, the chance to discover how light influences form, color, composition, movement, and shape. For me, a plein air study is a success if, in the process, I learned something useful that I can employ going forward in my studio. Each discovery we make is a step toward the ultimate goal of artistic expression. ■

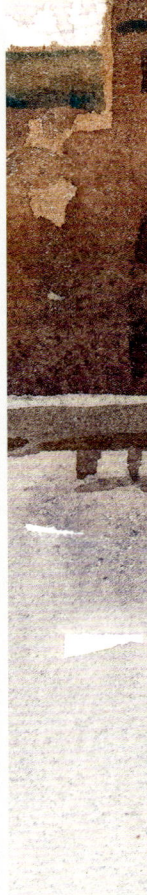

STOCKHOLM FERRY   *2023, watercolor on paper, 5.5 × 7 inches*

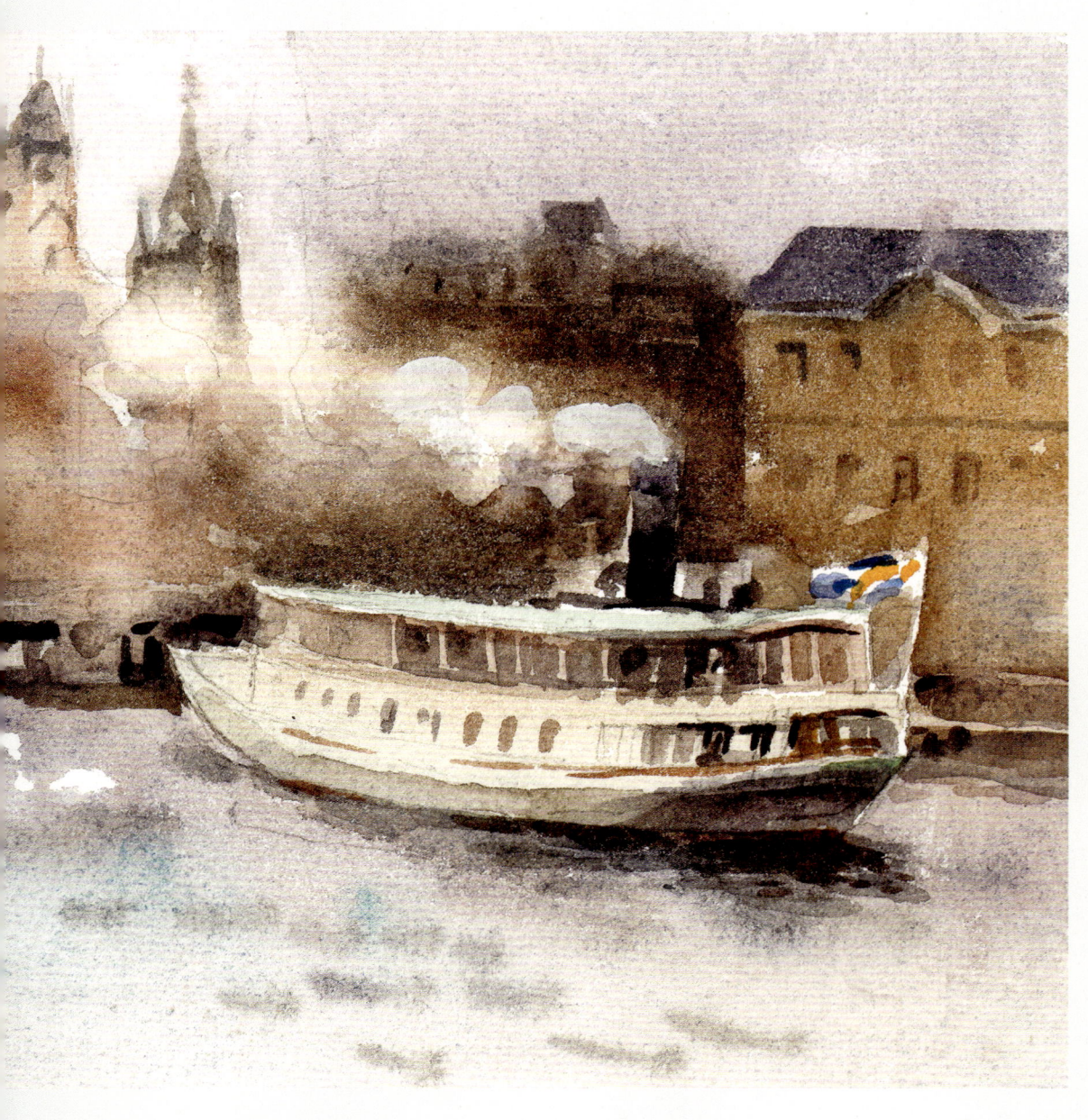

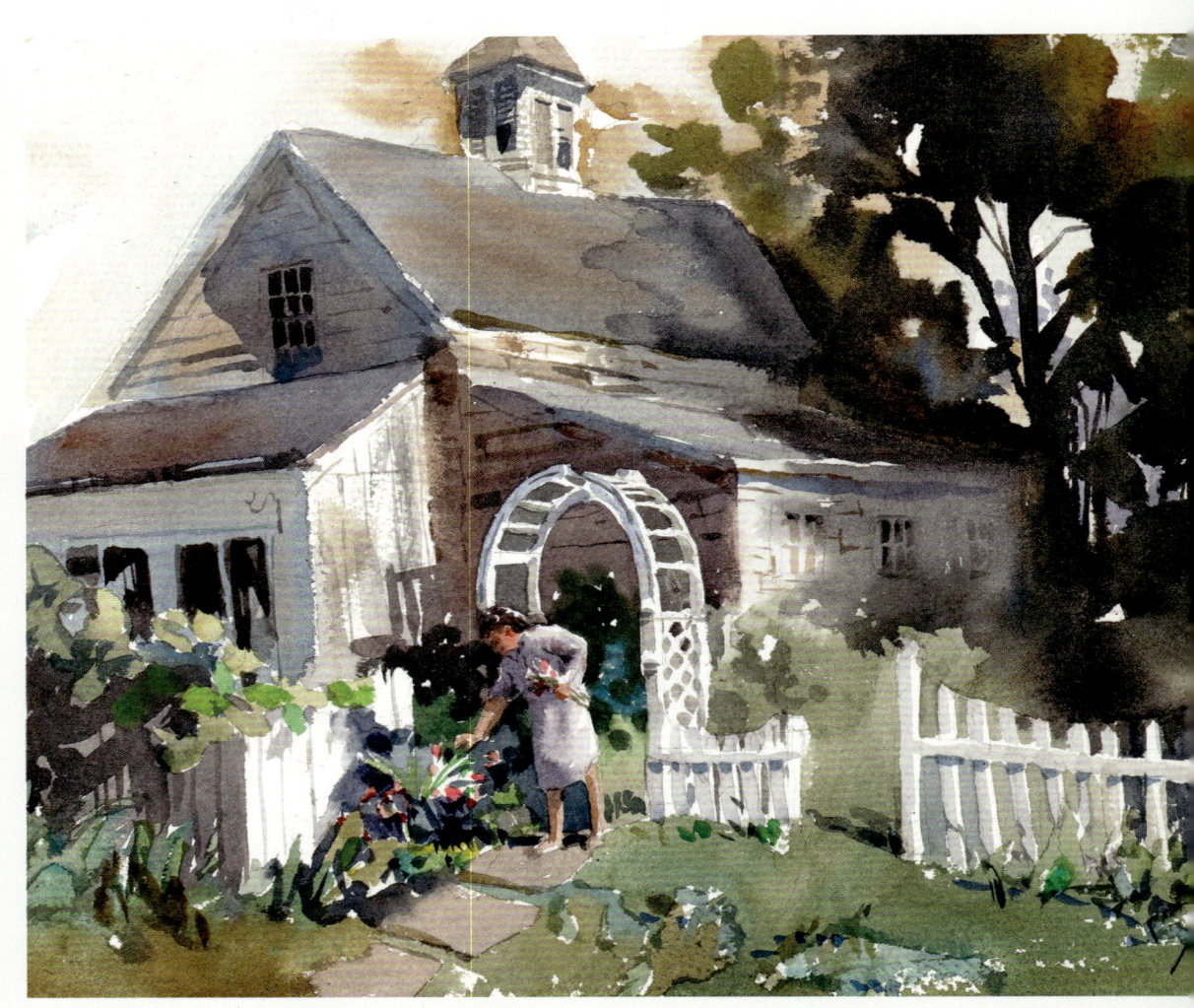

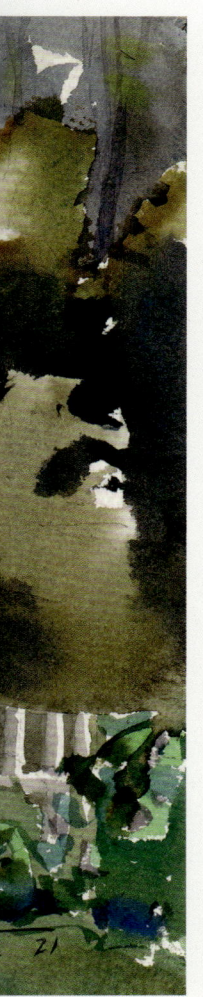

New England is one of my most favored summertime destinations, if not for the lobster rolls and the sunsets, then for the chance to paint the rocky coastline and small fishing villages. For over twenty years I have returned biannually to teach on Cape Cod, accompanied by my friend Carol, who serves as chief navigator, fun concierge, and, if need be, model. She isn't the only one of my friends who has been pressed into service to satisfy a creative whim. Many of my friends and family have been cajoled on the spot into modeling for me: Betsy, Tim, Bob, Aunt Connie, Sarah, Charlie, Arnie, Tracy, Donna, Susannah, Sharon, Lily, Diamond, Annabelle, Raymond, Jennifer, and countless others.

I prefer to plan the model's pose and costume in advance, although location, the person's demeanor, and lighting may necessitate a change to accomplish the desired feeling. Scavenging through thrift stores frequently turns up interesting clothing or props that can further an idea. Sometimes a perfect background will arise seemingly out of nowhere, with the only thing needed being the immediate addition of a willing figure. Once, I was late to an out-of-town birthday party in my honor because the sunlight coming through the lace curtains in the hotel room was too good to pass up. I rushed down the hall to Donna's room, dragging her back to my suite to pose nude in the waning light. One time Carol came to visit, only to spend hours sitting on the edge of the bathtub while I sketched her. For one of my children's books, I coerced my neighbors to dress up as scarecrows in formal attire and to waltz in a nearby field.

Somehow my friends are still willing to take a chance and go for a walk with me, well aware that at any moment I might beg them to pose by a white picket fence.▪

MAINE GARDEN   *2021, watercolor on paper, 9 × 14 inches*

Summertime offers the perfect opportunity to be outside to sketch or paint in one's own neighborhood. Home isn't far away, the terrain is familiar, and traveling on foot decelerates the whole experience to one that is more intimate, immersive, and contemplative. When we slow down, we see and experience things that we might otherwise miss. Our senses come to the fore, and busy, analytical thoughts are forced to recede.

I've discovered that no matter where I stop to paint, life happens by. It might be a dog trotting down the street, or a teenager on a skateboard that I decide to add to my composition. Once, when I was painting on Church Street in Charleston, my friend Jamee sailed by on her bicycle, her black cape billowing behind her. I called out for her to come back and convinced her to pose for a few minutes so that I could add her into the picture.

Another time, while painting an 1800s plantation-style house on Montagu Street, the owner spotted me and walked over and asked if I would like a tour of his home. I was delighted with the offer, but explained I needed to finish my painting before the light

6 MONTAGU   *2023, watercolor on paper, 14 × 10.5 inches*

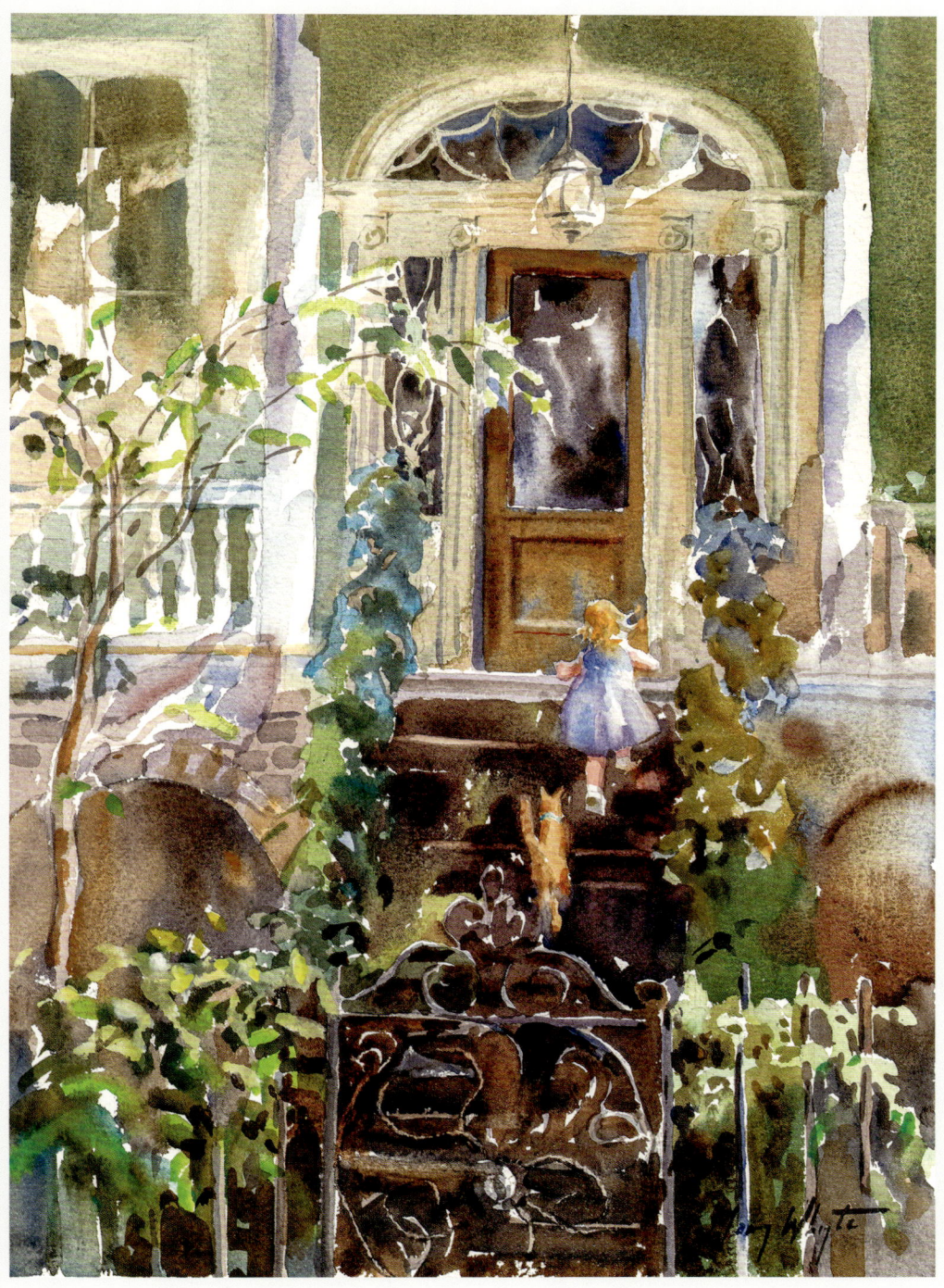

"I've discovered that no matter where I stop to paint, life happens by."

changed. He said to knock when I was done. As I watched him walk up the front steps to his home, his orange cat scampered up behind him. Just a few minutes later, a little blonde girl in a blue dress came skipping down the street. I was enchanted by her, too, so I included both the little girl and the cat in the painting.

Life happens by indeed, especially when painting out of doors. So do challenges. I have been confronted with bad weather, mosquitoes, swarms of bees, crowds of tourists, stalled trash trucks, and a dog mistaking my easel for a fire hydrant. I've accidentally dropped a favorite brush and watched it float downriver, had sea gulls carry off my lunch, and had a watercolor left drying on a nearby picnic table used as a placemat. Ask any plein air painter and they will tell you stories. My stories started when I was a teenager.

When I was eighteen, I climbed over a fence to a field overlooking a dairy farm. At the very top of the hill was an apple tree, ideal for shade from the bright sun, and, since there wasn't a soul in sight, the whole scenario held the ingredients for a perfect afternoon of painting. When I was halfway through my watercolor, a bell clanged in the barn, and a slow stream of cows came lumbering out of the building and started making their way slowly up the hill. As soon as the cows spotted me, they raced in my direction. Not knowing whether I might

be trampled, I grabbed as much of my gear as I could and scrambled up the tree. The farmer must have seen the circle of cows staring up into the tree, and my legs hanging down, because the bell sounded again and the cows turned and headed back to the barn. I quickly clambered down and, as fast as I could, ran to the edge of the field and jumped back over the fence.

Painting outdoors has encouraged a few other uninvited visitors as well. A few years later, when I was an art student in Rome, I frequently painted in city parks. I usually sat on the ground, careful to keep my wallet and bag securely tucked under my legs. One afternoon two women dressed in full skirts, fringed shawls, and gold bangles swayed over to me and sat down, one on each side. The older one motioned to my painting, crooning "Que bella," as the one on the other side snatched my wallet from under me, quickly shoving it under her skirt. I shouted at her, "Give me back my wallet!" She motioned that she didn't understand English. I screamed at her again. She glanced around the park, then shrugged her shoulders. Surely, I thought, she would understand a simpler language, so I showed my teeth and roared as loud as I could like a lion, inches from her face, reaching under her skirt and grabbing back my wallet. Both women froze, wide-eyed, mouths open. For a second none of us moved and I thought we might burst out laughing. Instead, the woman who'd grabbed my wallet leaned forward and made a fierce roaring sound back at me, before the two ran off.

Sometimes the unexpected produces a positive result. Once, on a painting trip to the California coast, I was able to find a secluded beach near Laguna where I could stand my portable easel on the jagged rocks to paint the water and sea foam swirling around me. Tiny shorebirds on spindly legs joined me, skittering across the rocks.

I heard it before I saw it. I was painting with my back to the horizon when I turned just in time to see an enormous rogue wave coming at me. I held my breath, grabbing my easel and supplies, and crouched low to hold on just as the wave slammed into the rock and crested high over my head, obliterating the light. A moment later I stood up and was surprised to see I was still holding everything. When I looked at my wet watercolor, I could see that the salt water had imparted a beautiful texture to parts of the painting. I have since duplicated that effect several times in my studio using sprinkles of salt and a spray mister. ∎

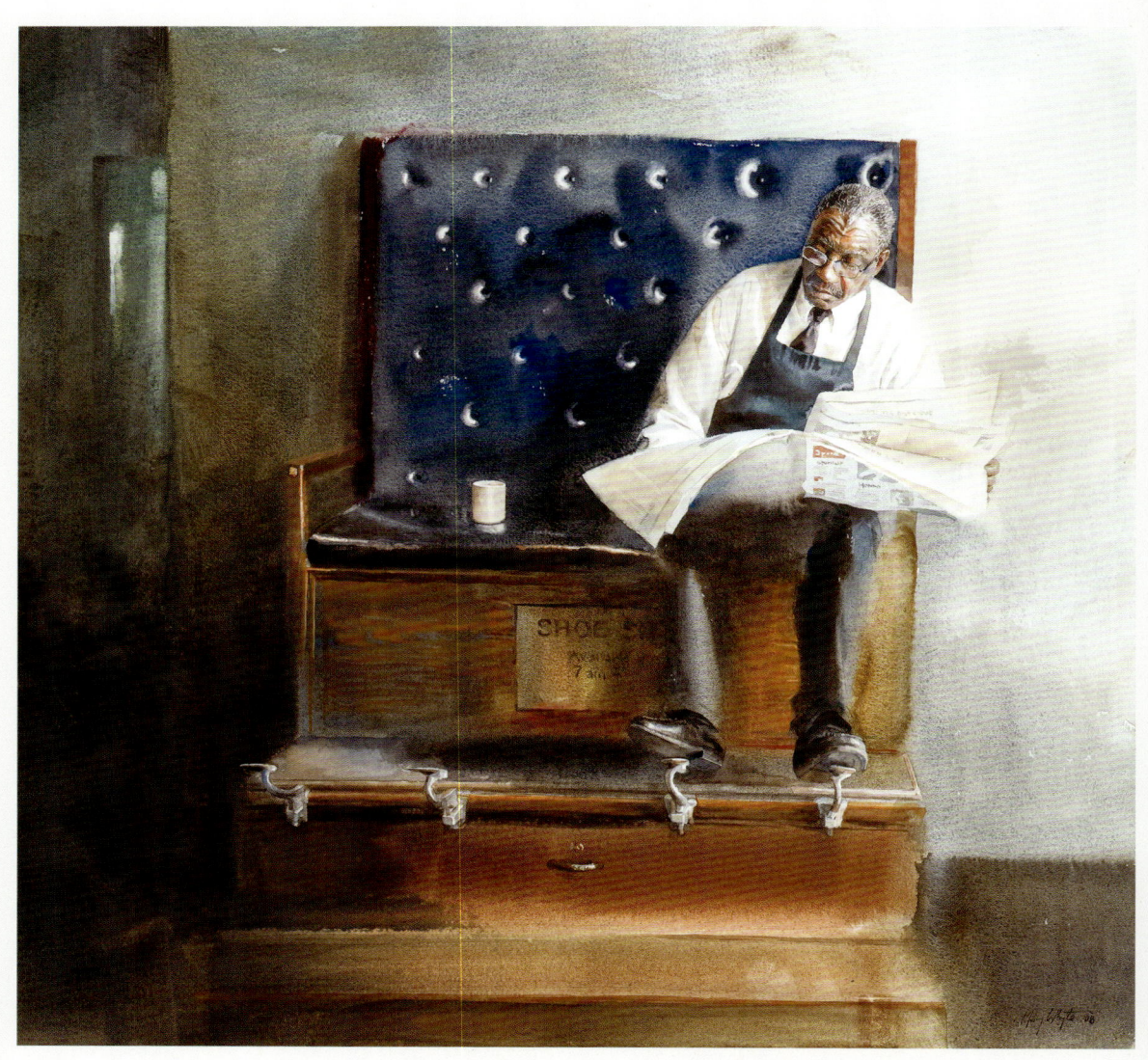

One of my favorite places to paint plein air will always be New Orleans. The Big Easy is just that, especially for artists. A city of human theater, its "anything goes" attitude makes it the perfect place to set up anywhere and at any time to paint. I've painted in dark, crowded night clubs, alongside mime performers on Bourbon Street, and in busy outdoor cafes such as Cafe Du Monde (*The News at Cafe Du Monde*) without anyone ever asking me to move or leave.

At one of the huge hotels on Canal Street I met Noah, then in his seventies, who had been shining shoes since he was five years old. It was midweek and business was slow, so Noah was a willing subject. I set up my easel next to his stand where he stored his polish, rags, and brushes. Streams of conference attendees and tourists moved past me as I sketched him reading the newspaper in his black apron and perfectly pressed white shirt. A few passersby paused to glance at my painting but most just stepped around me, eyes on their cellphones. One man patted me on the back and handed me a dollar bill.

I have found that most people are respectful of an artist at work, at times even protective. When I was in Stockton, California, I got permission to paint in the city's homeless shelter. The cafeteria was the size of a basketball court, with long tables set up, each with ten or twenty people eating lunch. I set up my easel near the middle of the room, and within minutes several of the men had designated themselves in charge, creating a barricade of folding chairs around me, and holding their arms out like traffic cops. "She's an artist," they announced, preventing anyone from getting too close. "She's working." For the rest of the afternoon, I was able to paint without interruption. Guardian angels come in many forms.∎

SHOE SHINE   *2008, watercolor on paper, 25.25 × 23 inches*

Several years ago I made a special trip to the Midwest. After picking up the rental car at the Kansas City airport, I unfolded the map of the state and spread it out across the steering wheel. Moving my fingers along the straight lines that indicated counties and highways, I finally located Lebanon, Kansas, the exact geographic center of the United States. I was on a self-assigned mission to discover and paint the folks of "Middle America," the very heartbeat of our country. I had five days to find them.

In Mankato, a town east of Lebanon, there was one main grocery store, two diners, a few shops on the main street, and a Sinclair station where the owner himself pumped the gas and did most of the auto repairs (*Kansas*). After I had been in Mankato several days, I drove out to the station and found Lloyd in stained overalls, standing under a lift and reaching up to the underbelly of a rusted Ford.

"Do you know where I can find the Red Rooster Cafe?" I asked, coming around

RED ROOSTER CAFÉ   *2021, watercolor on paper, 24 × 31 inches*

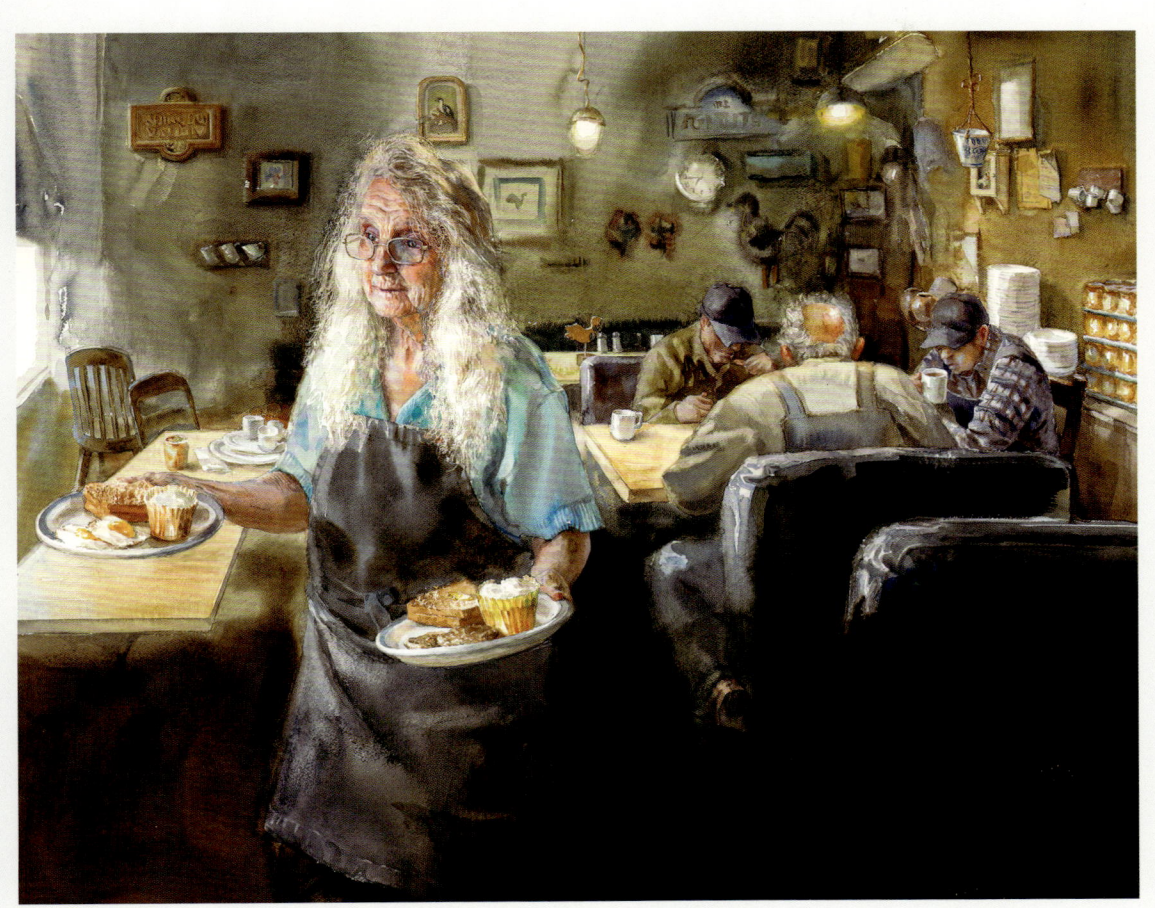

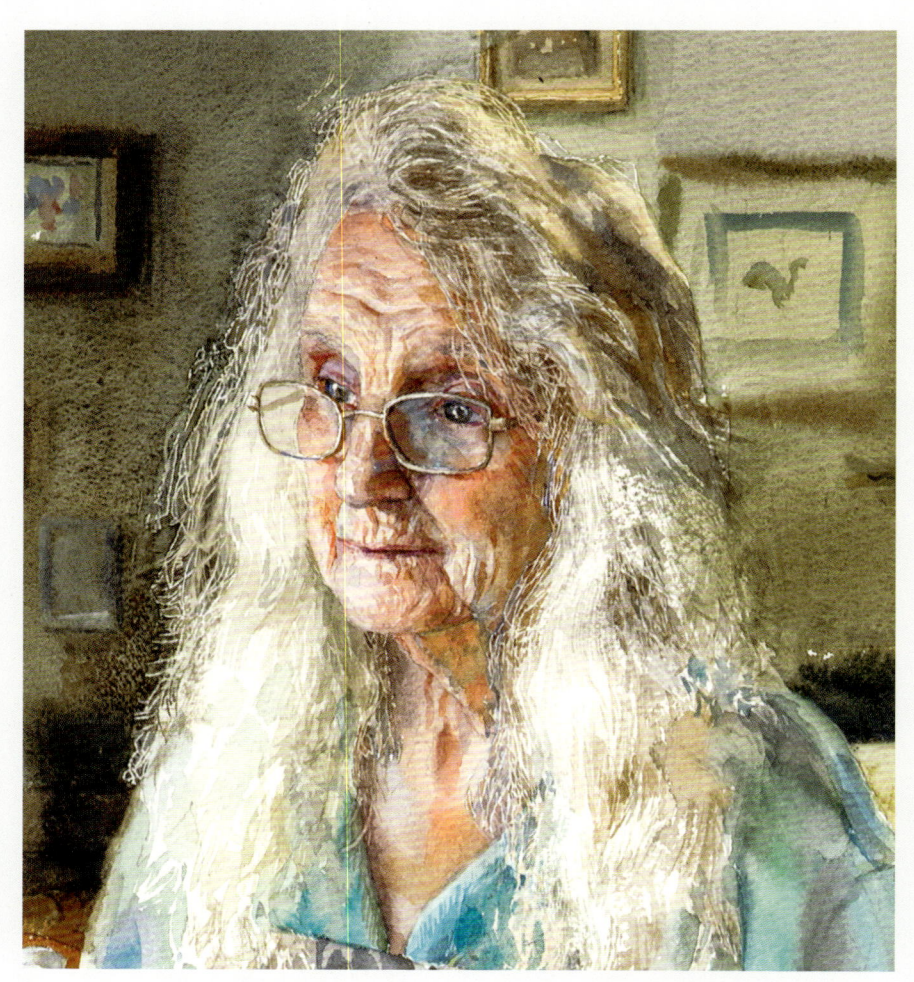

to the side and bending down so he could see me. Earlier that morning I had spotted a small handmade sign that was placed in the center of the town's intersection. It read *Monday Nite Special: Meatloaf & Two Sides $8.95.*

Lloyd motioned south down the highway with his wrench, and said I would find the diner behind some parked trailer trucks. "Can't miss it. Best breakfast around. Biscuits and gravy, waffles, chicken fried steak, whatever you want."

The owner of the Red Rooster Cafe was Avis Isaac, who'd spent decades serving breakfast, lunch, and dinner. At eighty years old she was still getting in before sunup to fire up the grill and start the bacon. That morning there were four men seated at a table near the kitchen, hunched over their cups of coffee, empty plates pushed aside, ball cap brims pulled low over their eyes. I slid into the corner booth and opened the menu.

The men's voices lowered as they brought their heads closer together. Occasionally one would steal a glance in my direction. More discussion. I studied the menu, holding it higher, in front of my face. Scrambled eggs, toast, coffee . . .

"You new here, aren't yeh?" one said, swinging his arm over the back of the chair and turning toward me. "Aren't you the storyteller?"

Word travels fast in a small town, especially when you don't live there. I smiled. "I guess that would be me," I replied, holding up my sketchbook.

"Yep," he said, "We heard you was in town. And that you was real tall."

After a while the men pushed their chairs back and rose to leave, giving a half wave to Avis, who was putting pies into the display case. As the bell on the door jingled behind the foursome, the one who had spoken to me turned back and nodded, touching the brim of his cap. ▪

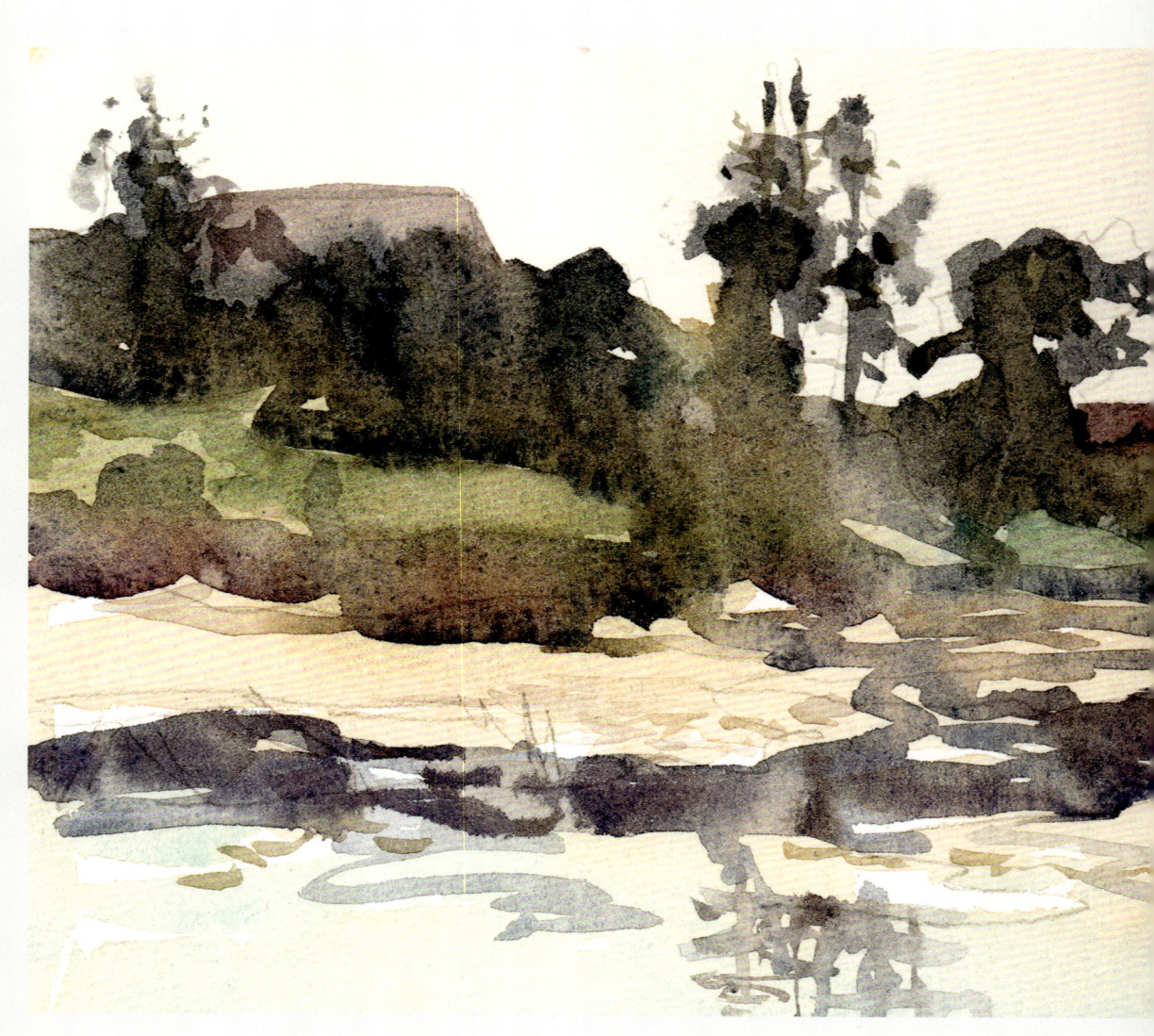

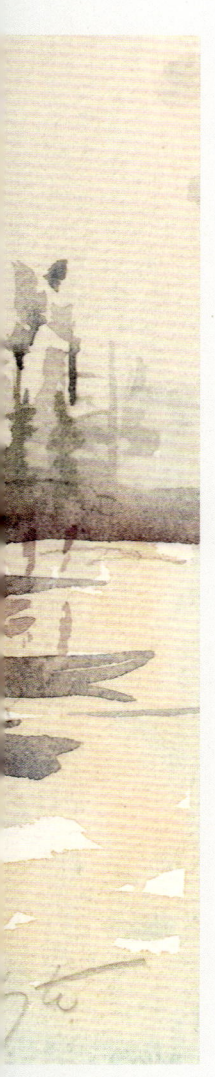

Generally, I prefer the solitude of painting alone so that I can choose my location and work at my own pace. However, for many years one of my best painting companions was my golden retriever, Boomer. He would accompany me on solo painting trips to Pennsylvania and Maine, always affable and eager, whether for a long drive in the car or an afternoon's painting excursion in a canoe. He was trained to lie completely still wherever I was painting, squeezing himself in between my feet and the easel, head on his paws, eyes open, ears and nose on full alert. He turned out to be a good taskmaster, reminding me to keep painting sessions short, preventing me from spending too much time on the painting and making it muddy by overworking it. When he sensed it was time to go, Boomer would let out several loud sighs. If that didn't work, he would groan. There were many times I should have listened to him and stopped working before I ruined the painting.

Boomer hated to be left behind and would let me know it. Often I would return home to find laundry strewn about or items removed from the waste basket, torn up and left by the studio door. He really got me back during a trip to Pennsylvania. I wanted to paint on a farm that had livestock and knew it might be risky to take a dog. I could feel his eyes on me as I closed the door behind me.

When I returned to the house I was relieved to see nothing was awry. Until I entered the room I used as a studio. On the floor, chewed and ripped into pieces, was a five-foot major watercolor I had just finished that morning. Boomer sat in the doorway.

I pointed to the painting. "You really thought it was that bad?"

I started the painting over the next morning and finished it two weeks later. It was better.∎

MAINE MIST   *2023, watercolor on paper, 5 × 7 inches*

The cell phone is always thrust into my face, just inches away. Behind it is a parent or grandparent, breathless and beaming, scrolling rapidly through images, zooming in, so I can't possibly miss any detail. "And she's only ten years old! Imagine! Such talent! Certainly, you must agree!" Whether by an enthusiastic relative or artists themselves, I am sometimes asked if I think a person has talent and is therefore likely to garner accolades and dazzle the art world.

Talent plays only a very small part in our potential. Being able to draw the likeness of a pear at a young age is not necessarily a harbinger of greatness to come. It is the gratification inspired by drawing a pear that leads to a desire to learn about perspective, light, form, color, technique, composition, and eventually to the ultimate goal of self-expression. Between talent and success is a lot of perseverance.

Talent is what they say you have only after you have done all the hard work. Often when people ask me to assess their talent, what they are really asking is if I think their effort will be worth it. Will spending money on classes, forsaking a steady income, and committing to years of practice guarantee success? Only the artist can decide whether the investment of time, education, and hard work will fulfill the need to create art. The artist plants the seed of possibility and then puts it into action. Future success is enhanced only by effort.■

CATHEDRAL HYDRANGEAS *2023, watercolor on paper, 15.5 × 13.5 inches*

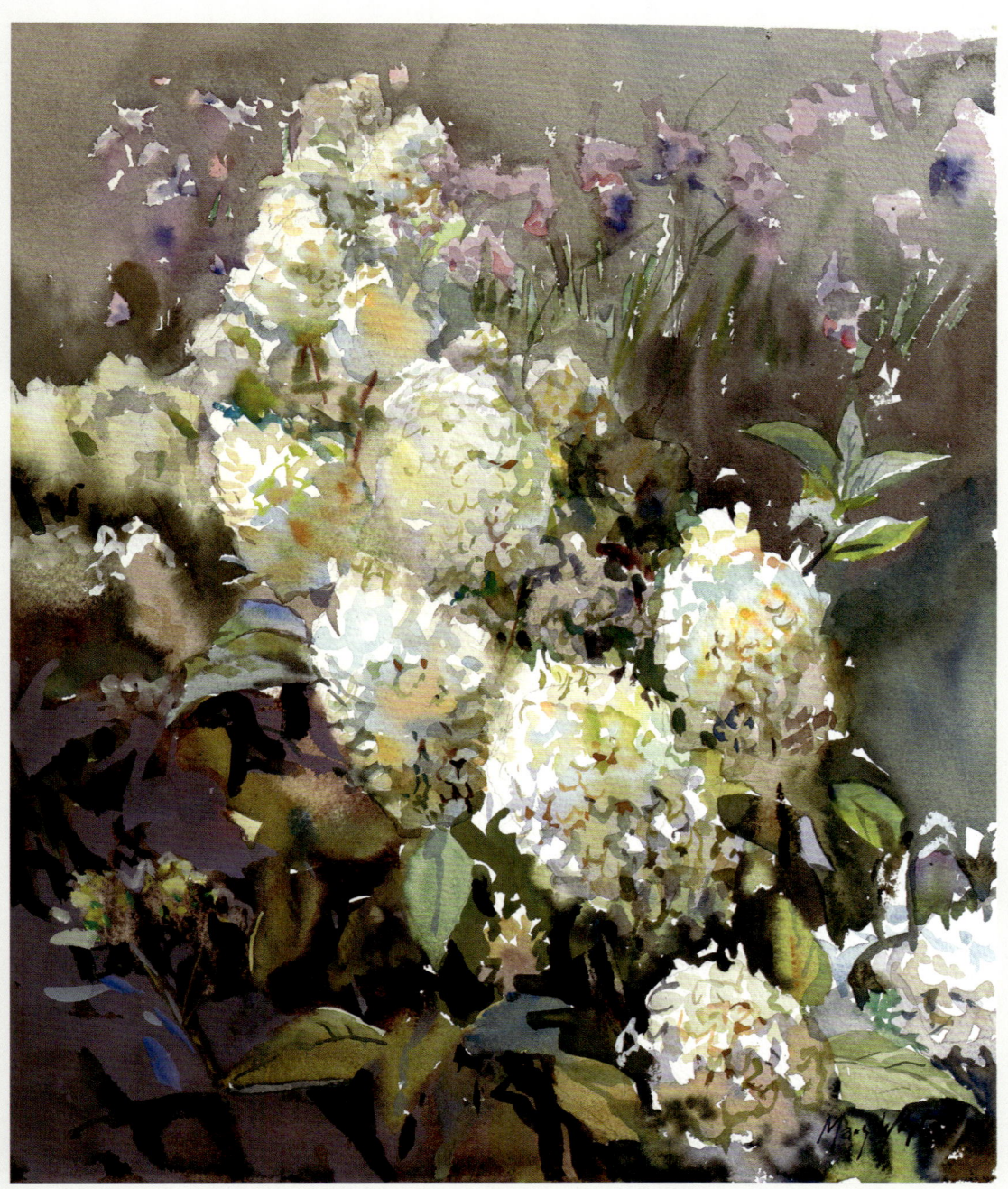

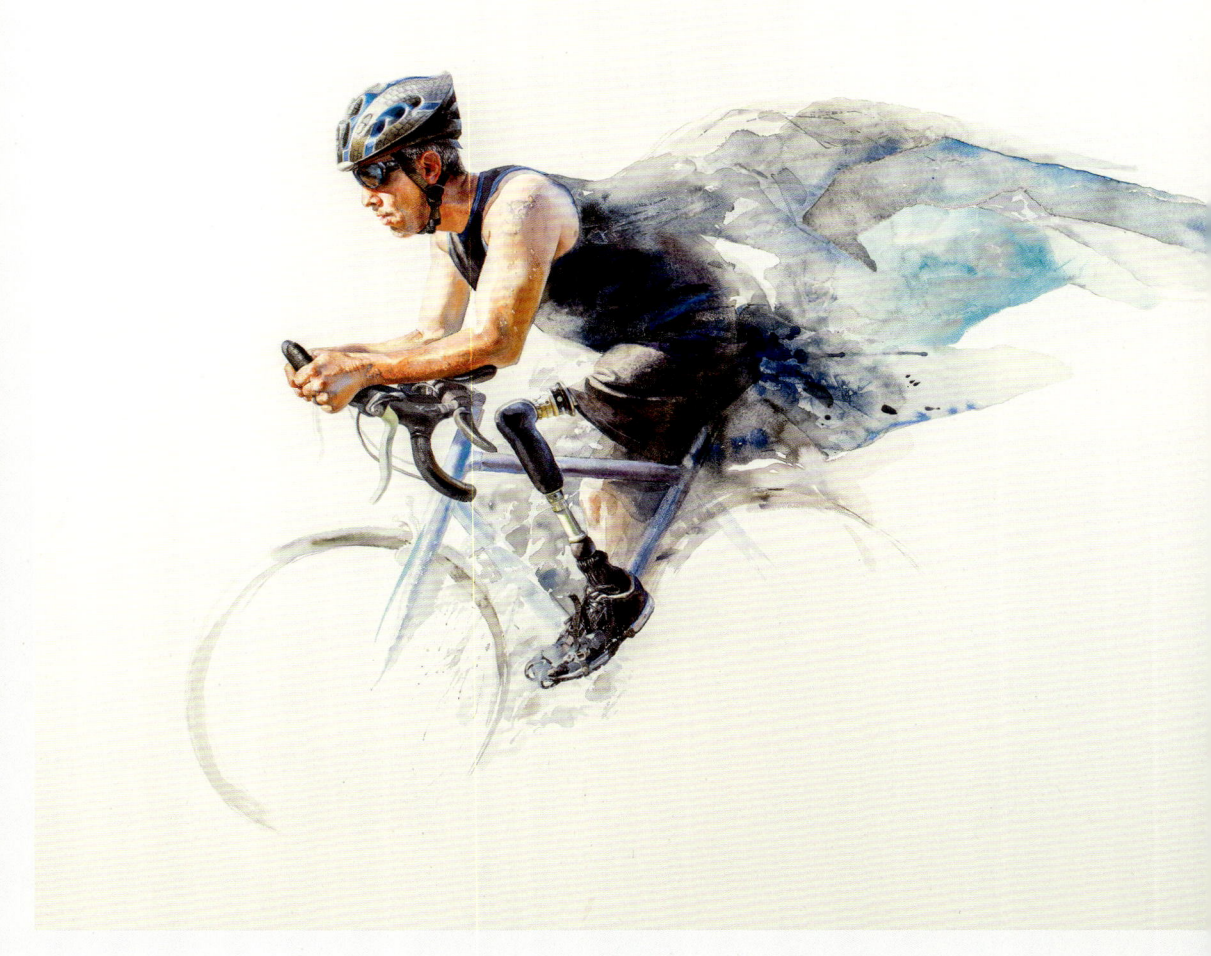

I've been absolutely terrified
every moment of my life and I
never let it keep me from doing
a single thing I wanted to do.

—GEORGIA O'KEEFFE

Many years ago a woman approached me at a conference and said, "I've been following you and your work for quite some time and have finally figured out the difference between you and me."

"Really?" I said. "Tell me."

"You're just braver," she replied.

There may be some truth to her observation, as bravery is often the only thing that stands between starting and accomplishment. Fear is the one thing that keeps many artists from realizing their best dreams, even more so than a perceived deficit of talent or opportunity.

ARCHANGEL   *2018, watercolor on paper, 39.375 × 58.375 inches*

"Fear is the one thing that keeps many artists from realizing their best dreams, even more so than a perceived deficit of talent or opportunity."

You may be afraid to begin a painting because you worry it won't turn out or that it won't be good enough to get into the local show. What if no one likes what you do, much less buy it. Perhaps your family feels you are wasting time and money. Maybe you are thinking you are too young and inexperienced to compete with the big guys. Or that you're too old and will never catch up and be as accomplished as your favorite artist. The voice in your head is saying, *Who am I to think I can even do this?* Until you change the audiotape in your head, every step you attempt moving forward will be hampered.

Several years ago, a friend of mine was fortunate enough to retire early. As a successful businessman, John had always dreamed of being an artist. When time off from his job permitted, he visited museums, collected art, read books on art history, and took classes. The day he retired fear set in.

"All these years I have been telling everyone I want to be an artist," John confided in me, "and now that I have the time, I am terrified that everyone will expect me to really be one."

For many artists, the thought that others will expect you to achieve a certain level of accomplishment can be paralyzing. My suggestion to John for moving forward was simple: "Just tell everyone you are an art *student*." It was an easy solution that immediately took the pressure off and gave John creative liberty. John was free to be an artist without worrying about the expectations of others. He could make art that was good or bad and in the meantime grow into his own brand of expression without fear that others might think he wasn't qualified to identify himself as a "real" artist. And grow he did. John Thompson is now represented in some of the country's finest art galleries and serves on the boards of several art and educational institutions.

The summer I graduated from art school, I experienced fear just as John did. I was finally away from school and free to work on my own, but I still heard the pedagogues in my head steering, influencing, and ultimately discounting my ideas.

For a while I tried working in ways that I thought would have found approval from my former instructors. I experimented with monotypes, oil paintings, acrylics, pastel, egg tempera, and charcoal. Although it was several years before I would gain the confidence and experience to express my own personal vision, little by little the work grew into what looked and felt more like me.

As an artist, getting past fear requires determination. If your idea and desire are important enough to you, you will find a way. As Vincent Van Gogh said, "If you hear a voice within you say 'you cannot paint' then by all means paint, and that voice will be silenced."

Creativity takes courage because it involves stepping away from what is familiar and doing something that is different. It means venturing into uncharted territory and making something that is completely new, unproven, and unfamiliar. The very concept of being creative means that you move past barriers and obstacles, all for the self-fulfilling purpose of doing more.

To be able to nurture your artistic vision, you must ignore the naysayers, whether they are real or imagined, and accept that criticism is part of the growth process. You must break away from the predictable pack, knowing that you will occasionally miss the mark and risk having to start all over again. You have to be willing to be the total amateur in the room, the last one picked for the team, or the one whose dog really ate their homework. In other words, as an artist you must be willing to accept the challenges and pitfalls that come with the territory and use them as fuel for moving forward and growing into your best work. Success and failure are the bookends of our lives. It's how we navigate through the middle that counts.■

> Don't think about making art,
> just get it done. Let everyone else
> decide if it's good or bad, whether
> they love it or hate it. While they
> are deciding, make even more art.
>
> —ANDY WARHOL

Criticism cannot be avoided when you put your art out into the world. All of us would prefer parade-worthy acclaim. However, no matter where you go, someone will have a negative opinion about you or your work that may be difficult or painful to hear. As a fellow artist once said to me, "I'm willing to receive harsh criticism, just as long as it comes in the form of overwhelming praise."

Although one cannot control criticism, as artists we can use it for our potential growth, while always remembering that negative comments are only one person's opinion—and sometimes come from a lack of knowledge, jealousy, or insecurity. Unfortunately, for many people one scorching review can diminish the glow of a hundred positive comments. To avoid that kind of emotional detour, I limit looking at reviews and try to avoid self-scrolling altogether.

Regardless, healthy criticism is well worth receiving, especially when it comes from a respected, more experienced peer or professional. Looking back over my career, there were a few artists that I wish I had asked for feedback; I didn't, because I felt intimidated by their stature in the art world. It is my loss. Through someone else's fresh and learned eyes, we can gain valuable feedback that may be otherwise hard to find. We don't have to accept another's observations, but we would be foolish not to listen.▪

ARCHWAY, ITALY   *2024, watercolor on paper, 13 × 10.5 inches*

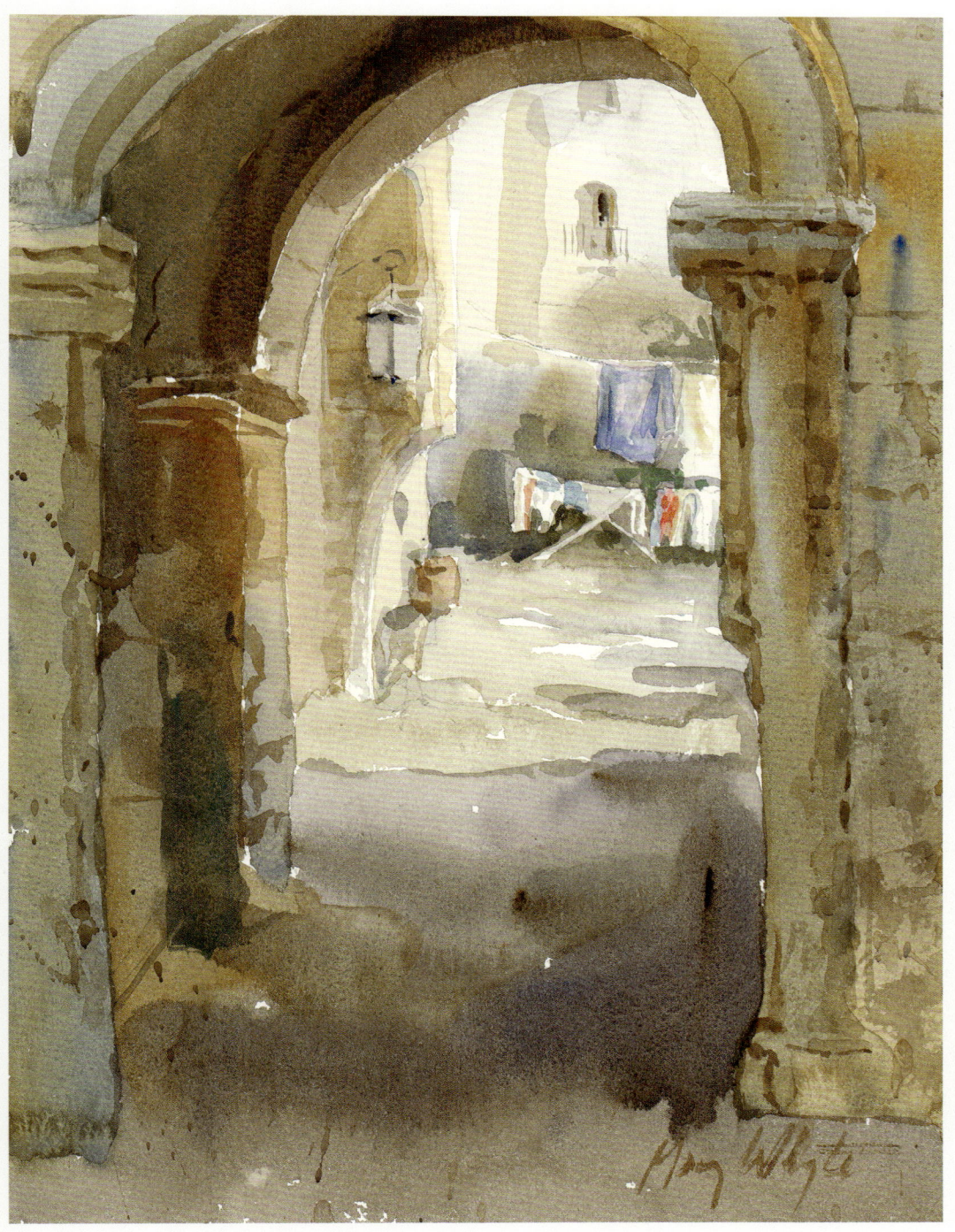

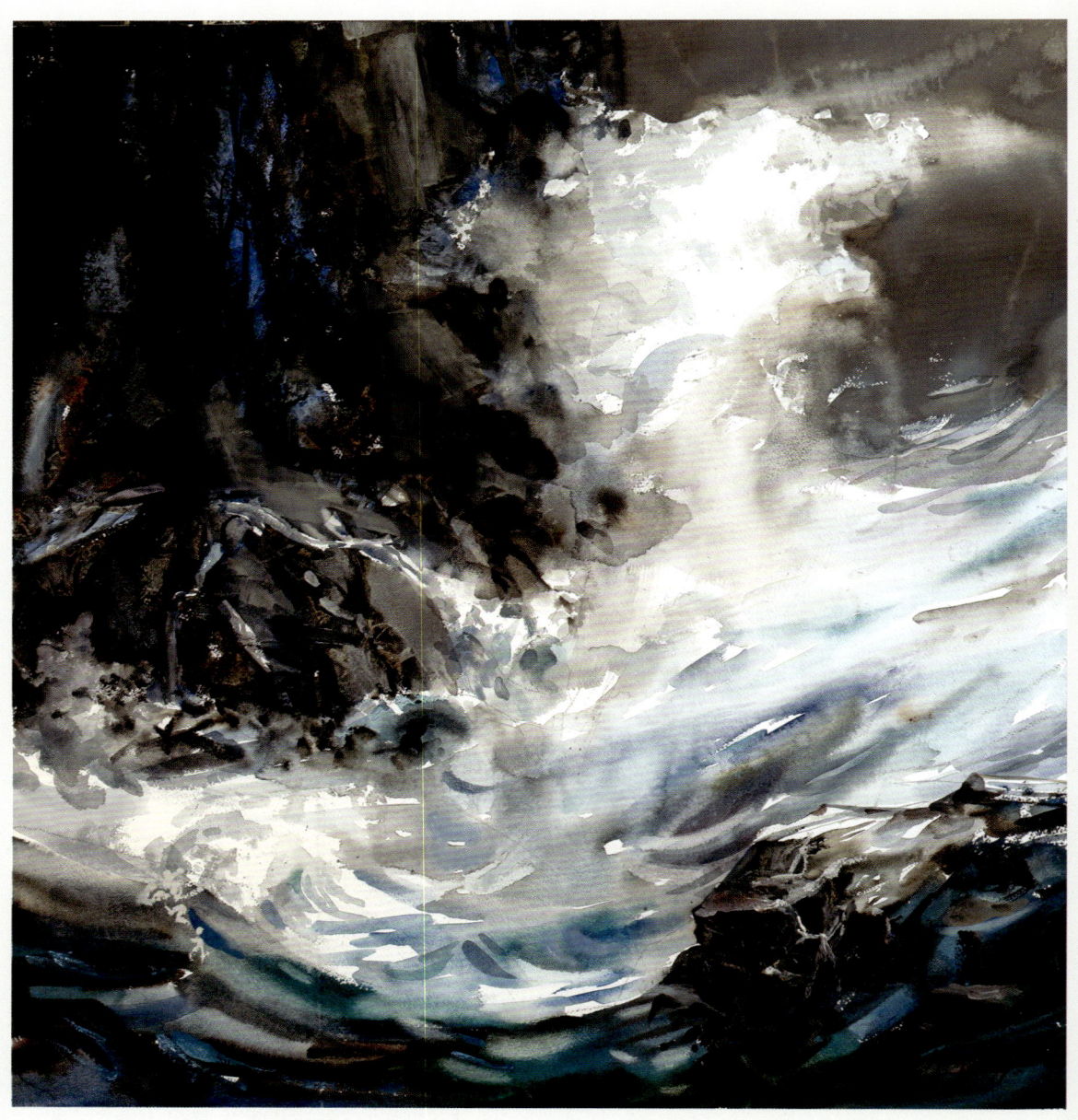

I am not afraid of storms, for I am
learning how to sail my ship.

—LOUISA MAY ALCOTT

Despite the challenges and failures life may throw an artist's way, favorable outcomes are possible, but they require strength of will. Artists such as Rembrandt, Van Gogh, Kahlo, and Picasso all produced some of their most profound work despite personal trials. Georgia O'Keefe acknowledged that all artists make bad work and encounter setbacks and that success comes only with time and persistence. As she told art historian Katherine Kuh, "Success doesn't come with painting one picture. It results from taking a certain line of action and staying with it."

The most important lessons I have learned as a painter haven't come from successes, but from colossal, crash-and-burn failures. Even with years of experience, many paintings end up in the trash. It's simply part of the process. Every failed attempt showed me something I needed to know going forward.

My friend Tom worked in risk management, selling insurance for most of his career. His personal mantra was "Every 'No' brings you closer to a 'Yes,'" a catchline I have adopted myself. I have since learned that every time a painting fails, a relationship ends, the sale falls through, or the dream is scuttled, there is the opportunity for something new and better. Going forward, I make every major failure the title of my next and best chapter, and every "no" the gateway to a "yes." ∎

CLIFFSIDE   *2023, watercolor on paper, 29 × 29 inches*

When I lived near Mennonite and Amish farms, one of my favorite events was the local county fair, which showcased hundreds of Amish quilts in spectacular colors and complicated patterns. Each quilt was made with tiny stitches that had required months of labor. Imperceptible to most people's eyes, each quilt included one imperfect stitch, the makers' way of acknowledging that only God is perfect.

Seeking perfection in one's life and art can be a recipe for frustration and disappointment. Aiming to create work that is without fault means constantly comparing and measuring yourself against the high-water mark already set by someone else. Unfortunately, the closer we get to another artist's level of perceived perfection, the more our work will look like theirs and less like ours. At some point we become stuck and cannot go any further in their steps; as Michelangelo said, "He who follows another will never overtake him."

I have seen too many students with potential give up because they fell into what I call the Pit of Perfectionism. In their mind their work fell short of their own impossibly high standards and will never measure up. Unfortunately, the goal of achieving perfection can itself become a repeating cycle of failure. Instead of pursuing what is exact, aim for what is expressive. Leaving work a little imperfect or a little messy can be the much-needed welcome for the spirit of humanity to step in. ▪

REMNANT   *2020, watercolor on paper, 23.75 × 21.75 inches*

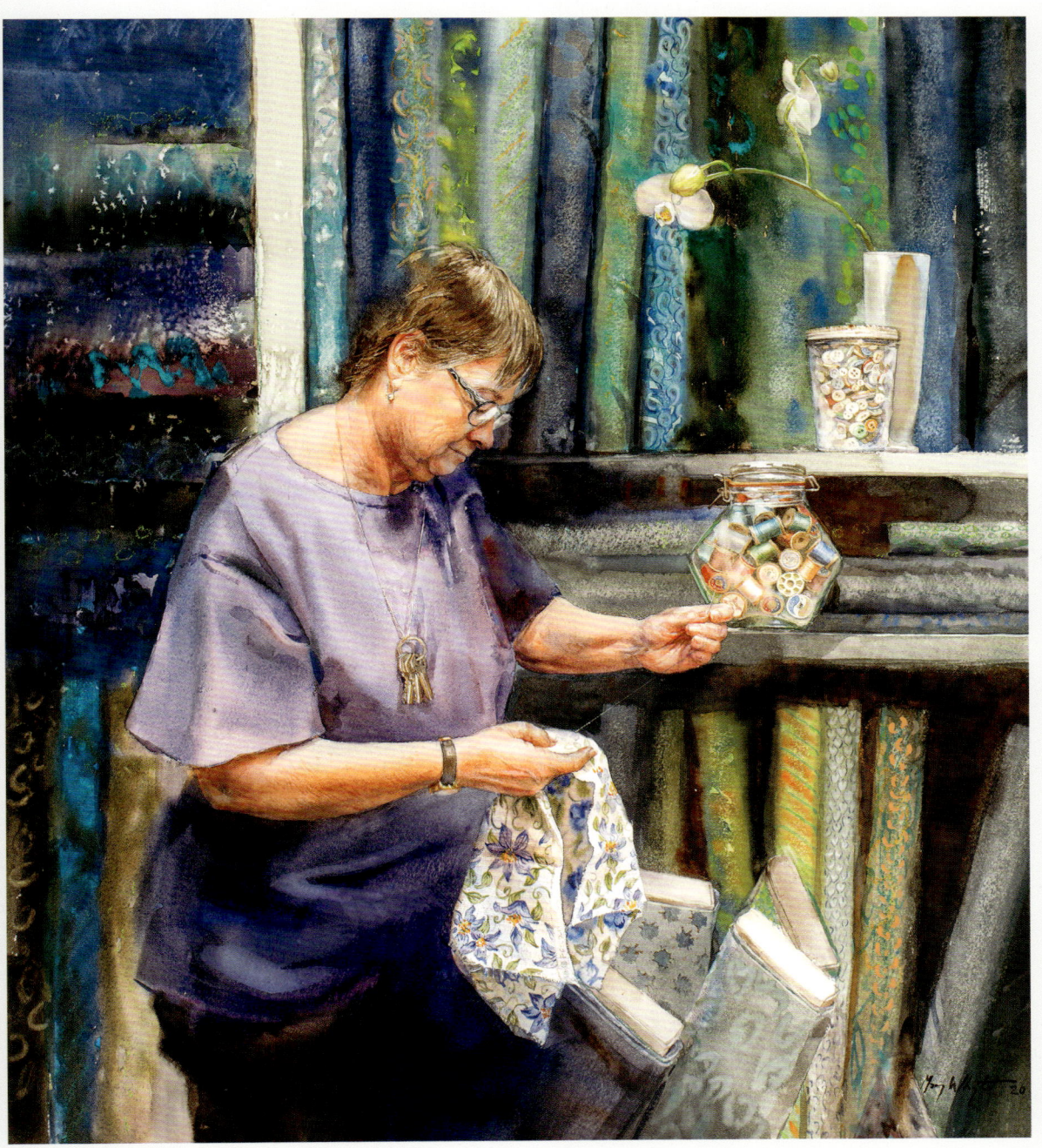

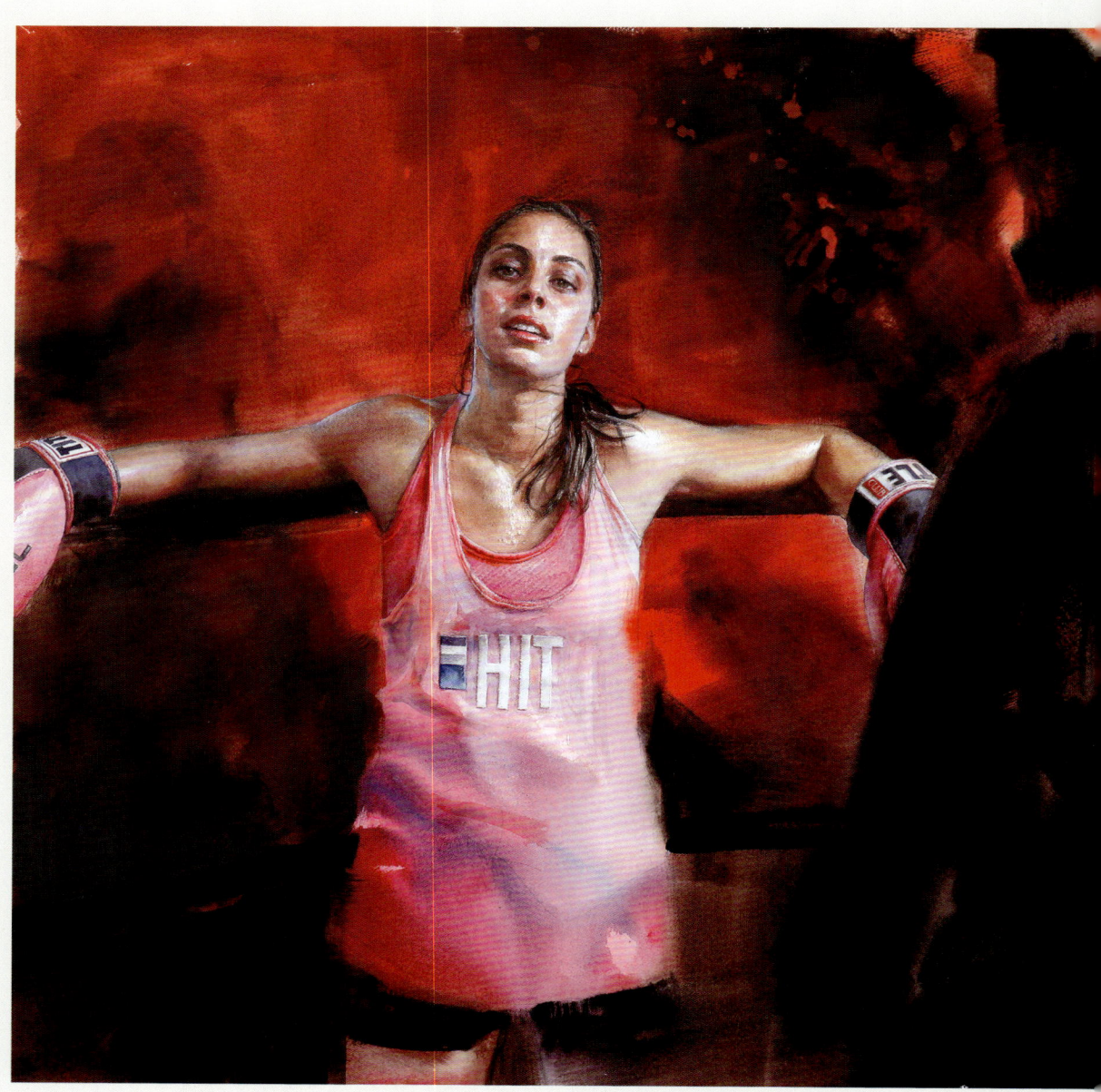

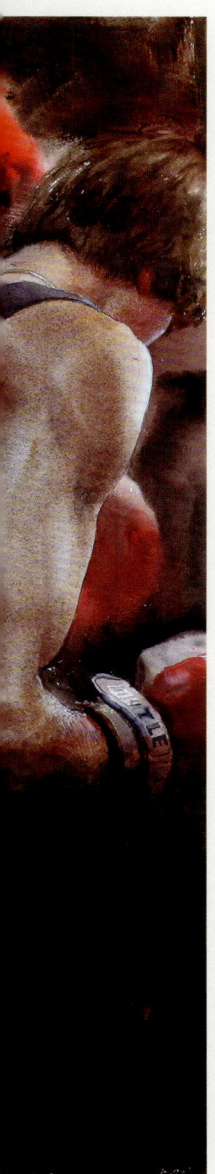

Wayne Gretzky, the former star ice hockey player and head coach, once said, "You miss 100 percent of the shots you don't take." His point is clear. When you make the attempt to accomplish anything you have at least a small success rate. If you don't try at all, you are guaranteed a 100 percent failure rate.

Fear can keep our best ideas locked in limbo, never to be realized. I remember a middle-aged student who showed me an idea for a children's book he had been writing and illustrating about a boy who ran away to join the circus. Certain his concept would be a phenomenal success, he told me the title of his story and handed me two beautiful watercolor illustrations.

"But," I said, turning the pages over to see if there was anything on the back, "Where's the rest of it? How does it end?"

"I don't know," he said. "I haven't done it yet."

When I saw him again several years later and inquired about the book, he admitted that he had stopped working on it and had put it aside.

You miss 100 percent of the shots you don't take.

For myself, the only paintings I regret were the ones I didn't do. They were the works I thought would require skills I didn't have. Sometimes I was afraid to ask a stranger if they would pose for me. Because of my lack of courage, who knows what I missed? Now, when presented with an opportunity I'm unsure of, I ask myself "Would I regret not having at least given it a try?" Since making the decision to be braver, my success rate has gone up considerably. ▪

ARMISTICE   *2014, watercolor on paper, 29 × 38 inches*

*"For myself, the only paintings
I regret were the ones I didn't do.
They were the works I thought
would require skills I didn't have."*

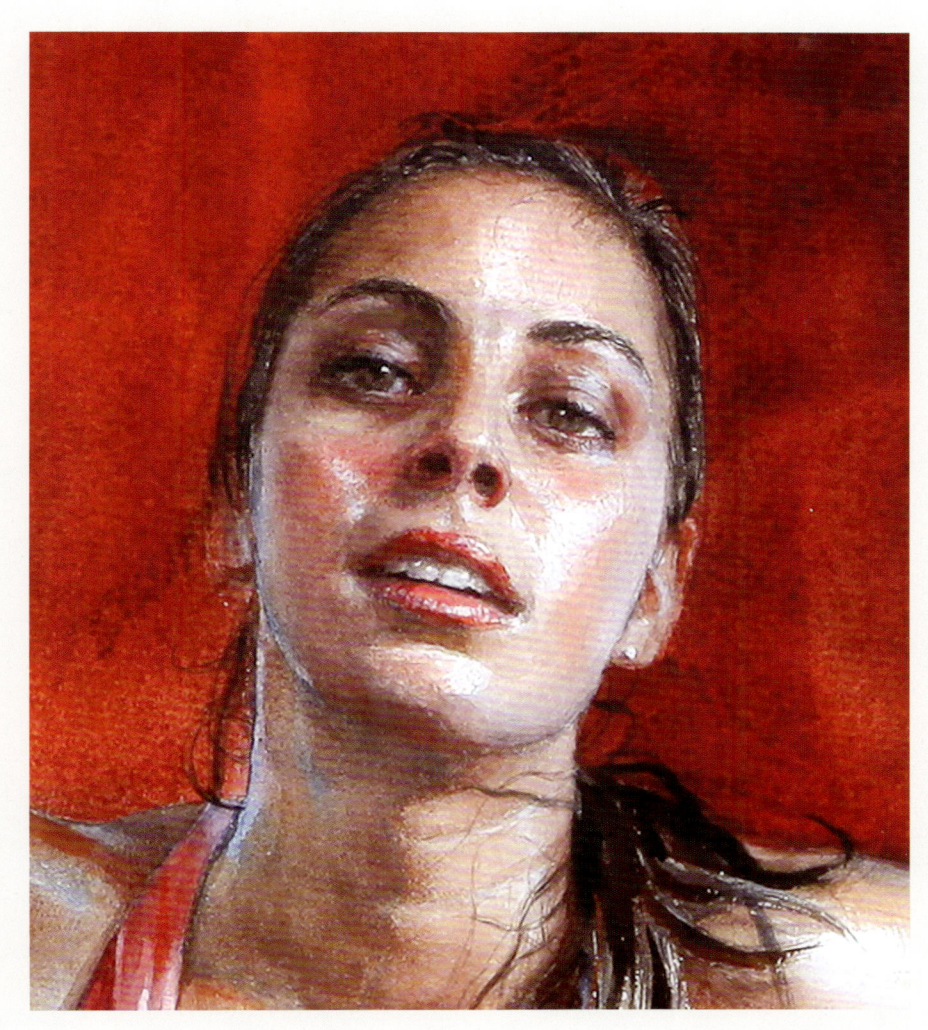

Staring at a blank canvas or paper while holding a paintbrush can be unsettling even for the most seasoned artists. Regardless, jumping into the abyss is what we were created to do. Although frightening at times, these plunges into unchartered territory can lead to some of our biggest breakthroughs.

When people ask me what my next painting is, I often say I have no idea, but that I'm really excited about it. Many of my paintings begin as a glimmer of an idea drawn on cheap typing paper. Sometimes I'll fill entire pages with murky shapes, erasing parts, then cropping areas out, folding the paper, redrawing, and then tearing it up before moving on to the next one. There may be dozens of small, crumpled sketches strewn around the studio before the right image begins to come into view.

Other times an idea will plunk down right next to me. Literally. Once, when I was sketching in a diner, a group of burly construction workers straggled in and sat down in the booth across from me. They wore frayed bandanas and were covered in fierce tattoos and black soot. The possibility for a future painting was just too good to pass up. I got up, walked over, slid into the booth and introduced myself. Forks stopped midair. With a bit of convincing, my gumption paid off, transforming into the painting called *Fifteen Minute Break*.

The truth is, most artists will tell you they have no clue where their ideas come from, only that they'll be ready for them when they do. As artists we just keep showing up. On time. Every day. Just in case a good idea happens by. ▪

FIFTEEN MINUTE BREAK   *2008, watercolor on paper, 58 × 38.75 inches*

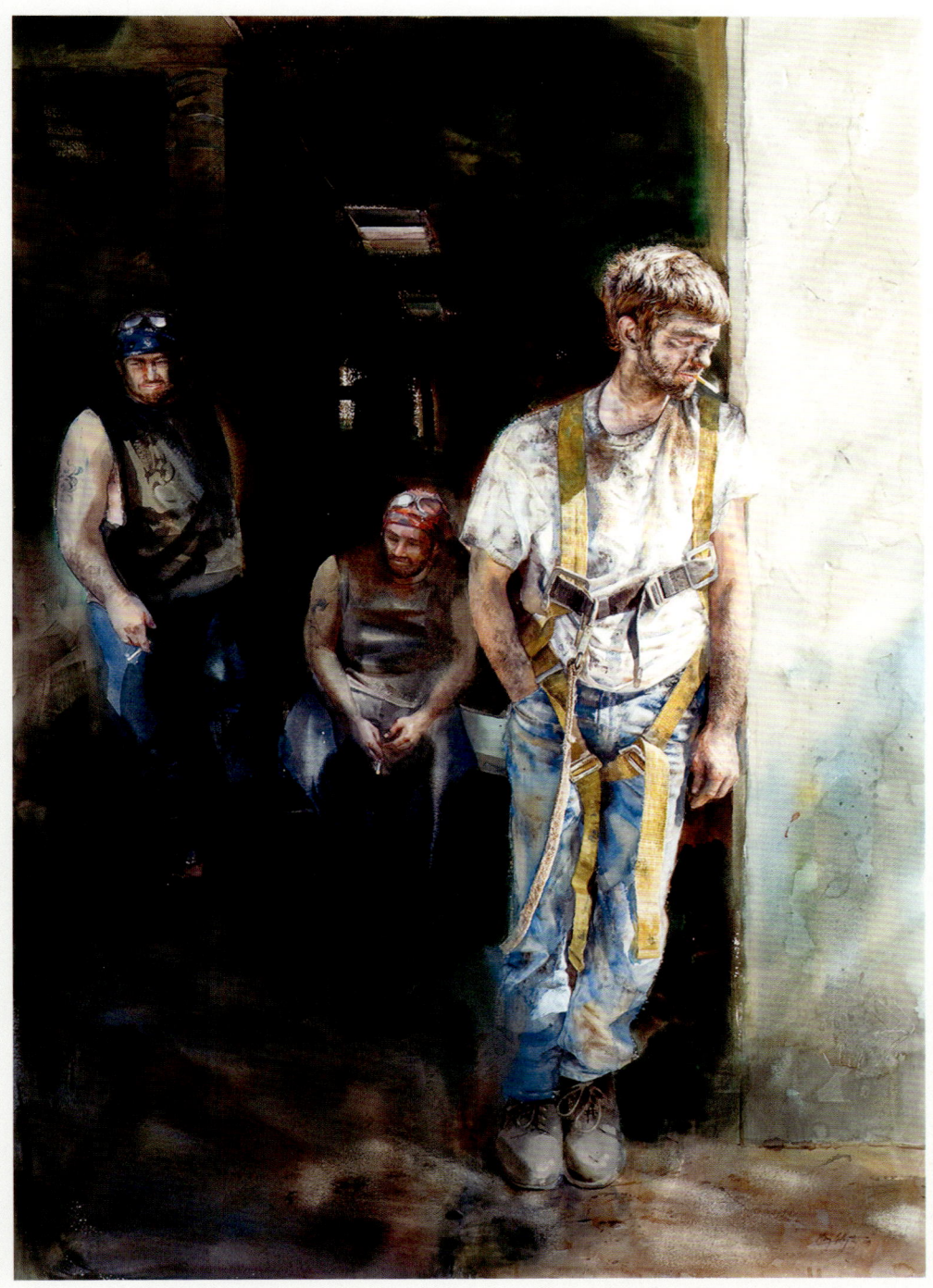

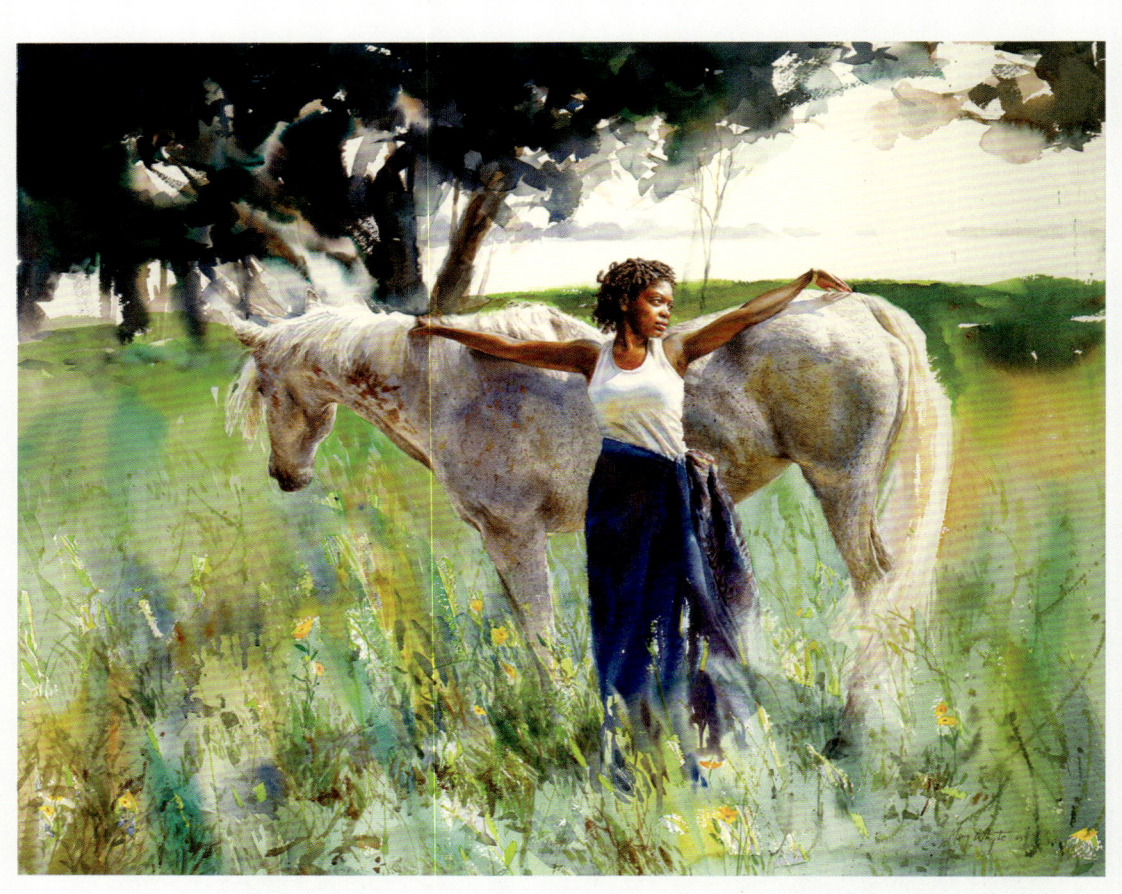

An artist need not travel far to find worthy subject matter. When I lived on Johns Island, I spent many years painting the landscape with its gnarled oak trees, tomato farms, and winding tidal creeks. The locals shrugged their shoulders at my enthusiasm for what they had known for generations, but were always amenable to letting me roam their fields and yards. When I first met this community, the people of Johns Island were shy, if not reluctant to pose for me. Yet after they saw portraits of themselves in books and magazines, the locals would sometimes appear wherever I was painting, idling their way, ever so nonchalantly, into my field of vision.

Tesha was always up for any idea I had for a painting, sometimes offering suggestions for unique settings herself, such as a hollow tree that she thought I would like, or a slow-moving marsh creek with a wide oyster bank. The best time for painting was early spring or summer, with the season's fullness of coreopsis, wisteria, and bee balm. In 2003, on the summer solstice, we led Rosie, an old training horse that belonged to my friend Marie, out into the field so that I could paint her as a backdrop to Tesha. It was a glorious June day, the air fragrant with honeysuckle. Far in the distance was a silver thread of the Bohicket River, and beyond that, Seabrook Island, where I maintained my studio for close to thirty years.

Over time my paintings of the people of Johns Island became even more personal. Friendships deepened. I found that the closer I stayed to home looking for subject matter, the more the watercolors *became* my home. The geographic perimeters of a small island community had expanded into a universe of expression. ∎

SUMMER SOLSTICE   *2003, watercolor on paper, 30 × 39 inches*

Fall

REACHING FOR SELF-EXPRESSION

A great flame follows a little spark.

—DANTE

Copying the work of the masters and practicing their techniques is part of the curriculum of many art schools. We are taught to study, emulate, and reflect. With enough time and practice, a proficiency of technique, concept, and composition is gained. Eventually, our work takes shape.

Most of what I have learned about painting results from study I did on my own. When I was in my twenties and thirties, there wasn't the smorgasbord of inexpensive or free online educational offerings we have today, and watercolor teachers capable of teaching a level higher than beginners seemed almost nonexistent. Taking an in-person class meant driving or flying to another state or country.

I spent a lot of time in libraries. Perusing the shelves of books about art, I discovered artists whose work had been previously unknown to me. Artists such as Anders Zorn, Henry Casselli, Childe Hassam, Maurice Prendergast, Gustav Klimt, and Edward Hopper would have a notable influence on my work. I already admired the watercolors of artists such as John Singer Sargent, Winslow Homer, and Andrew Wyeth.

For artists, learning never stops. No matter one's level of formal education, in the end, we learn more from our mistakes, experiments, and perseverance than we would from taking any art class. No art professor could have ever taught me how to express translucent steam rising from a pot of boiling water, the force of a wave slamming into a cliff, or the delight of a child twirling in her new dress. With persistence and determination, we become our own best teachers. ∎

EVOLUTION   *2016, watercolor on paper, 28.875 × 32.5 inches*

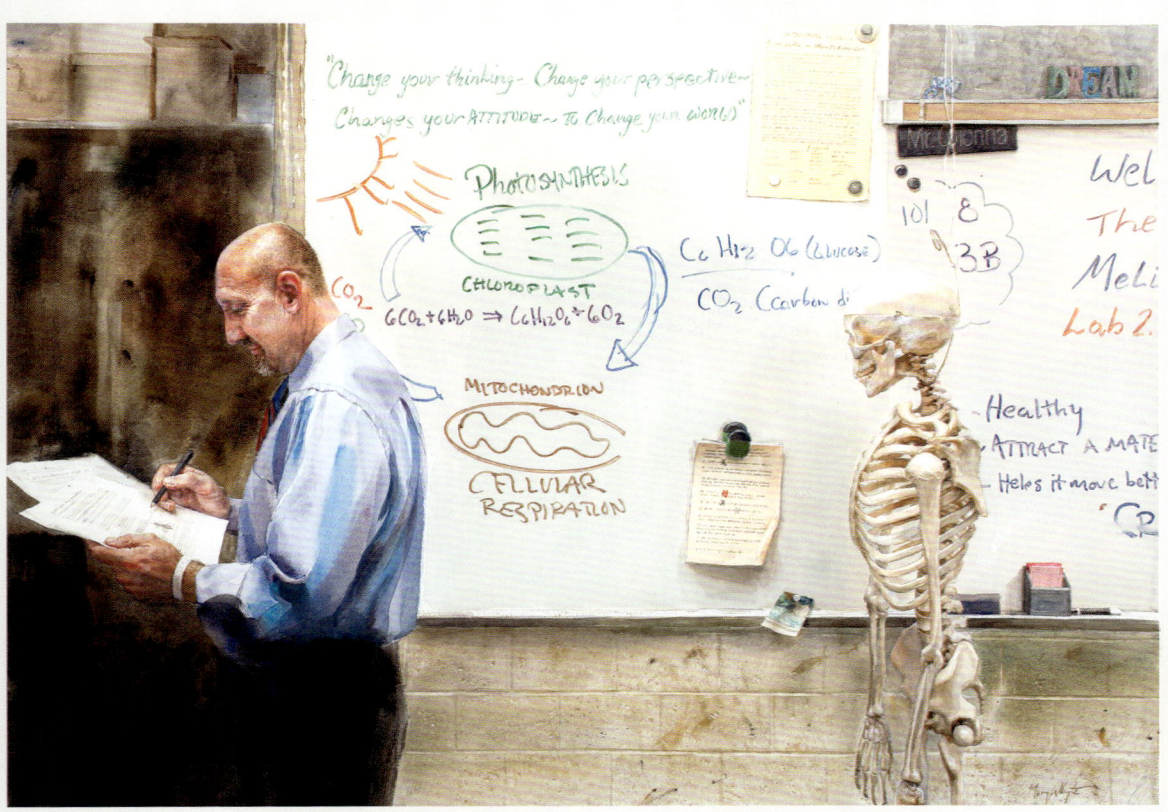

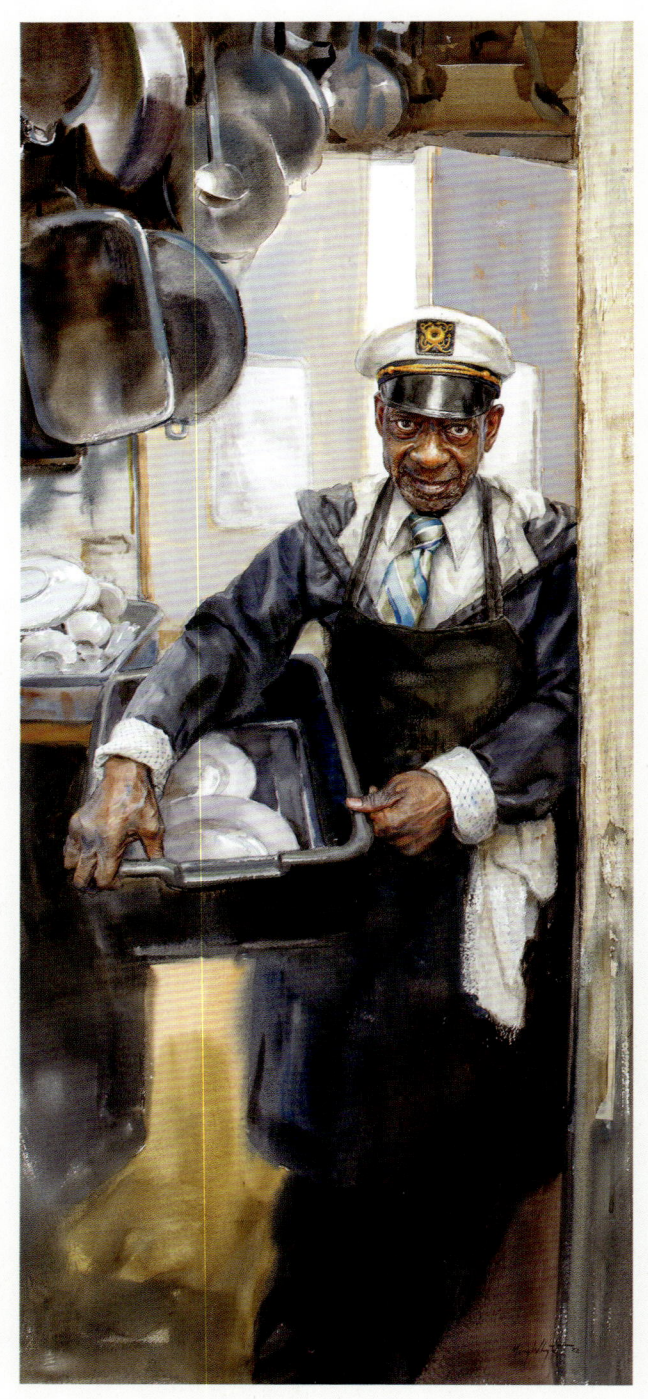

Professional ice-skaters make what they do look easy. In fact, anyone who is proficient at something makes what they do look effortless—as if, by chance, it just *happens*. No one is born with skill. It is gained through patience, determination, and practice. As famed football coach Vince Lombardi said, "The man on top of the mountain didn't fall there."

One day, looking out my studio window, I saw Sam. He was standing on the sidewalk, smartly dressed in a coat and tie and captain's hat, holding a wet dishrag. He had definitely caught my eye, and with a little sleuthing I learned that he was a dishwasher in a nearby restaurant. It was an intriguing idea for a painting I couldn't pass up.

Sam had been trained as a dishwasher in the Navy. Now in his seventies, his chosen work was still in the kitchen washing dishes. The fact that Sam had done this type of work for so long made him a dishwashing machine. He adeptly balanced heavy racks of clanking dishes on his shoulder and empty stew pots on his hip, evenly spinning between sinks and stacks of dirty glasses. Snapping the dishrag over his shoulder, and elbow-deep in suds, Sam proudly told me he was the best dishwasher who ever lived, and his captain's hat proved it.

Sam confirmed for me that whether it's dishwashing or painting, both time and practice are required to develop real skill and that aiming for excellence can be both painstaking and rewarding at the same time. Go Sam. ∎

CAPTAIN *2022, watercolor on paper, 57.5 × 26 inches*

Other than the investment of time, I believe there are two key components to becoming really good at something. One is skill and the other is passion. No matter what we seek to do well, whether it is golf, tango, speaking a new language, or playing the violin, we must first put in the necessary hours of training to become an expert. Getting up the learning curve can sometimes feel like a long slog. Not so if passion is involved. The road to mastery will seem easier and much more engaging if what we have chosen truly excites us and speaks to our heart.

As a portrait painter I am always interested in how my subjects ended up in their chosen profession. Surprisingly, many say it was by accident. Whether they are a doctor, farmer, accountant, or hair stylist, theirs is often a story of starting out in one direction and ending up going in another.

Somewhere along the way, they bumped into their passion.

Even artists are challenged when finding their niche. They may know they want to *be* an artist, but what *kind* of artist? What is the *feeling* they want to express in their work, and *how*? As one student put it, "I'd be a really good painter if I just knew what to paint."

The best way to find a unique path is to experiment and try a lot of different things. Take classes. Go to the library and take out obscure books. Attend poetry readings, concerts, plays, and art shows. Try your hand at acrylics, oils, pastel, watercolor, printmaking, photography, pottery, jewelry making, or glass blowing. Take cooking, tap, or gardening classes. Sooner or later you will find the medium, messaging, and subject matter that truly stirs your heart. It may take a while to find your passion, but if you persist long enough, you will.▪

STUDIO ENTRANCE   *2024, watercolor on paper, 10.5 × 8.5 inches*

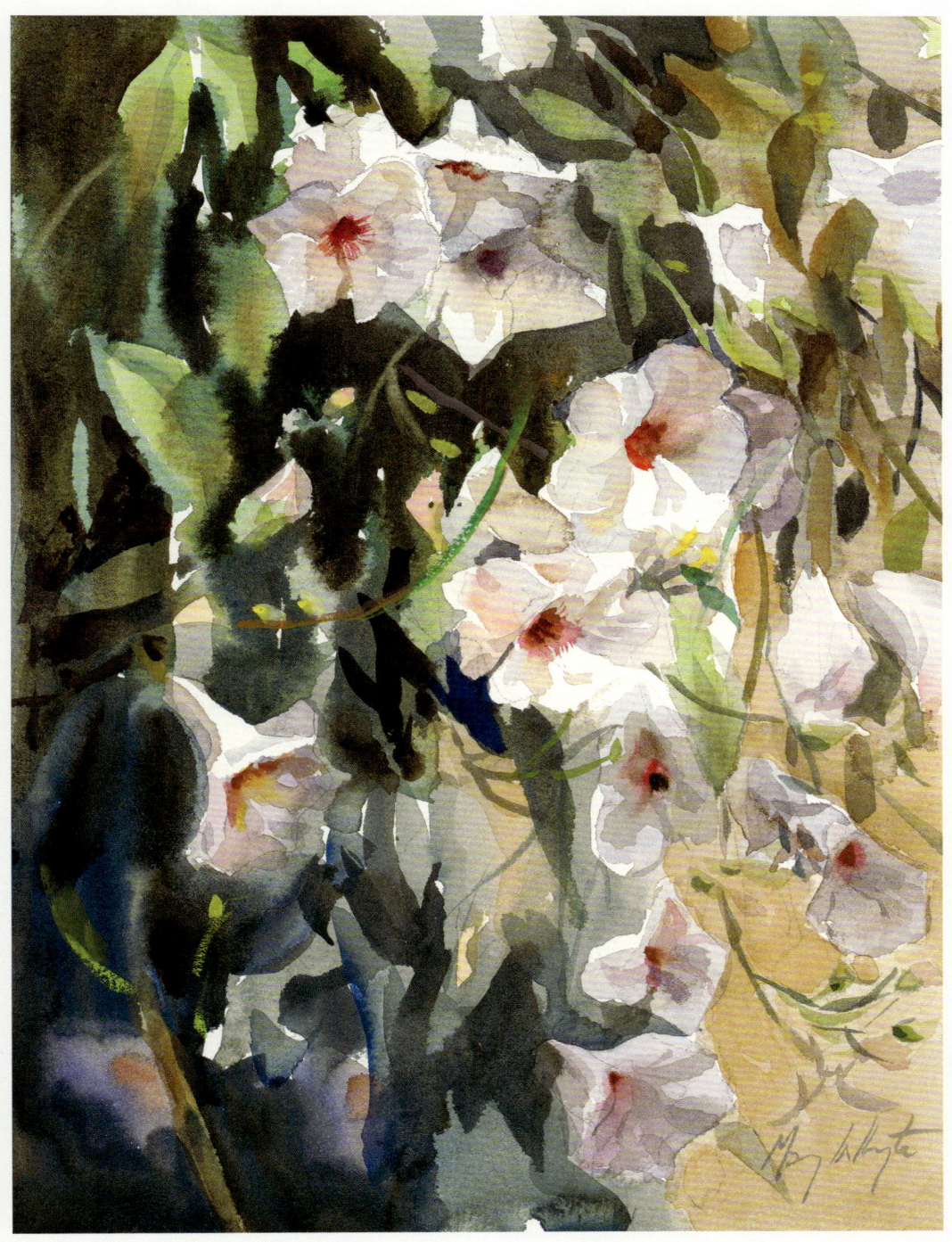

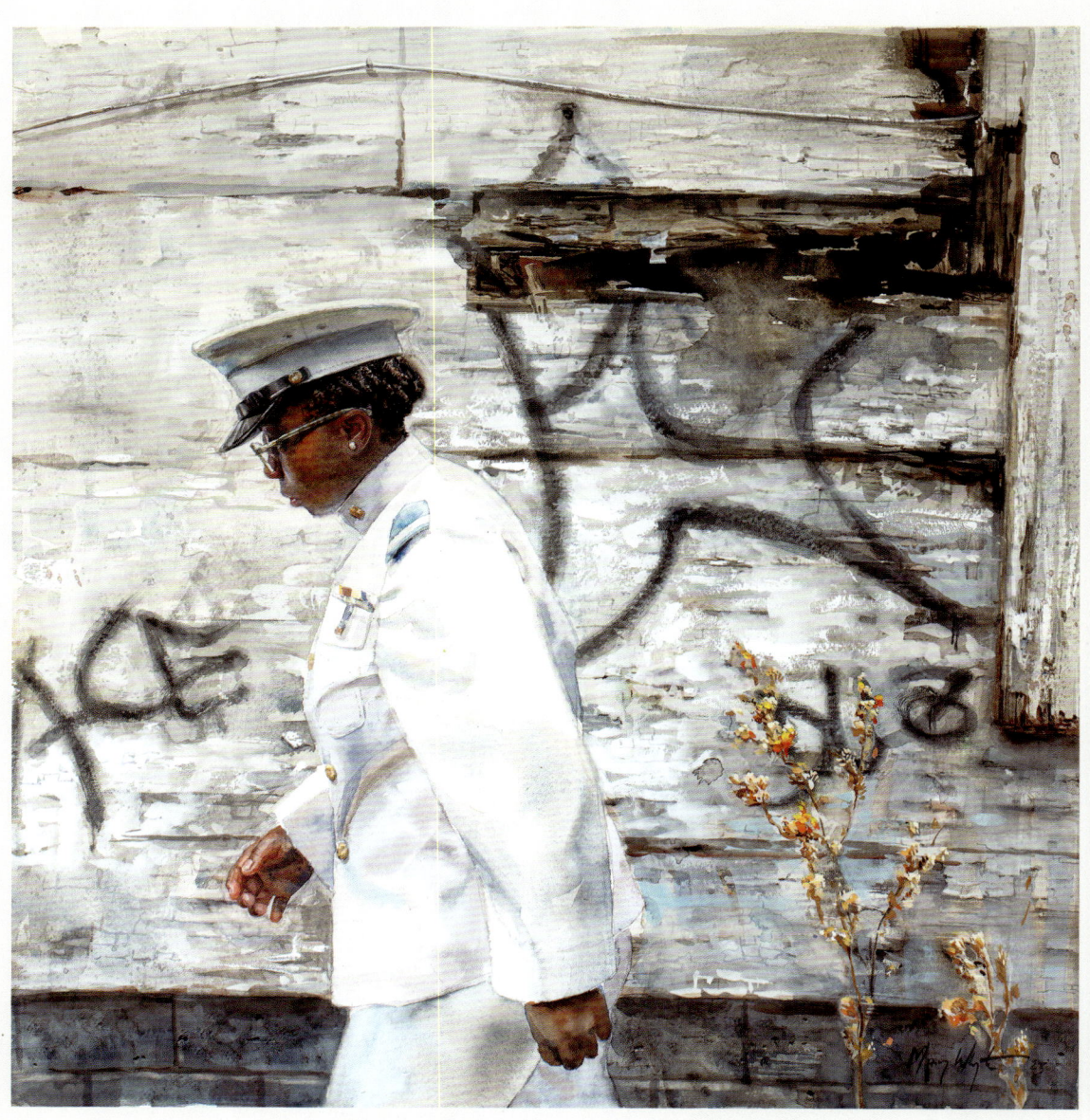

Knowing what to create and how to express it is most often dictated by the heart. We follow our yearnings and passions, always moving in the direction of what is pleasurable and feeds our inner joy. When we get off track trying to make our work look like someone else's or painting strictly to please others, the joy quickly fades.

People have always been the inspiration for my work. The age of the person modeling for me never really mattered. Lilly was less than four years old when she first became the subject of one of my paintings. From the time she was four until she graduated from The Citadel in Charleston, I created dozens of watercolors and drawings of her.

Lilly always seemed to understand what I wanted her to do and was willing to be flexible. Whether posing holding an umbrella, picking flowers, holding a heavy pot of lilies as tall as she was, sleeping in a colorful quilt, showing off a new dress (*Twirl*), or blowing out the candles on a birthday cake, Lilly was determined to do what I asked of her and made our time together fun. Each painting was interesting for me to do, spurring me on to the finish, and each left me looking forward to the next one, whatever that might be. ∎

CADET   *2023, watercolor on paper, 22 × 22 inches*

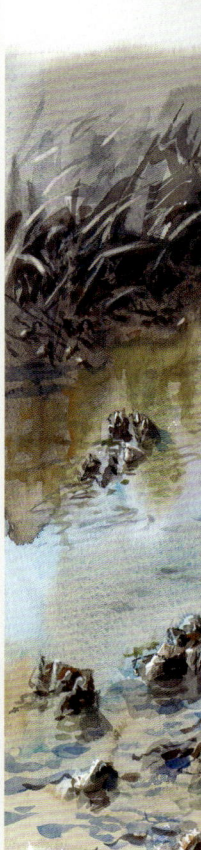

My first gallery and studio were located together on the second floor of a dingy office building in Ambler, Pennsylvania. A closed door was the only thing that separated the public from my personal workspace. Only it didn't. Friends and browsers off the street frequently wandered in to chat and to see what I was working on. My studio soon became a mecca for the bourgeoisie and bored, and in time I realized I wasn't getting any work done at all. Eventually, I posted a sign outside the door with my strict working hours, stipulating that I wasn't to be disturbed until after 5 p.m. Even my mother had to wait until the end of the day to call me.

OYSTER BANK   *2023, watercolor on paper, 29.75 × 38 inches*

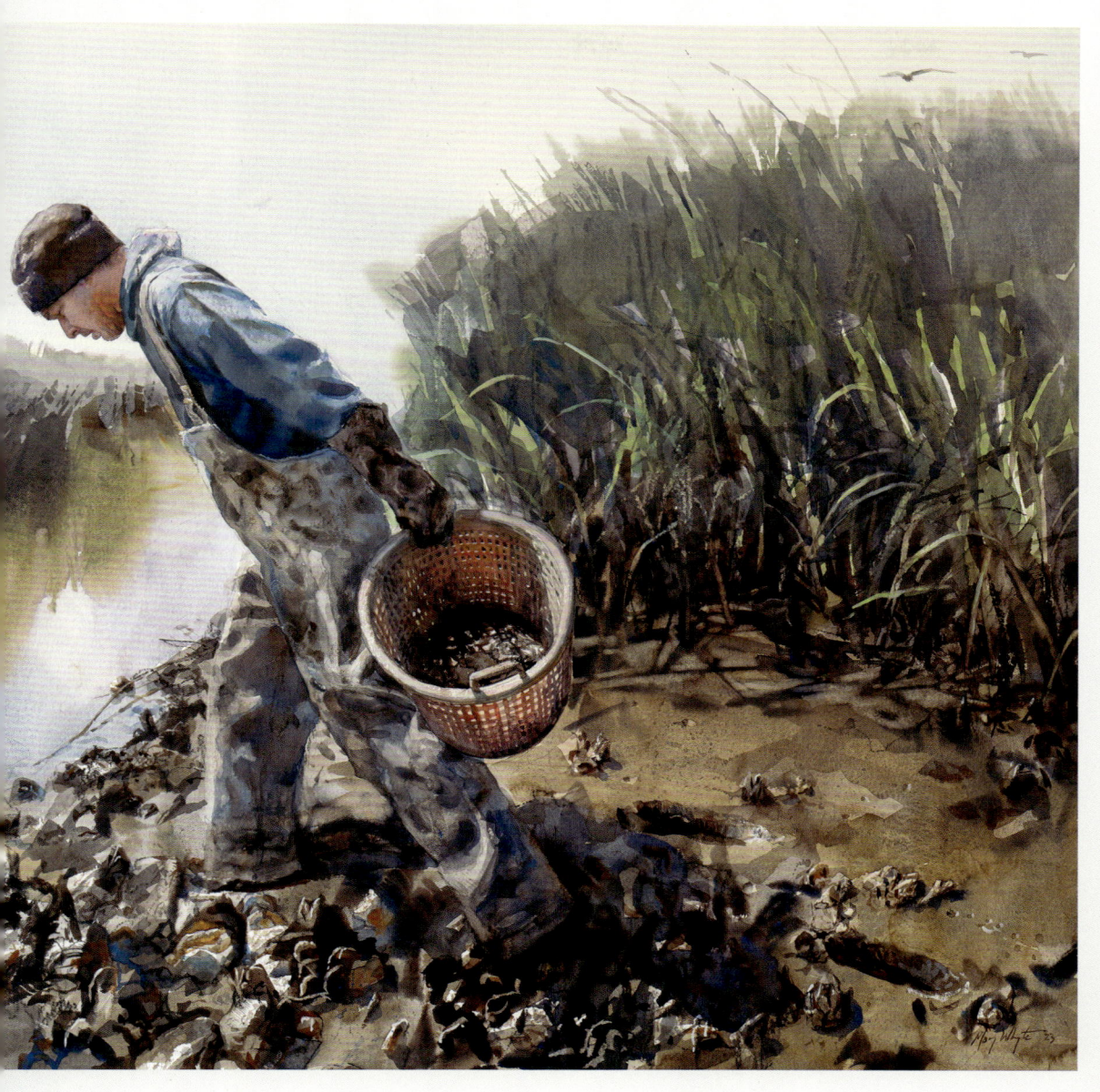

The result of my newly declared focus was twofold. Besides being able to concentrate uninterrupted, I discovered that I was now being referred to in the community as a professional artist. When I finally treated myself and my time in the studio seriously, others did as well.

The takeaway is simple. Although it may require enormous discipline, it is paramount to dedicate regular hours in the studio if you want to accomplish your goals. Every day, you must act, plan, work, and think as if you are a professional artist. As Aristotle said, "We are what we repeatedly do. Excellence, then, is not an act, but a habit."

Making a habit of your work time can be a challenge with daily distractions and responsibilities. The laundry needs to be done, your boss needs a report, the house needs to be cleaned, the dentist and plumber need to be called. The interloper called life must be negotiated with every day.

The best guidance I ever received regarding time management came from my friend Jan Fritsen. At the time I was frantically trying to complete several paintings within a very short deadline for an exhibition in China. The pressure to turn out my best work left me fraying at the edges. A seasoned educator, relationship author, and career coach, Jan's advice to me was simple, and I still adhere to it: Say No and Make an Appointment.

The "say no" component meant that I had to turn down all offers and requests that would compete for my time and distract me from my goal. No, I couldn't meet my neighbor for lunch and an afternoon of shopping. No, I couldn't paint a small painting for the charity auction. No, I couldn't do all of the public relations or housework by myself. Some chores had to be delegated to others so I could focus on my painting.

The "make an appointment" part of Jan's instructions meant that I actually had to write down in my calendar designated studio time, in the same way that I would schedule an unbreakable appointment with my doctor or attorney. After penciling it in, if I received a subsequent request for my time, my answer was that I already had a commitment.

Becoming good at anything requires discipline. It requires long, dedicated hours gaining the proficiency that can lead to untethered expression. It also requires sacrifice. In order to say yes to one thing, we must say no to something else. It is what we give up that makes room for what we take up. ∎

"*When I finally treated myself and my time in the studio seriously, others did as well.*"

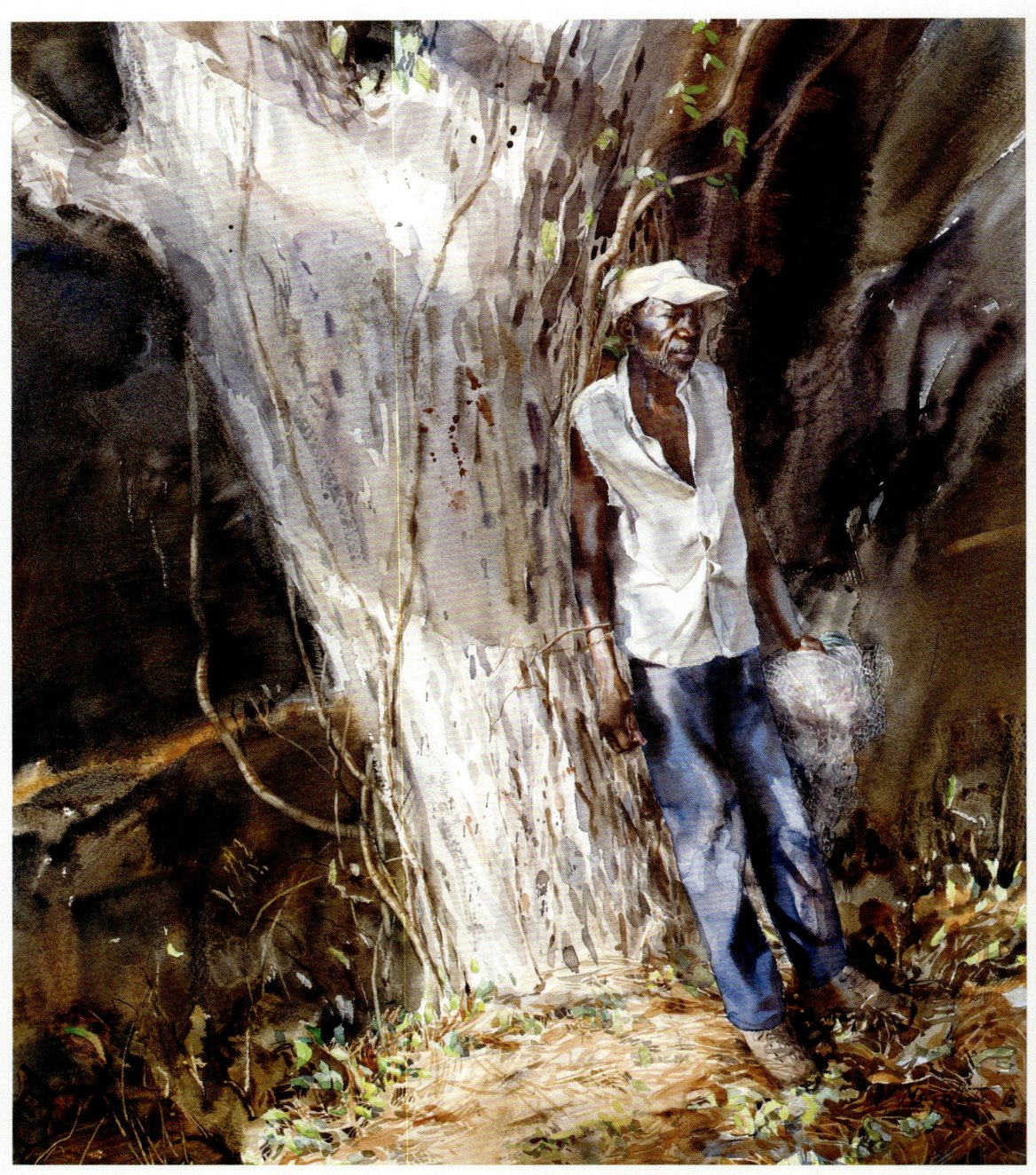

At times in my career, I have had to go into "radio silence" so that I could meet a deadline. I would hole up in a remote location that only my family and closest friends knew about, a secluded place where I could spend several weeks concentrating on nothing other than the work at hand.

Once it was a cabin in Vermont. Another time it was an upstairs apartment in rural Iowa. An empty mill worker's house in Simpsonville, South Carolina, a tavern house in the Pennsylvania countryside, a carriage house in Philadelphia, a house on the coast of Maine, a B & B in the middle of Kansas. Each time the goal was simple: immersion without distraction.

Adhering to good work habits creates the opportunity for our best work. It means maintaining a daily routine, prioritizing goals, avoiding distractions, staying fit, and being organized. When I am home, I do my best to maintain a strict schedule. I begin my day at 6 a.m. with breakfast, exercise, and reading inspirational essays or scripture. If I have a few extra minutes, I like to study the work of artists I admire. By 9 a.m. I am ready to fully focus on painting until late afternoon, after which I turn my attention to business and correspondence until dinnertime.

My friend Joe Paquet, an accomplished landscape painter, has often said that being able to spend his days painting is a gift. I think most artists would agree. Not to be squandered, this precious gift we have been given is worth protecting and holding in the highest regard. We may not always be rewarded with financial or critical success, but striving for excellence in our daily routine and work habits will bring us much closer to the mark and to the satisfying goal of self-expression. ▪

CORNER OF THE WOODS *2018, watercolor on paper, 22.5 × 19 inches*

One of the advantages of being an artist is that subject matter for creative expression is always close at hand: in our home, the nearby landscape, or the view from our apartment. Wherever we go, near or far, we are sure to discover interesting and meaningful ideas to be explored.

I have been fortunate to paint with gifted artists all around the world and have marveled how the pros can size up a scene and pull off a jaw-dropping rendition with little apparent effort. I remember painting with an older Chinese artist who would complete a beautiful watercolor in less than an hour, then turn his stool forty-five degrees to do another painting. Within an afternoon he had rotated his stool a quarter turn four times, coming away with four admirable works. He didn't bother to get up and seek out a different location each time. Instead, he stayed in the same place and fixed his gaze in four different directions. No matter where he looked, he found and transcribed the beauty he saw there into a beautiful painting.

When I travel alone, I prefer to paint subject matter that is different from anything I might find in the Lowcountry of South Carolina. What I am trying to learn when I am painting is how the light works in a particular setting. If, as artists, our goal is to paint light on form, we must observe the difference between the way light washes softly across a face and the way it skitters across a stand of wind-blown Mexican sage. Each brings its own lesson, offering an opportunity for creative expression. ∎

MEXICAN SAGE   *2024, watercolor on paper, 13.75 × 10 inches*

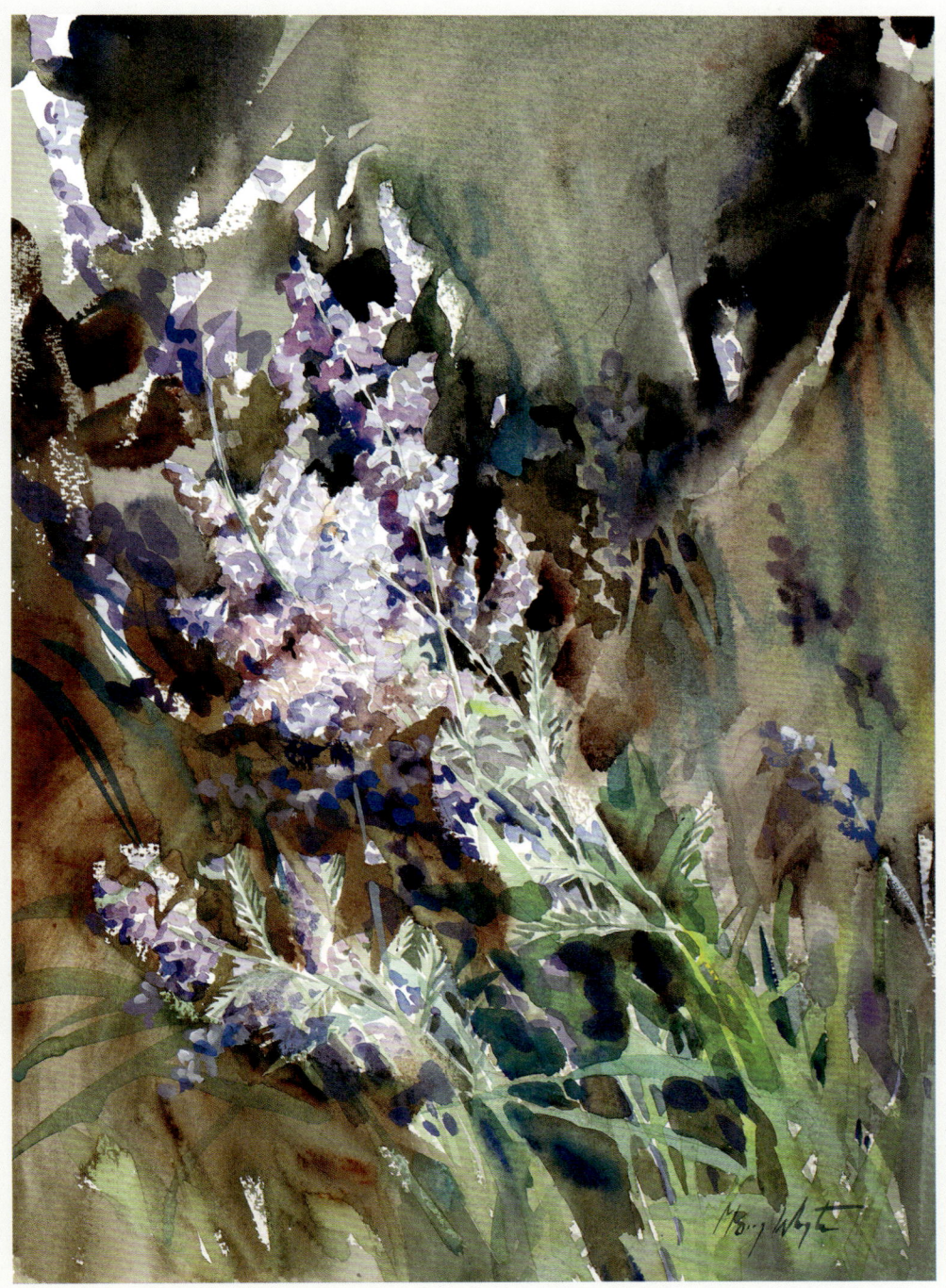

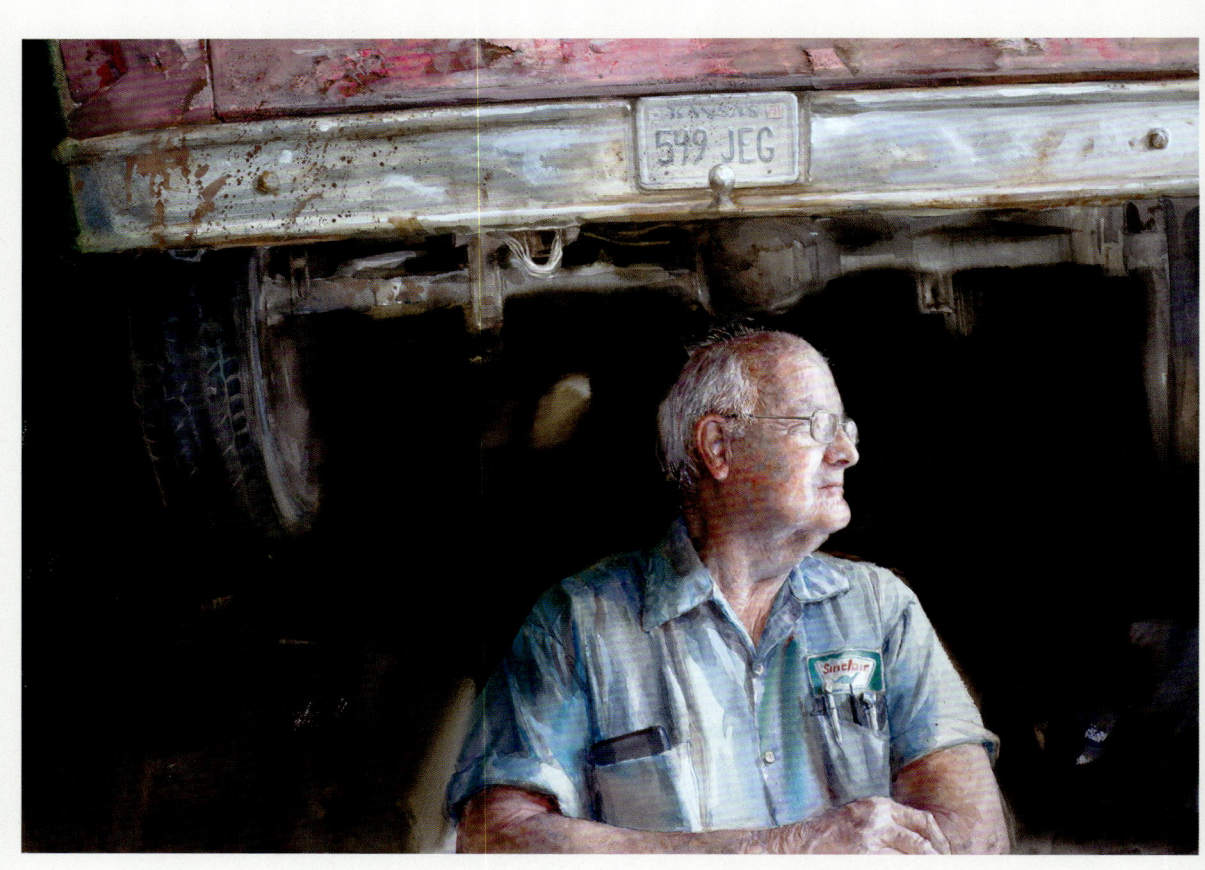

> I have made my world and it
> is a much better world than
> I ever saw outside.
>
> —LOUISE NEVELSON

I've had coffee with the President and beer with a hog farmer, and on both occasions I recognized that each of us had been anointed with a unique ability in life. Neither of us could have done the other's job. I've learned, too, that artists are often viewed differently by others, since what we do seems to come magically out of thin air. To others we are wizards, with a mystifying, unattainable power. Christopher, a highly accomplished doctor and hospital director from Philadelphia, once said to me, "Mary, I have written computer programs, earned my pilot's license and learned to play the violin. I've mastered French, Spanish, Mandarin Chinese, and ballroom dancing. I have traveled the world, am a certified Bridge Master, and have taught medicine and psychiatry. The only thing I can't figure out is how to paint." I can't explain it either, but I told him jokingly that it was because he just wasn't as smart as me. I already knew that each of us are bestowed with distinctive capabilities that are to be embraced, appreciated, and developed, including the remarkable and unexplainable gift of being an artist.∎

KANSAS   *2024, watercolor on paper, 19.5 × 29 inches*

> The aim of art is to represent not
> the outward appearance of things,
> but their inward significance.
>
> —ARISTOTLE

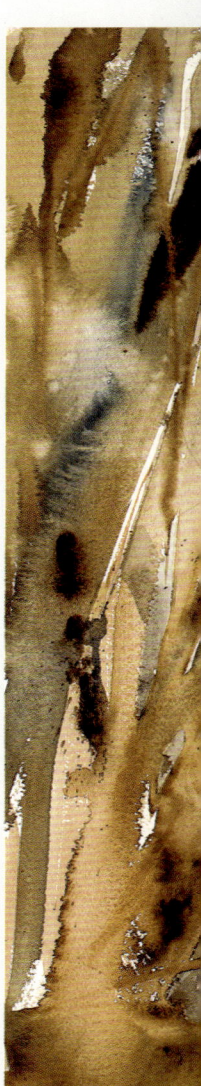

As artists, each piece we create is an accounting of a reality only we know. We paint the pictures, write the poems, or take the photographs we do, not to be part of the world, but to invite others into *our* world. Surprisingly, works based on our most intimate and personal surroundings are the ones most likely to become universally understood. I have found that my most recognized images are the ones done closest to home. Paintings of the marsh, landscape, neighbors, and close friends are the truest and most honest portrayal of the world as I know and feel it.

I know of several artists who do all their paintings within a stone's throw of their home. One reclusive artist I know lives in the rural Midwest and does sizable paintings solely of her back yard. Although some might not give her neighborhood a second glance, it is her total world and a wellspring of inspiration. The weathered chair under the pear tree in winter, the tipped, empty flowerpots by the back step, the spent garden covered with frost—all are transformed by her hand into lush works of art. Hers is proof that a small plot of dirt can be spun into a universe of beauty and connection.

A painting, no matter the subject matter, should be constructed like a musical composition, and unfold that way to the viewer. Using color, shape, and line to move the eye around the image, the artist creates the visual equivalent of sound. We play our music for all the world to hear from our small corner of the garden and invite all to enter. ▪

CATTAILS   *2022, watercolor on paper, 20 × 29 inches*

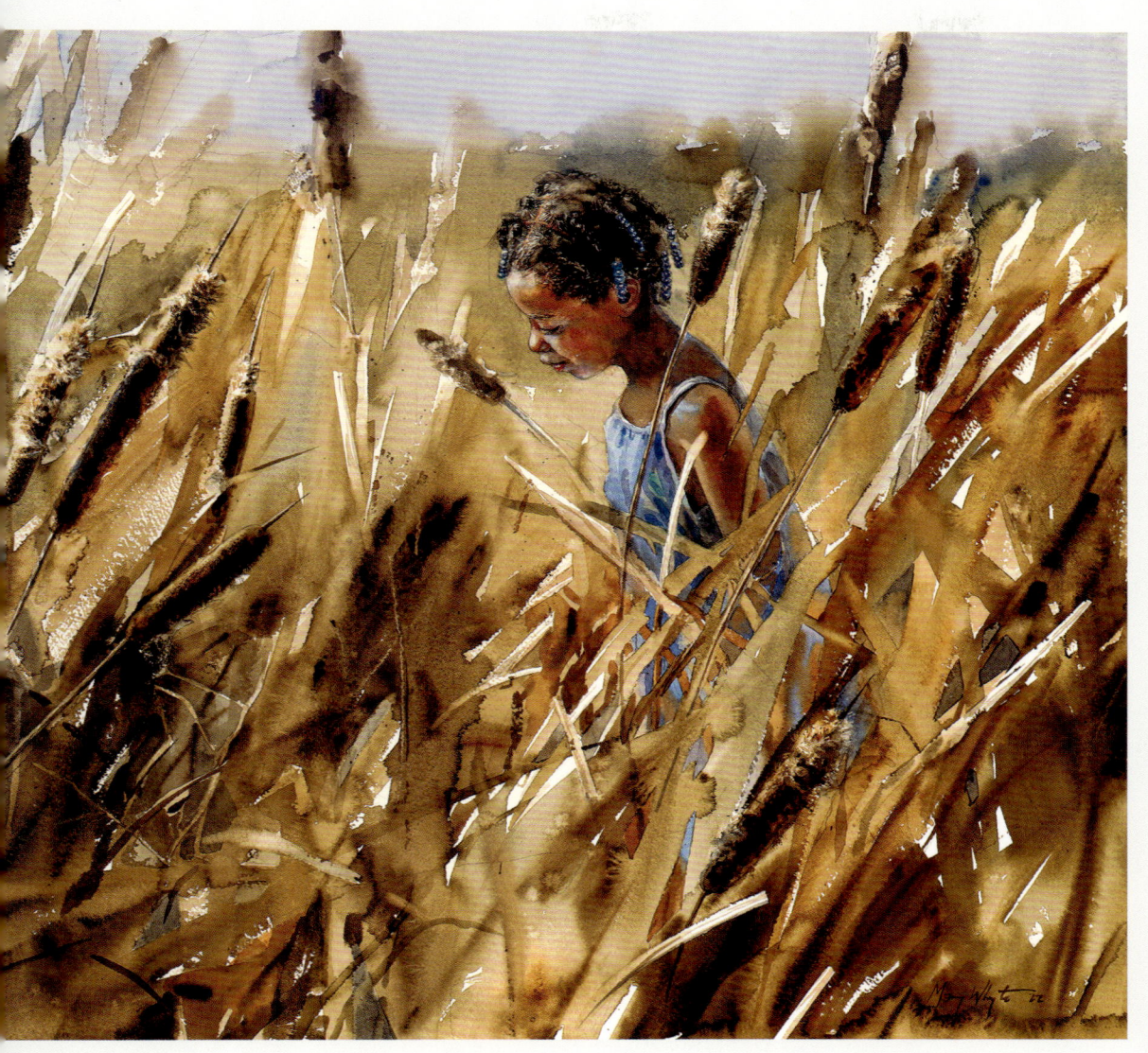

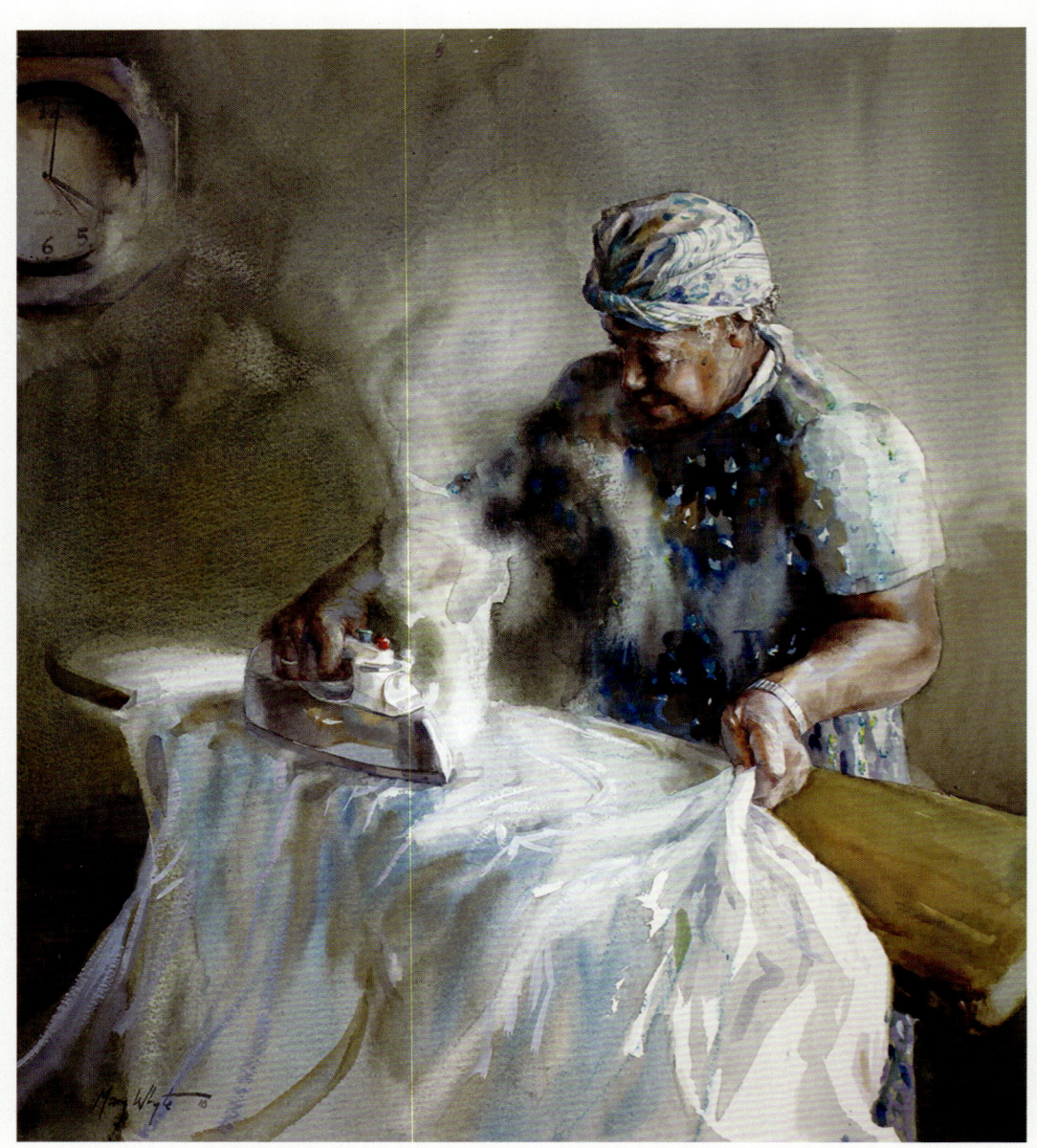

At a dinner party someone asked me what I collect: antiques, coins, weathervanes, thimbles, perhaps? My answer was "ideas."

As creators, we are in the business of collecting ideas. Ideas come filtering through the subconscious all the time, nudging for an audience. Some ideas seep in barely noticed, like a crack of light under a door. Other ideas gently tap us on the shoulder while we are doing something mundane such as making the bed or walking the dog. Each notion, no matter how trivial, odd or insignificant, is a whispered suggestion of a path yet to be taken.

Students sometimes lament that they don't have experiences or ideas good enough to be turned into a painting. Theirs is not the glamorous or exciting existence they see others romping through on social media, so they get trapped into doing predictable and unoriginal art. When you see your life as ordinary, why would you expect others to be interested in your ideas or what you have to express?

The core elements of what we might perceive as an unexceptional life in ourselves can be what ultimately resonates strongest with others. A seemingly everyday occurrence of a pair of muddy boots by the back door, a half-eaten bowl of cereal left on the kitchen table, or a toddler reaching up to be held can elicit memory and strong empathy in viewers. Our most personal and deeply felt experiences will always find a human connection through art. Although the viewer may not be personally familiar with the subject we have portrayed, they will recognize the emotion.∎

IRONING   *2009, watercolor on paper, 29 × 27 inches*

As artists we take hold of an idea, then wrestle with it and wring everything out of it until we've used it up. In the first years of the twentieth century, Claude Monet created nineteen canvases depicting the houses of Parliament. Painting at different times of the day, he explored and extravagantly portrayed how changing light and atmospheric conditions affect form, color, and mood.

Many of my own ideas for paintings were used again and again before being exhausted. I spent nearly thirty years painting the women of Johns Island, their families, and secluded way of life. After three decades I could see that the island was changing, with housing developments, golfing communities, and shopping centers erasing the once familiar landscape and history. Life for the folks of the Hebron St. Francis Senior Center, where I once went almost every Wednesday, has become different, too. The days of quilting, farming, canning, Gullah speak, and lavish hats worn to church are disappearing. Their world has changed, and my paintings have changed with it.

From time to time, I have returned to Johns Island and have been able to meet the descendants of many of the women I once knew and painted. Living just across the road from where Alfreda once tended her garden are her daughter, granddaughter, and great-granddaughters. Although the youngest ones never knew their great-grandmother, I had. Alfreda's life force is in them and has been portrayed in several paintings including *September Litter* and *Eden.* Although life on Johns Island and elsewhere has changed, my mission to paint the people and places of our times remains. ▪

SEPTEMBER LITTER   *2023, watercolor on paper, 21.5 × 18.5 inches*

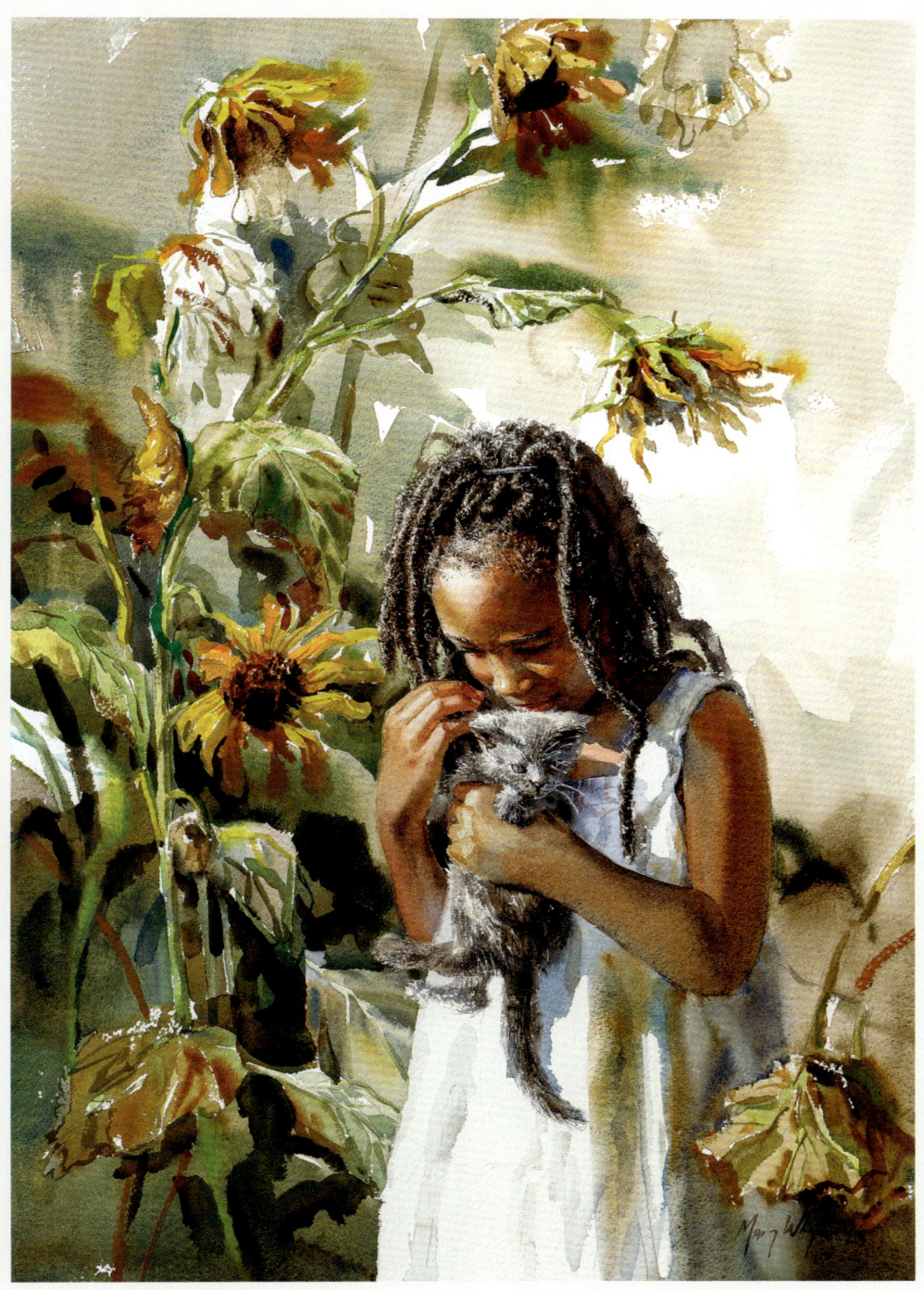

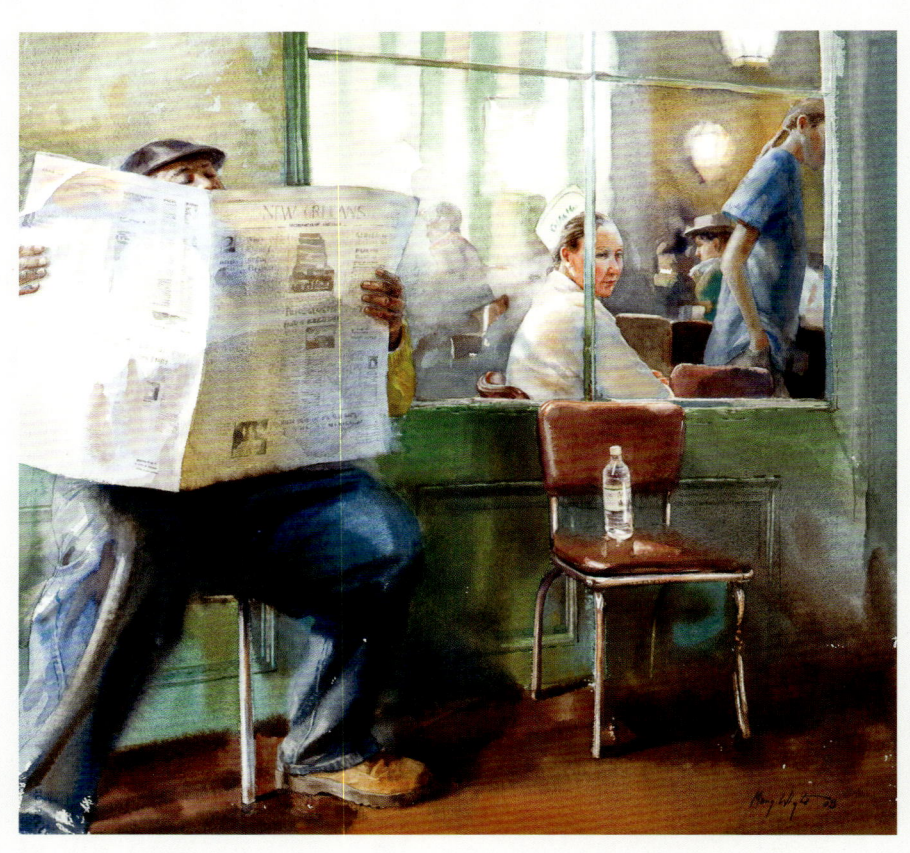

Great ideas cannot be acquired, only forfeited. Each day hundreds of ideas, thoughts, and notions occupy center stage in our minds, if only for a nanosecond. Some return again and again. Deciding which idea is worth pursuing is a gut response. As one artist friend of mine put it, "It's when I feel the hair on the back of my neck stand up, I know it's a good idea."

Many of my ideas have literally walked in the door. More than once I have been in a cafe, hotel lobby, or grocery store when an individual came in, riveting my attention. Immediately, my mind's eye saw a glimpse of a painting, the first glimmer of an idea to be grasped and held closely. If circumstances do not allow me to do a painting right then, the memory of the idea stays in my mind and will trail me until I can put it on paper. Drawing from my imagination and memory, I am able to reconstruct the essential elements of the experience and how it sparked my emotion. No Photoshop-, Artificial Intelligence-, or computer-generated imagery can do that.

As artists we need not go far looking for worthy concepts. Unless we choose to ignore them, our very best ideas will find us and track us down, nudging us until we take notice.∎

THE NEWS AT CAFÉ DU MONDE   *2008, watercolor on paper, 31 × 32.75 inches*

For me the hardest thing to paint is something I am not familiar with or have never seen before. When I was younger, I attempted a few paintings of sail boats, a subject of which, as a Midwesterner, I had very little knowledge. Predictably, the results were mediocre. Had I possessed an affinity for sailing and known firsthand about rigging, heeling, jibs, and wind conditions, I might have produced works with more credibility and life.

Painting the figure demands knowledge and comprehension of human anatomy. Traditional art schools and ateliers generally require several years of drawing from nudes and plaster casts, intended to help the student become familiar with the skeleton, muscles, and movement. The goal is to become so versed in anatomy that it can be reconstituted from memory.

Doing an entire painting of a person from life is ideal for an artist but rarely for the model. Poses are difficult to hold for more than thirty minutes at a time, and most models are not professionals, capable of maintaining a graceful or asymmetrical gesture that looks natural. Often, too, the light and background may change. The perfect setup is rarely available, so artists are left to create their own.

Every work of art is an invention, both in its concept and in its making. For the painting *Sweeper*, I used drawings of the man's head from a previous painting and made up the background using my studio as reference. Looking in a mirror, I worked from my own hand gripping a broom. ▪

SWEEPER   *2019, watercolor on paper, 21.5 × 21.75 inches*

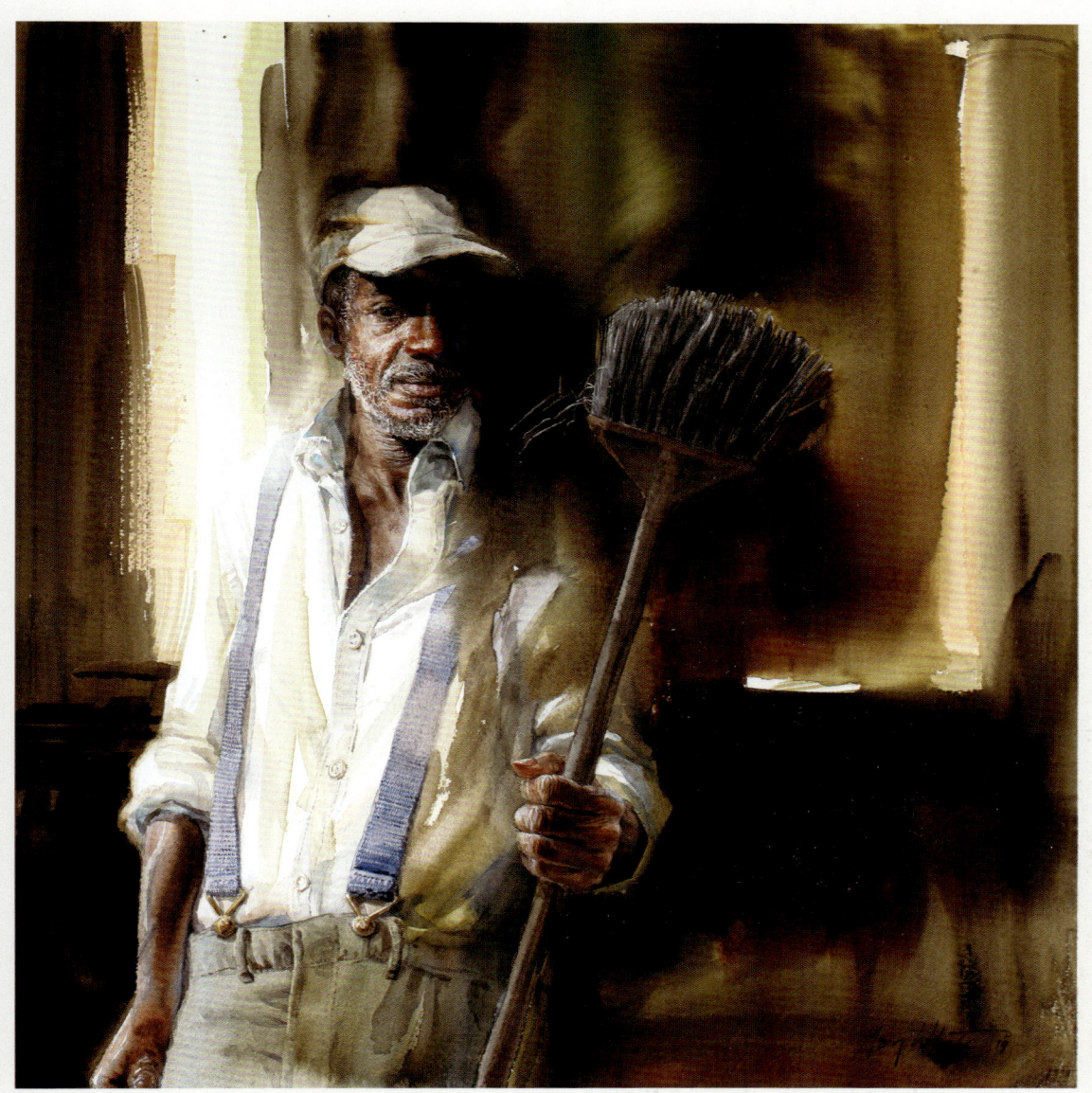

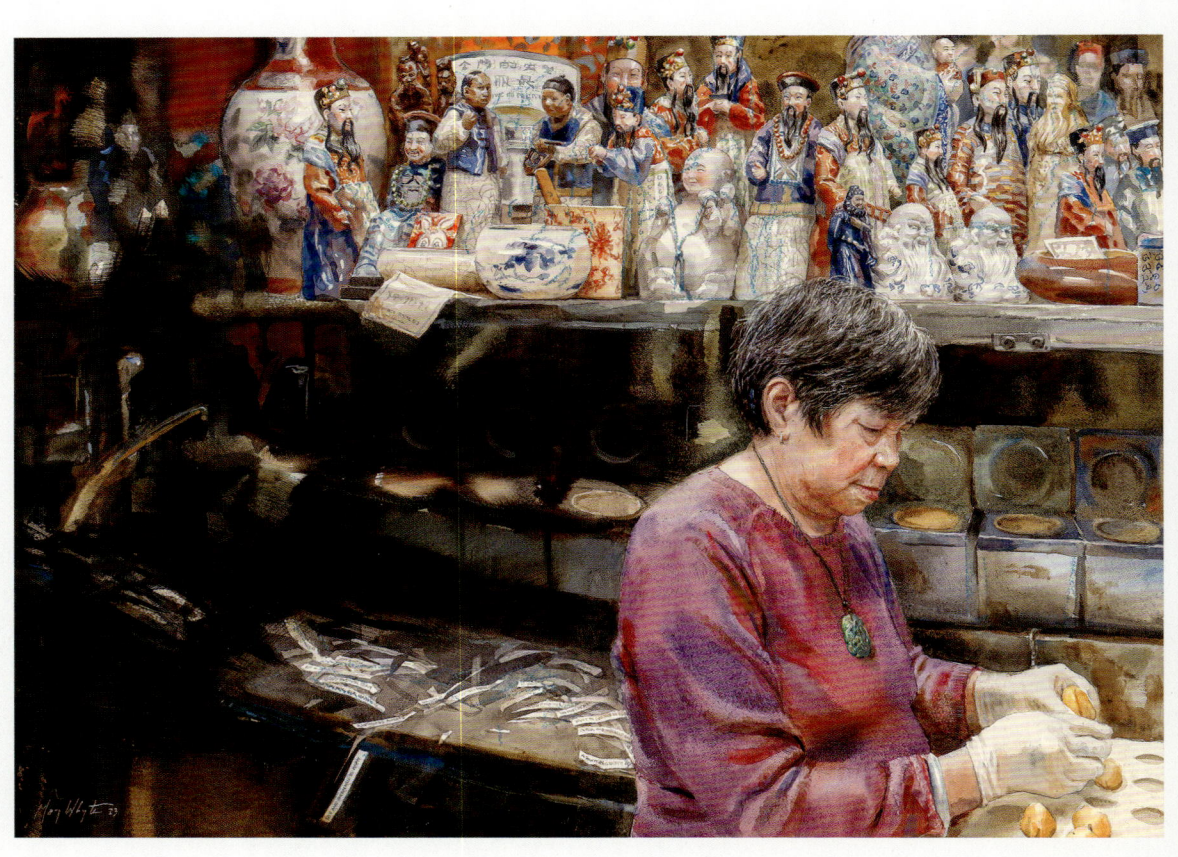

Taped to the wall of my studio I have a small sign that reads:

Establish the mission
Develop a plan
Work relentlessly
Hope for a little luck

I have often wondered which of the four items on the list plays the biggest part in achieving success. In my own life I have had more than my share of what many might deem extraordinarily good luck. Opportunities for exhibitions, books, interviews, publicity, and commissions have been abundant. Looking back, though, not one of the opportunities would have happened without a lot of planning, hard work, persistence, and readiness up front. Good fortune is often given the credit when it was the preparation for its arrival that made it happen.

Many years ago, I talked about writing a book about art but could never find the time. Nevertheless, I kept an ongoing file of notes, quotes, magazine articles, and newspaper

---

FORTUNE COOKIE   *2023, watercolor on paper, 19 × 27.5 inches*

clippings that might someday be useful. Every time I came across an interesting idea, I'd write it down and put it in the file. The "book file" grew.

A couple years after I started the file, I slipped and broke my right wrist. It was impossible to hold and manipulate a brush with my hand immobilized by a cast. When I asked the surgeon how long it would be before I could paint again, he said "Twelve weeks." At first I was dismayed at the thought of going so long without painting, but then I realized I could still type with one finger. I would peck my way through a book.

I typed a one-page synopsis and called my publisher. Because I was considered handicapped and not allowed to drive, their team came to me. I handed them my outline and then left to wait in the next room while they had a discussion. When I returned, they told me they loved the idea and wanted to publish it. When I asked how long I had to complete the manuscript, they said, "Twelve weeks."

When I started culling through my book file, I was surprised at how much material I had amassed. I discovered a good part of the outline and writing were already done. *Establish the mission* and *Create a plan* were in place. *Work relentlessly* was already part of my ethic, and I now had a twelve-week deadline to spur me on. All of the ingredients were there. Had I not had the outline and majority of the resource material already in hand, I wouldn't have been able to seize the opportunity and finish the book on time. *An Artist's Way of Seeing* was published the following year.

Many will argue that success comes down to being in the right place at the right time. Certainly, being able to influence one's potential outcome by having a solid objective, reliable resources, meaningful connections, and a step-by-step plan doesn't hurt. Regardless, I believe that nothing we ever strive to accomplish will have a favorable outcome without the overriding hand of Divine Providence. That and a tiny pinch of good luck.∎

"Good fortune is often given the credit when it was the preparation for its arrival that made it happen."

Those who dwell among
the beauties and mysteries
of the earth are never
alone or weary of life.

—RACHEL CARSON

Close to where I buy groceries is a building with a large mural depicting the globe and a well-known soft drink. The message reads "Everybody Chill." I have often thought that world peace might be more readily achieved if instead the sign proclaimed, "Everybody Paint." Perhaps we should just give everybody, including our world leaders, a set of watercolors. We'd all be so wrapped up in our painting that no one would have the time or inclination for war.

I like to describe painting as "The Great Escape." In it I have found hope, enjoyment, connection, and solace. For many artists the studio can be a place of refuge, where chaos gives way to a ceasefire and a few hours of calm. Even when paintings fail, sometimes bringing frustration, there is something to be learned, moving the creator forward with expectation. With each detour we are redirected onto a new path, and a new chapter of possibilities begins.

Several times in my life I have relied on art to get me through a difficult time. When I was in my mid-thirties I was diagnosed with cancer. For nearly a year the rigors of surgery, chemotherapy, and radiation made it impossible for me to draw or paint. I was

BATTLEGROUND   *2012, watercolor on paper, 40.75 × 28.75 inches*

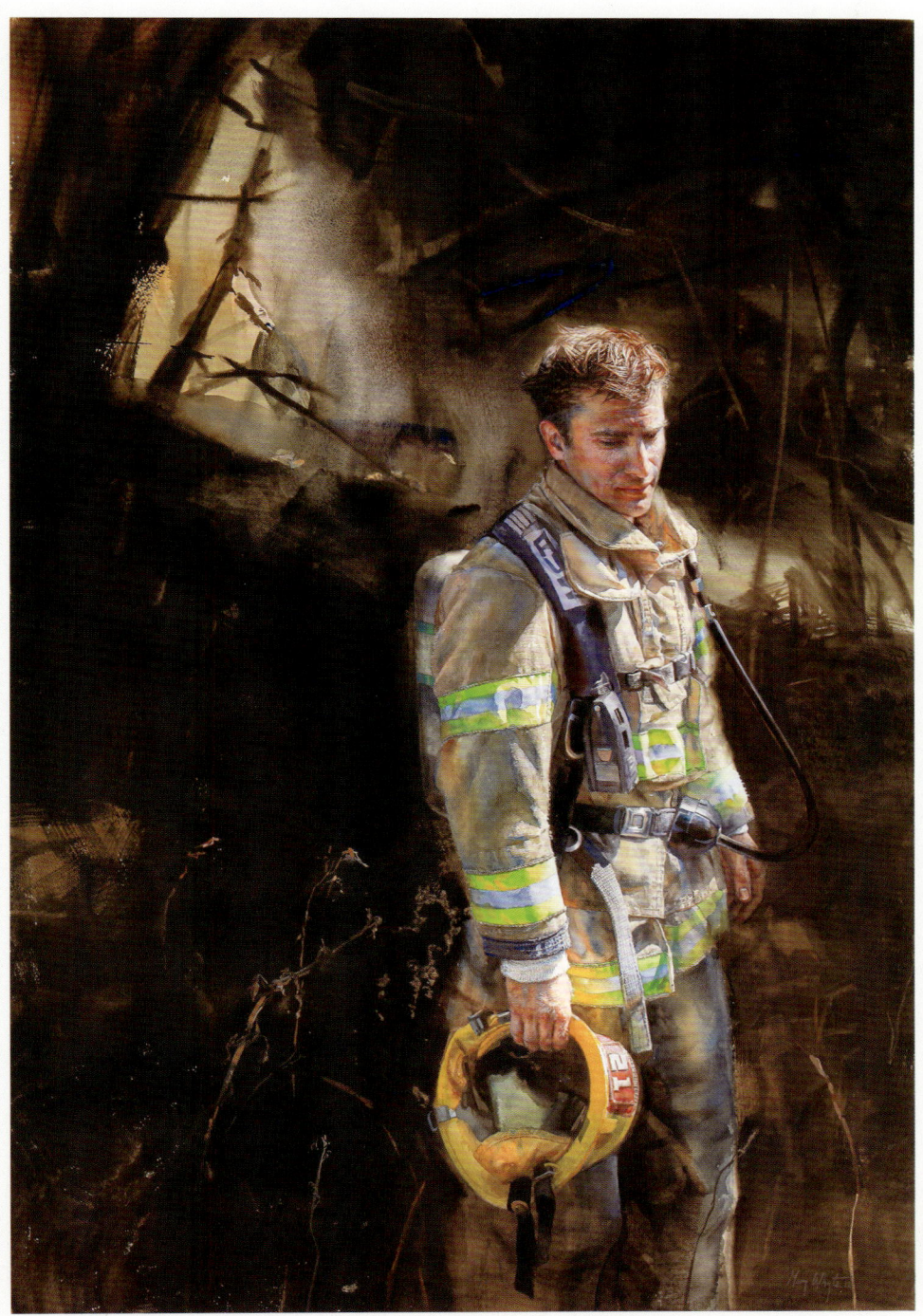

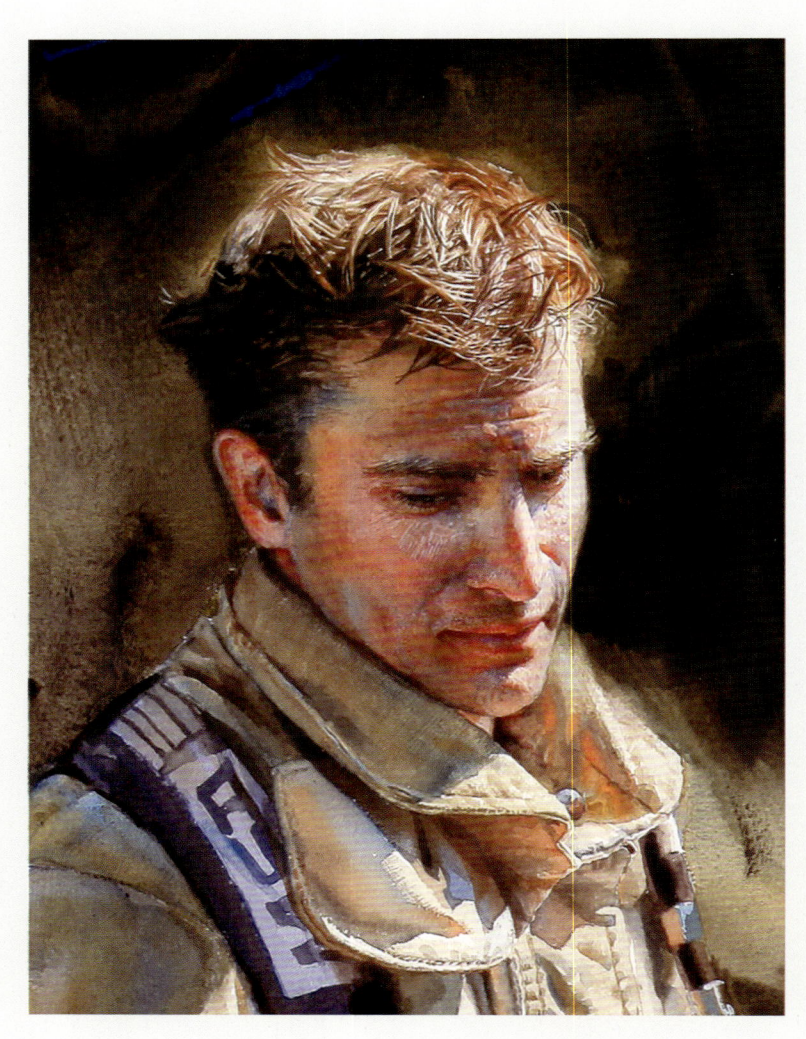

> *"Several times in my life I have relied on art to get me through a difficult time."*

totally limp and exhausted. To cheer me on, my friends planted a perennial garden outside my window as a sign of hope and renewal. Spring came, and eventually my painting returned, this time with more vigor and sense of purpose. To everything there is a season.

Art connects us to a sense of wholeness and well-being and can turn a bleak outlook into one of dreams. Self-expression can be a way of navigating a complex world, leading to a more fulfilling and meaningful existence. Experiencing a greater sense of beauty, self-worth, and connection can become the gateway to changing a life for the better. This in itself can be miraculous.

Several years ago, I exhibited my work at the newly built Nebraska Medicine Fred & Pamela Buffett Cancer Center. The centerpiece of the modern ten-story building is the Chihuly Sanctuary, showcasing a soaring installation by the famed glass artist Dale Chihuly. The permanent installation of Chihuly's art, as well as the work of several other artists, is an important aspect of the center's mission to go beyond simply curing a disease. They strive to heal the human spirit with an environment of hope and resilience, as well as by offering art experiences that help to reduce pain perception, anxiety, stress, loneliness, and depression.

When I was at the center I was asked to teach two drawing classes. My first group of students were doctors and researchers.

Each was given a sketchbook and led out into the garden to draw with me for an hour. As expected, many of their renderings were tight and precise. After all, these were physicians and scientists whose practice and expected outcome is built on a platform of accuracy. I knew of a study that had been done of doctors looking at art. When physicians spent ten minutes looking at a painting before going into the operating room, they often reported feeling calmer and more focused.

After the doctors left, a group of hospital patients were escorted into the garden. Many were slumped in wheelchairs, pushed by an attendant. Wearing hospital gowns and head scarves, the patients appeared thin and frail. I started by showing them how to draw a daisy, using big, simple lines. Then holding the pencil at a low angle to the paper, I showed them how to add shading. I gently emphasized that this was to be their own interpretation. It was their own work of art.

The results were moving and confirmed the research on how participating in art can reduce the stress hormone cortisol as well as the perception of pain. When they had finished their drawings many of the patients smiled. One woman, who previously had difficulty holding the pencil, proudly held up her drawing saying, "I feel better! For the first time, I actually feel better!"

To everything there is a season. ▪

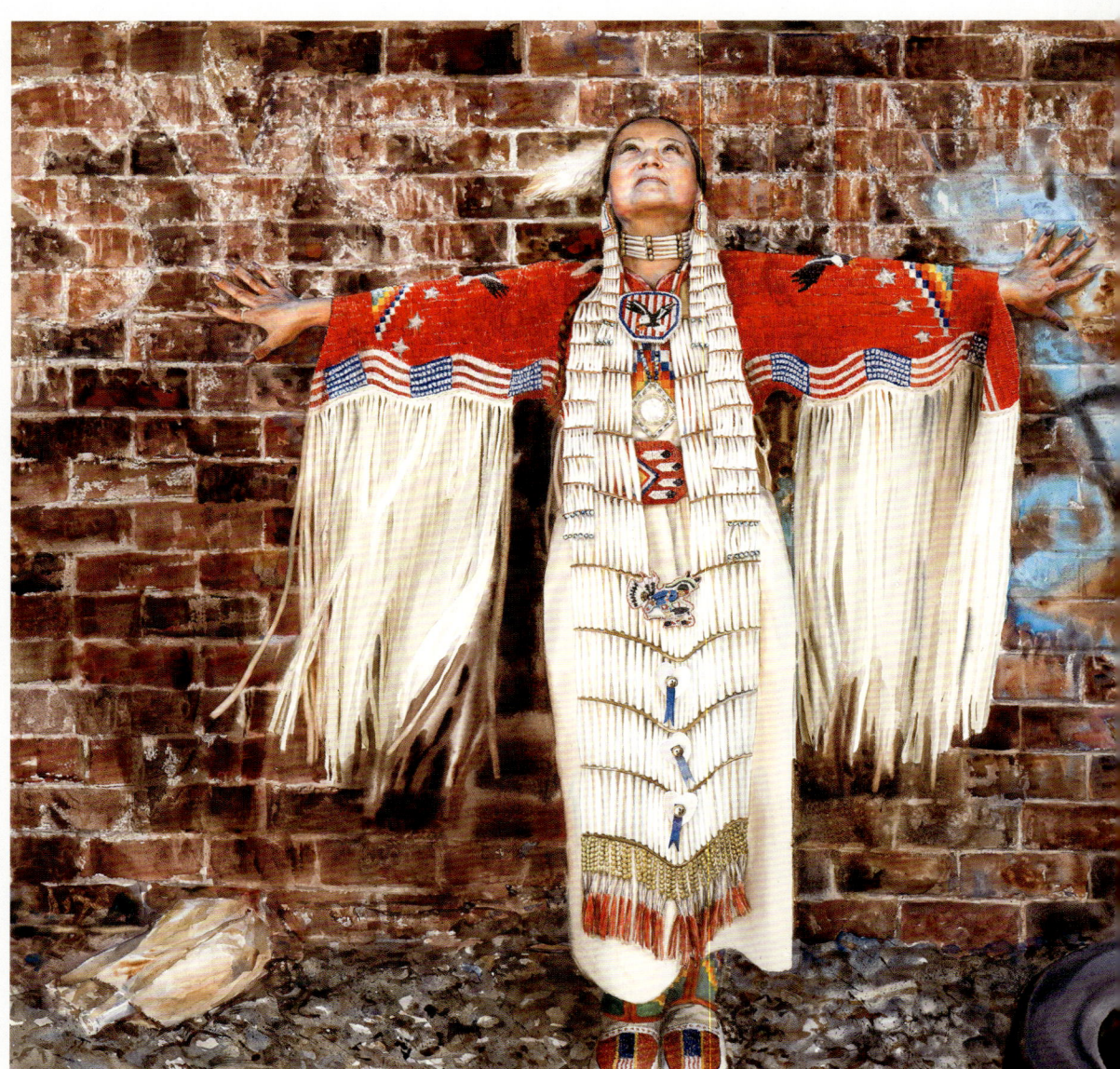

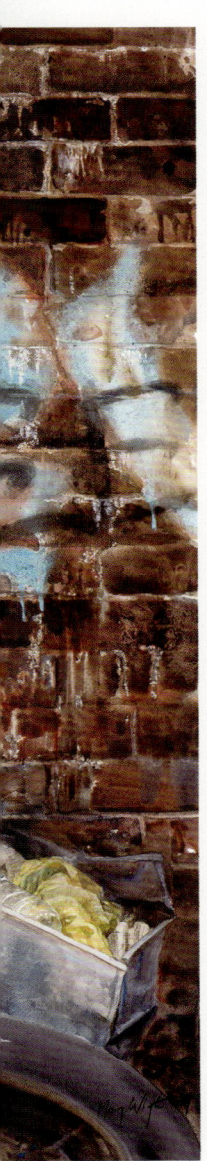

For a couple of years, I rented studio space on the third floor of an old warehouse. Just below me on the second floor, another artist, Dan, worked full time doing illustration and commercial art. From time to time, we would meet in the hallway to chat and compare notes about work and making headway in the art world. "Success as an artist," Dan said, "is simply a matter of hanging in there long enough." I have to agree, as there have been many times I have seen promising artists throw in the towel too soon.

AMERICA   *2017, watercolor on paper, 40 × 53 inches*

I prefer to work on large projects without public knowledge so that all decisions about what, whom, or where I paint are purely my own. Such was the case in 2010, when I embarked on a nationwide journey that took more than seven years to complete and was carried out almost entirely in secret. My goal was to paint a true and honest portrait of America, depicting a veteran from each of the fifty states in their current environment. Showing our diverse population, the fifty large-scale watercolors depicted veterans of all ages, backgrounds, and vocations, and from all five branches of the military.

By year six I had been to nearly every state. Travel costs, hotels, model com-pensation, framing, insurance, stress, and storage fees were mounting. My marriage ended. The large personal commitment that I had made with no guarantee of success made me question the wisdom of my venture. I might have quit were it not for the small voice in my head urging me to *just keep going.*

I persevered, and *We the People* turned out to be the most surprising and fulfilling adventure of my life. The experience allowed me the privilege of meeting, painting and honoring many of our country's veterans, as well as seeing all fifty states. It also solidified for me the value and reward of persistence, determination, and hanging in there long enough. ∎

"I prefer to work on large projects without public knowledge so that all decisions about what, whom, or where I paint are purely my own."

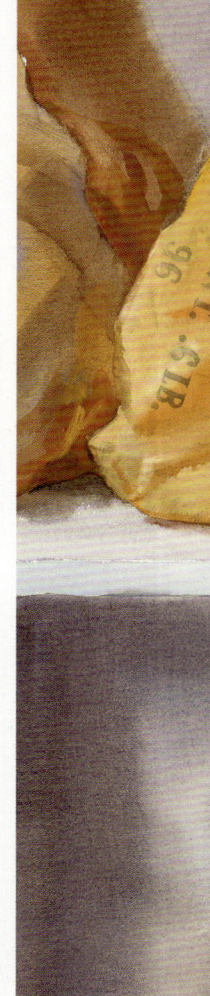

I started my secret fifty-state veterans project by drawing a map of the United States and taping it to my studio wall. Next to it I wrote a list of all the types of Americans I wanted to include: a dairy farmer, rancher, tattoo artist, astronaut, businesswoman, truck driver, window washer. My plan was to meet with each veteran, do the preliminary sketches, take notes and photographs, and then color in that person's state on the map with yellow. After each painting was completed, I would paint over the yellow with red, so that one day I would finish with a solid crimson map of the country.

I quickly realized the map was the easy part. There were two major hurdles. The first challenge was finding and contacting the

SPECIAL DELIVERY   *2015, watercolor on paper, 27.75 × 40.25 inches*

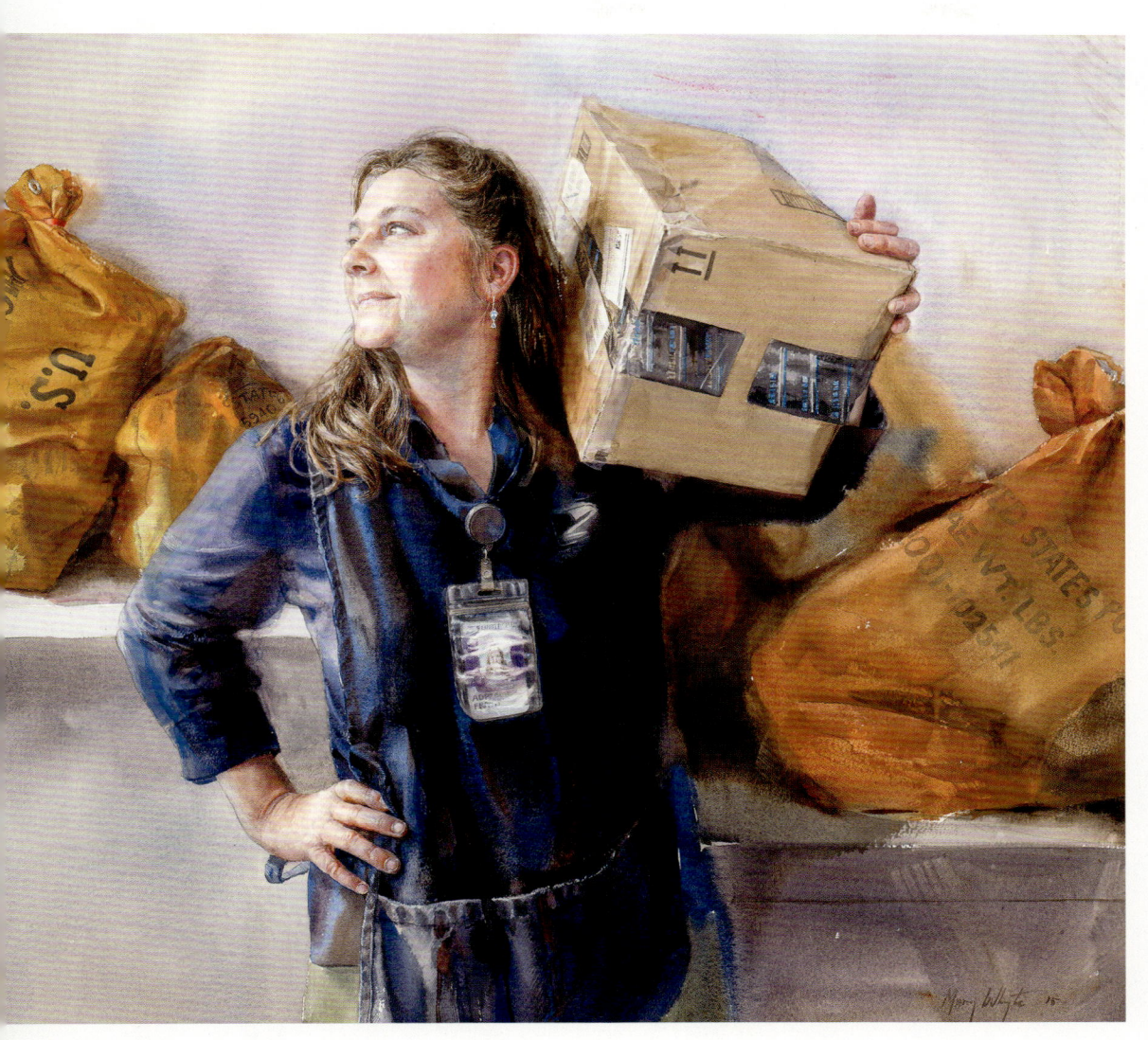

> *"I hope that every veteran who comes to view the collection will see himself or herself in the paintings."*

veterans. Locating a truck driver might be easy, but finding one who is also a veteran proved to be really difficult. With veterans representing only 7 percent of the adult population, it seemed, at times, like trying to find a golf ball in a cornfield.

I spent hours on the internet searching for veteran-owned businesses and making phone calls. Most of the time my calls were never returned; people may have thought it suspicious that a supposed artist from South Carolina wanted to come and paint their portrait. Veterans Administrations and government organizations turned out to be less helpful because of HIPAA regulations protecting privacy. As it turned out, my greatest resource was often found in small towns. I would roll into a sparsely populated municipality and head to the chamber of commerce. There, I discovered, the local officials were eager and proud to tell me about their veterans and to make introductions.

The second hurdle was traveling to all fifty states on a limited budget. To get to the midwestern states I rented an apartment for a month in Woodbine, Iowa, and then went on day trips to the four surrounding states. Other paintings were managed by coupling destinations with teaching and speaking engagements. To get to my veteran in Alaska I scheduled a weeklong workshop aboard a Norwegian Cruise ship that left Vancouver and sailed north up the Inside Passage. During daytime hours, twenty

students and I were given one of the large restaurants to use as our classroom, with several of the ship's musicians and vocalists posing for us.

Heading north, the ship made scheduled stops in a few ports, allowing passengers to get off for an afternoon of exploring. When the ship docked in Skagway, I slipped away from the group and headed into town to the small wood-frame post office. Several weeks prior, over an exchange of emails and phone calls, I had arranged to meet with the town's postmaster, Adrianne, who had served four years in the Air Force and posed for the painting *Special Delivery*.

Generally, I had only enough time with each veteran for photos and a quick sketch. I then brought the material home to my studio where I would complete the portrait, have it framed, and put it safely in storage. One more state colored in red.

I kept the project a secret because I wanted full reign on who I painted and how. My goal was to find and paint everyday veterans who had served largely under the radar, not high-ranking officers who had earned numerous medals. I also wanted to keep my mission quiet because I wanted to make sure I could finish it before unveiling to the public what I hoped would be seen as a fresh and noteworthy idea.

When asked what I hoped viewers would take away from seeing the exhibition *We the People: Portraits of Veterans in America*, my answer was and remains threefold. First, I hope that every veteran who comes to view the collection will see himself or herself in the paintings. That within the spirit of the work, each will see their own face and know that they matter.

Second, I hope that through the portraits, the American public will recognize the worth, value, and ongoing contribution of our military and veterans, while holding them in the highest regard. Each portrait depicts a unique and real individual who made a commitment and a sacrifice for the rest of us. Each made a pledge to uphold and to fight for the freedom we enjoy.

Last, with this exhibition, my hope is that people of all ages and abilities will be inspired to take a brave step forward and reach for what is impactful and meaningful, not only for themselves, but for others. Having a cause greater than self can be the most rewarding ambition of all. ∎

When the exhibition *We the People* began touring, I had the opportunity to speak with many veterans. Curious to see the paintings, many service men and women were visibly moved, relaying to me they had rarely felt this kind of recognition or appreciation from anyone, and certainly not coming in the form of a watercolor portrait.

Many service people expressed a desire to learn how to paint, as they could sense the pleasure and meditative calm that engaging in art might bring. I knew firsthand the feeling of well-being I derived from painting and wanted veterans to experience it as well. It was the desire to share this wonderful gift of art that led me to create the Patriot Art Foundation.

Through online classes, partnerships with local Veteran Administration facilities and small mentoring groups, the foundation is teaching veterans how to paint at their kitchen tables. While learning the basics of watercolor at home might not sound like much, the results are sometimes astonishing. Not only do many of our veterans end up creating works they are mighty proud of, the change in their confidence, self-esteem, and sense of connection with others can be life changing. Through the healing qualities of art, veterans are given a much-needed way to express themselves when words can't and to provide a way to navigate a sometimes-difficult world with creativity, purpose, and joy. As one veteran, Ralph, told me, "Art is the only thing that stops the voices in my head." Another vet, Carla, explained, "It saved me. I hit a really deep spot, and it was the art therapy that pulled me out. I get stressed, and art is the first thing I go to. The problem still exists, but it doesn't affect me anymore."

Art opens the door to whole health, not just for veterans, but for all of us. ▪

VETERANS DAY   *2022, watercolor on paper, 13 × 14 inches*

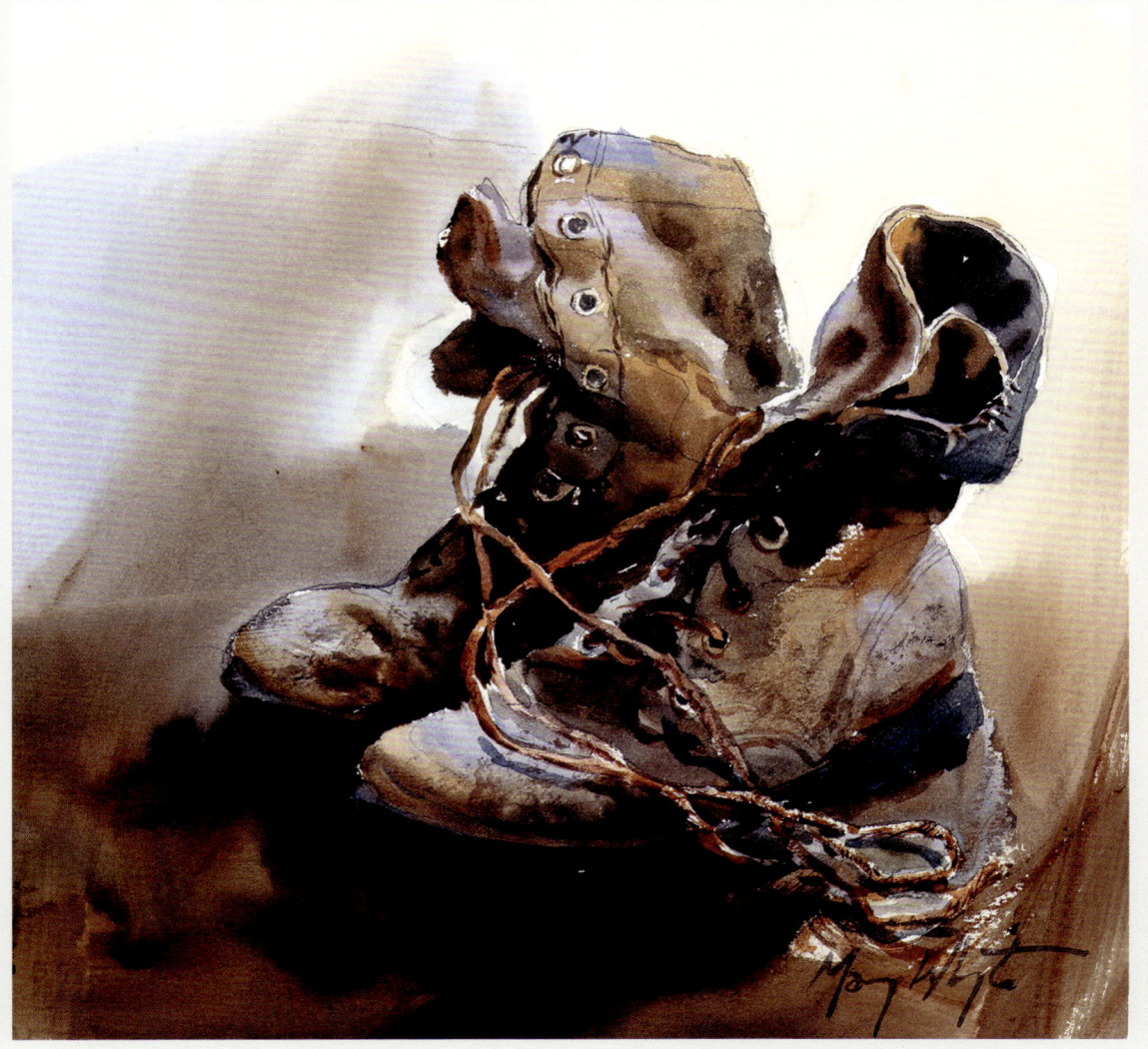

Winter

PROOF OF A LIFE WELL LIVED

To be an artist is to believe in life.

—HENRY MOORE

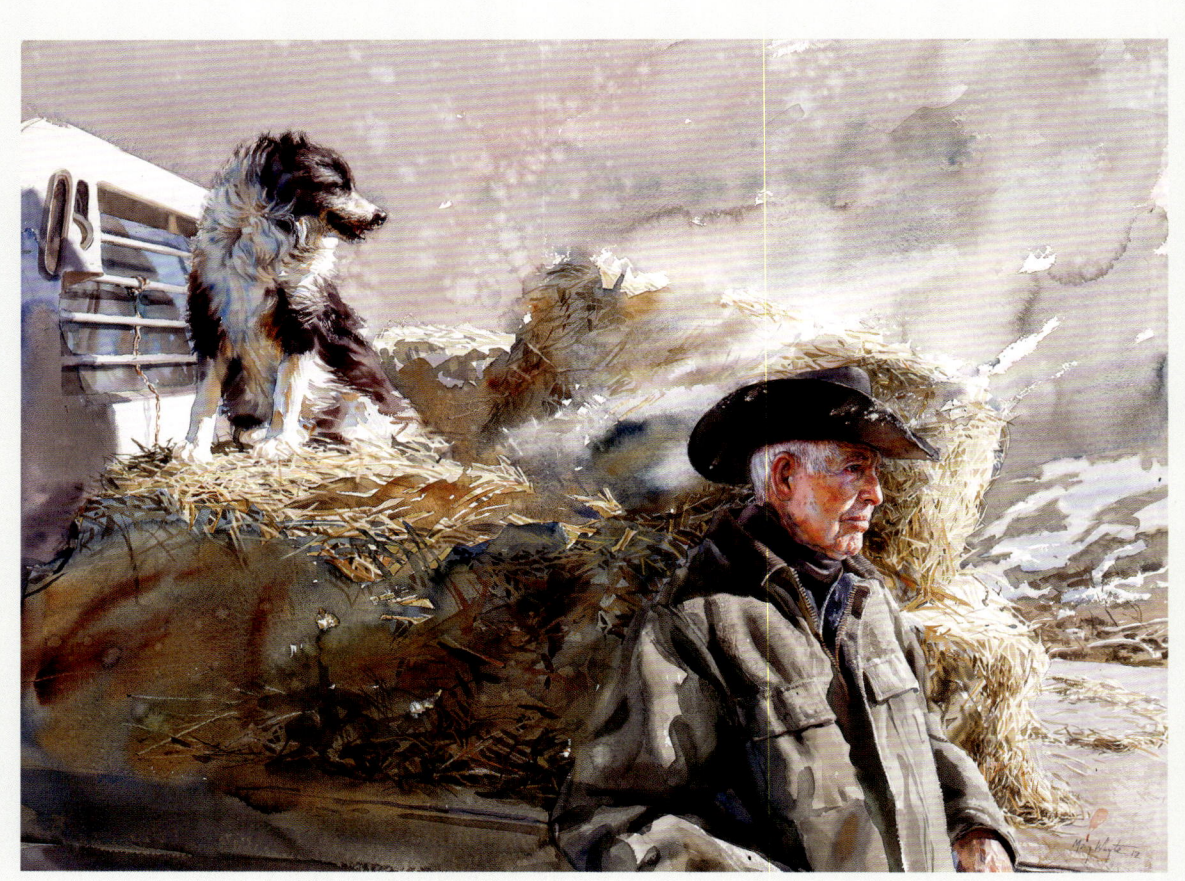

Watrous, New Mexico, is a long way from Charleston. Sprawled across high plains, Dogie's grazing land rolls into the distance like a faded Navajo blanket. Softened by wind and time, the original ruts made by wagons heading west on the Santa Fe Trail are still faintly visible.

Dogie is the kind of man who can fill a doorway before he gets there. Even taller in his boots and hat, the rancher would have broken the ice off the troughs and fed and tended to the herds of quarter horses long before his wife Joyce Ann had flipped the first pancake.

Dogie and Joyce Ann invited me to stay with them, which may not seem unusual, except that before I got there we had never met. They were told an artist was looking to paint a veteran who is a rancher and extended the invitation. I assured them that I wouldn't interfere with ranch work and drove the 550 miles from Scottsdale, where I had been teaching, up to the high-altitude plateaus of Watrous.

Being invited to stay in the home of someone I have never met has happened many times over my career. I can't think of many other vocations where this kind of openness and trust in a stranger might occur. I suppose we artists are seen as a harmless lot, a clan of wayward vagabonds more interested in painting the family silver than stealing it. Regardless, each time I have been invited to a stranger's home, I have come away having made a new friend, and increasingly grateful to be an artist.▪

FLURRIES   *2012, watercolor on paper, 23.375 × 31 inches*

When I was in art school, I never seemed to fit in. While many of my fellow students were creating gigantic abstract expressionist works or rolling naked in pigment and transferring an imprint of their body onto the canvas, I was doing small paintings of my mother's blue and white teacups. I set the cups on the windowsill in my apartment and did studies of the sunlight moving across their translucent surfaces. I took special interest in the hand-painted designs on the cups and watching how the delicate colors changed with the light. Most important, I remembered my mother drinking tea from them.

My art professors were not impressed.

For years after I left art school, I continued to depict the china in my paintings. Sometimes the cups, saucers, and plates were featured prominently in a still life composition. Other times a single piece might be found as a seemingly random note hidden in the background. Somehow that china kept finding its way in.

We may never be able to explain why certain objects spur happiness within us. Perhaps it is solely what or whom the article represents. While we may seek to surround ourselves with items of beauty, it is the inner significance of the object that matters most. As artists we paint what is most meaningful to us and lifts our spirit. Our mission isn't so much to paint a replica of the thing itself, but to give rise to its essence. In doing so, we pave the way for our most joyful state of being, the very thing that makes freedom of expression and art possible.■

BEES   *2024, watercolor on paper, 11 × 9 inches*

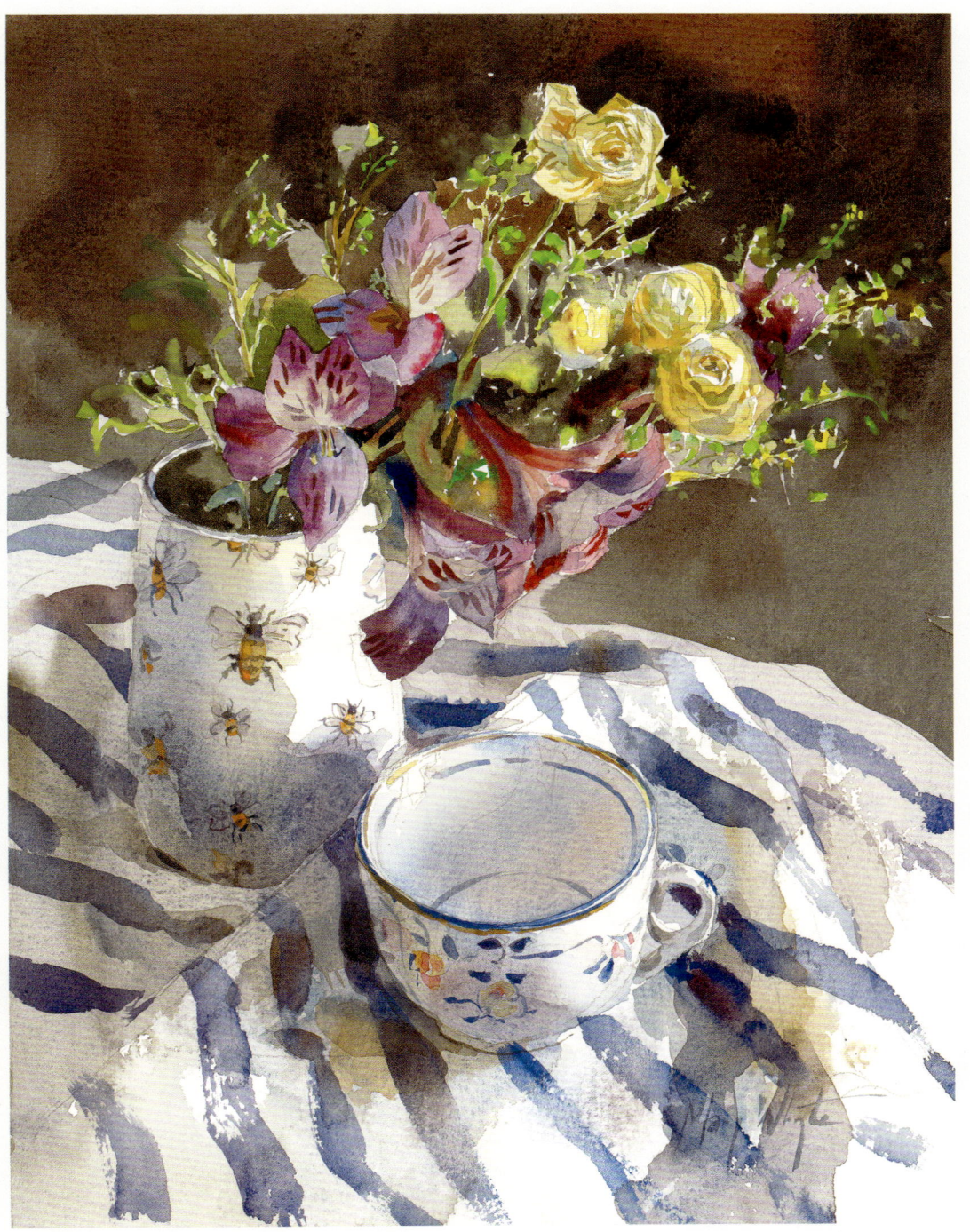

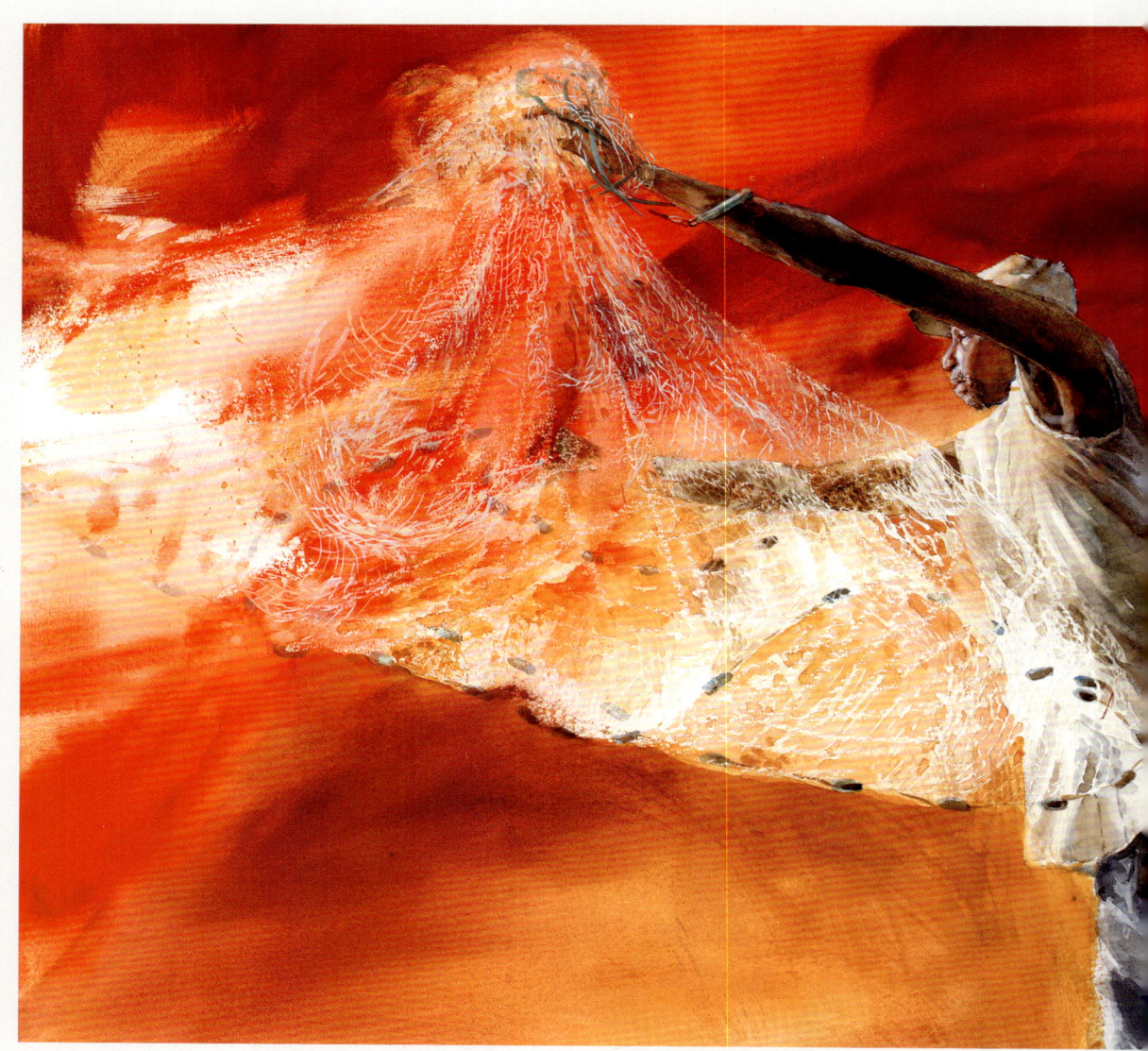

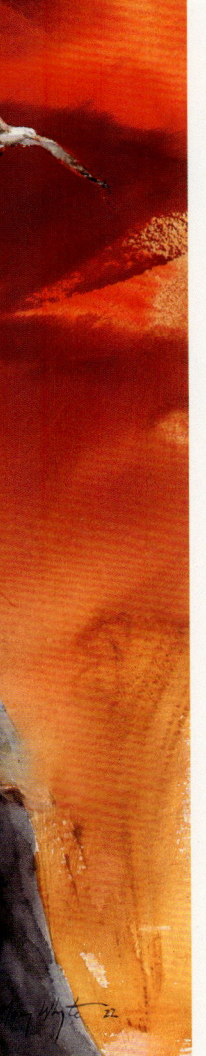

Every portrait that is painted
with feeling is a portrait of
the artist, not of the sitter.

—OSCAR WILDE

The marketing team was having trouble coming up with a title. A new biography about my life and work was about to go to press, and the publisher was struggling to find the right header, one that would sum up the book's contents, garner attention, and appeal to potential buyers. I sat at the end of the long table.

Possible titles were tossed back and forth among the group, followed by a discussion and laptops tapping furiously, checking to see if the idea had already been used. Nope. Already done. Nope, too wordy. Too vague. Too long. Too something.

RED TIDE   *2022, watercolor on paper, 20 × 28 inches*

Finally, the director sighed and turned to me, asking, "Mary, just what *is* it that you want people to know about your work?"

I thought for a moment, gauging my words, then said, "I just want people to know that my work is about more than a likeness."

The room went silent, eyes darting back and forth. The director bent over his laptop and typed rapidly. "That's it," he said, looking at his screen and holding his palms up. "More Than a Likeness: The Enduring Art of Mary Whyte."

The book was published the following fall.

That my work might be seen as more than a likeness became the overall message of the book and remains the ongoing mission of my life and teaching. I want my students and the public to know that art goes beyond merely making an exact copy of a person or a scene. We don't paint a likeness of a person; we paint what it feels like to be that person.

Over my career I have painted hundreds, maybe a thousand, portraits. Almost all of the commissioned portraits were of a person I had never previously met and in a place I had never been. All of the sessions were done on location and were limited to just a few hours— short enough not to overburden the model, but long enough for me to get a feeling for their character. After getting the initial studies and photographs I might need as resource material, the majority of the actual painting was done back in the quiet of my studio.

The physical features of the sitter are merely the prop. Behind the face, hair, attire, and setting is a unique set of emotions worthy of expression. With thoughtfulness and compassion, we are able to tap into the model's inner nature because, no matter their current state of being, we have already been there. We are not only rendering a likeness of a specific individual, we are pulling back the curtain and revealing a representation of humanity. ∎

"We don't paint a likeness of a person; we paint what it feels like to be that person."

I have always loved quilts and how they come together to tell a story. Each section of fabric has a history. The remnant of a child's outgrown dress. A father's worn blue work shirt. A few yards of fabric left over from curtains. A bolt of irresistible color purchased at a yard sale. Most quilters start with a symmetrical design in mind and cut precise shapes from various scraps of solid and patterned fabric. The stitches are usually tediously small, necessary for holding the quilt layers together through multiple washings and generations. What I especially love is that one individual scrap of fabric cannot stand alone. All of the pieces must join together for the quilt to be strong and complete.

For many years I collected quilts and used them as props in my paintings. Over time my collection grew, with examples from the Pennsylvania Amish, the Texas Hill Country, and numerous friends who I knew spent many months completing just one. However, my favorite quilts were made by the women of Johns Island, who would patch a weekly impromptu jumble of colorful scraps together into an unpredictable design, all to a chorus of Gullah spirituals. Mustered together from an assemblage of fragments from old clothing, outdated designer sample books, and donations from the public, each quilt was a cock-eyed, haphazard fabrication of total joy.

As artists, we make our own assemblages. Each work is an innovation of idea, color, and design, pieced together from the remembered, the discovered, and the boundless.▪

JUBILATION   *2005, watercolor on paper, 20 × 29 inches*

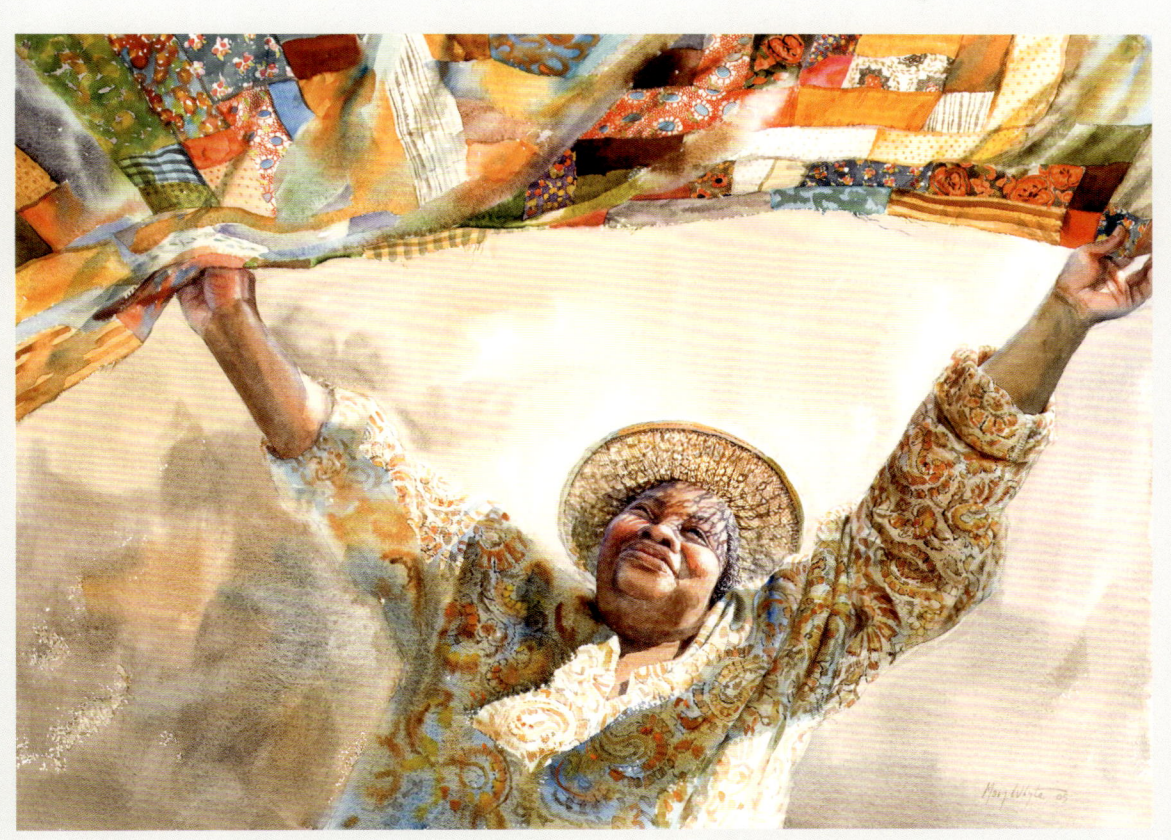

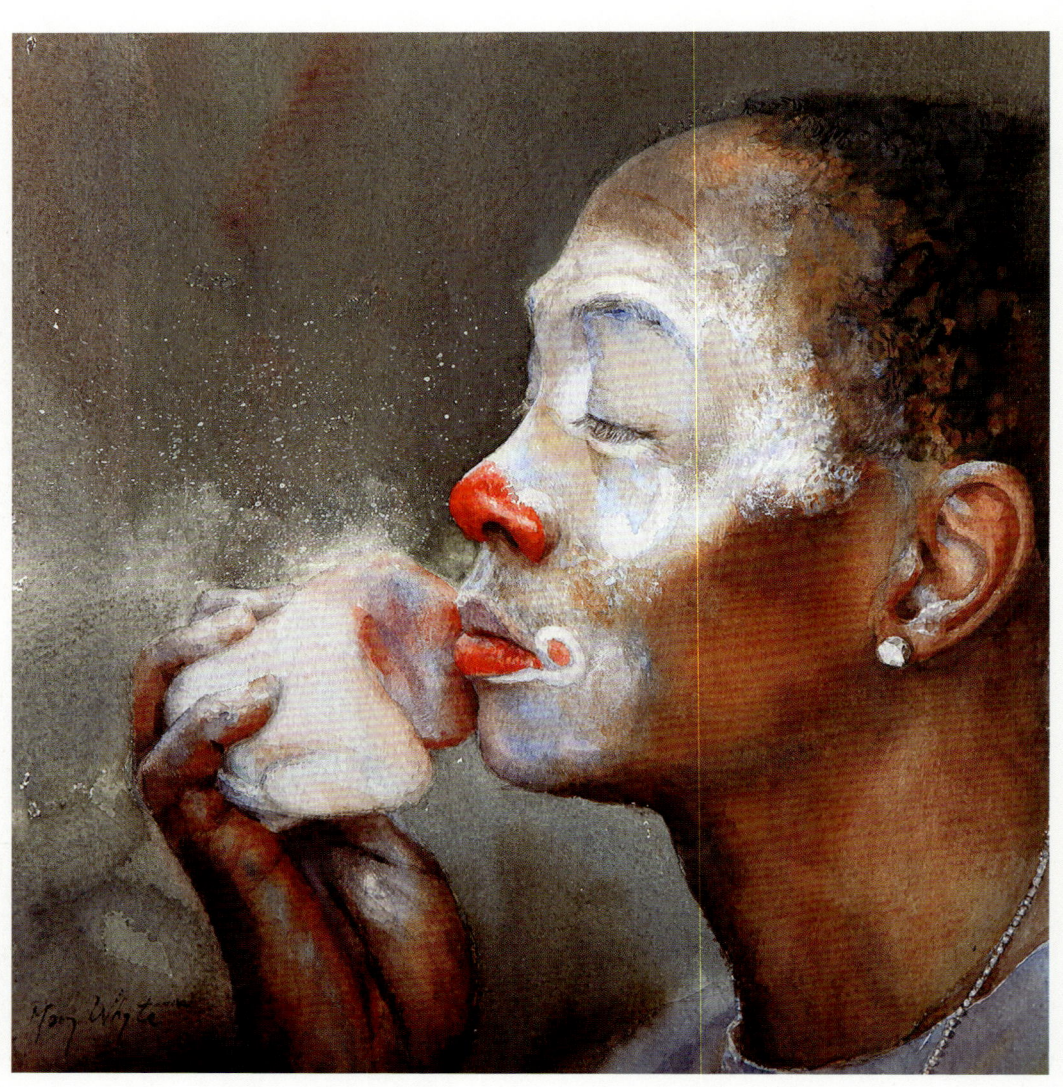

Several years ago, I had a student who I felt had real potential. Each watercolor she began in class was rolled out with enthusiasm and delight. Her abstracted imaginings of the figure were every artist's envy—a poetic and beautiful blend of shape and color coming together as pure magic.

And then she would wreck it.

Each time the student would get halfway through the painting only to begin reworking it. "I hate my style," she would tell me, furiously scrubbing out and painting over her work. She was convinced that her piece would never be good unless it looked like that of an artist whose work she greatly admired.

Each day I encouraged her to stop before the clouds of doubt and dissatisfaction set in and she reworked her painting into oblivion. In her mind all she could see was the work and style of the other artist. With each adjustment and correction the student made, she erased a little bit of herself. She had given up her creative birthright and handed it to another artist.

Each of us is born with our own style, which is as unique and individual as our thumbprint. With time, education, and experience, our style can be strengthened and refined but never deleted. The less we try to make our work look like someone else's, the more we give it the freedom to flourish and the chance to become completely and joyfully our own. Instead of asking if your style is any good, ask if you are being true to it.∎

POWDER   *2012, watercolor on paper, 9.5 × 9.5 inches*

When I was in my early twenties, I had my first solo exhibition at a gallery in Philadelphia. I was excited that one of my former instructors would be coming from New York to attend the opening. I spent months preparing for the show, producing a wide variety of works that included nudes, still lifes, chickens, barns, florals, landscapes, seascapes, and pen and inks. A week after the opening my teacher wrote me a letter congratulating me on successful sales but cautioning me on what he viewed as the "department store" look of my offerings. He warned that until I forged a recognizable style and consistent point of view, success in the art world might elude me.

It took me several years to identify the subject matter, style, and message I would claim as my own. In life and in art, I learned that we recognize our most earnest self by how it feels on the inside, not by how many "likes" it gets on the outside. Gradually, as artists do, I came into my own.

Over the years I have found that my technique has strengthened and my palette of colors has deepened, becoming more confident and expressive. Not surprisingly, the overall concept of my work today has many similarities to what appealed to me when I was young. Although the models and locations for my paintings have changed, the original starting point has remained. Decades later, so much of what I find myself painting is a faint echo of the people and places I remember as a teenager growing up in the rural Midwest. There is no other way to explain how over fifty years later I would find myself in a barn painting a woman holding a chicken, hundreds of miles from Ohio.▪

SOLSTICE   *2024, watercolor on paper, 24.5 × 20.5 inches*

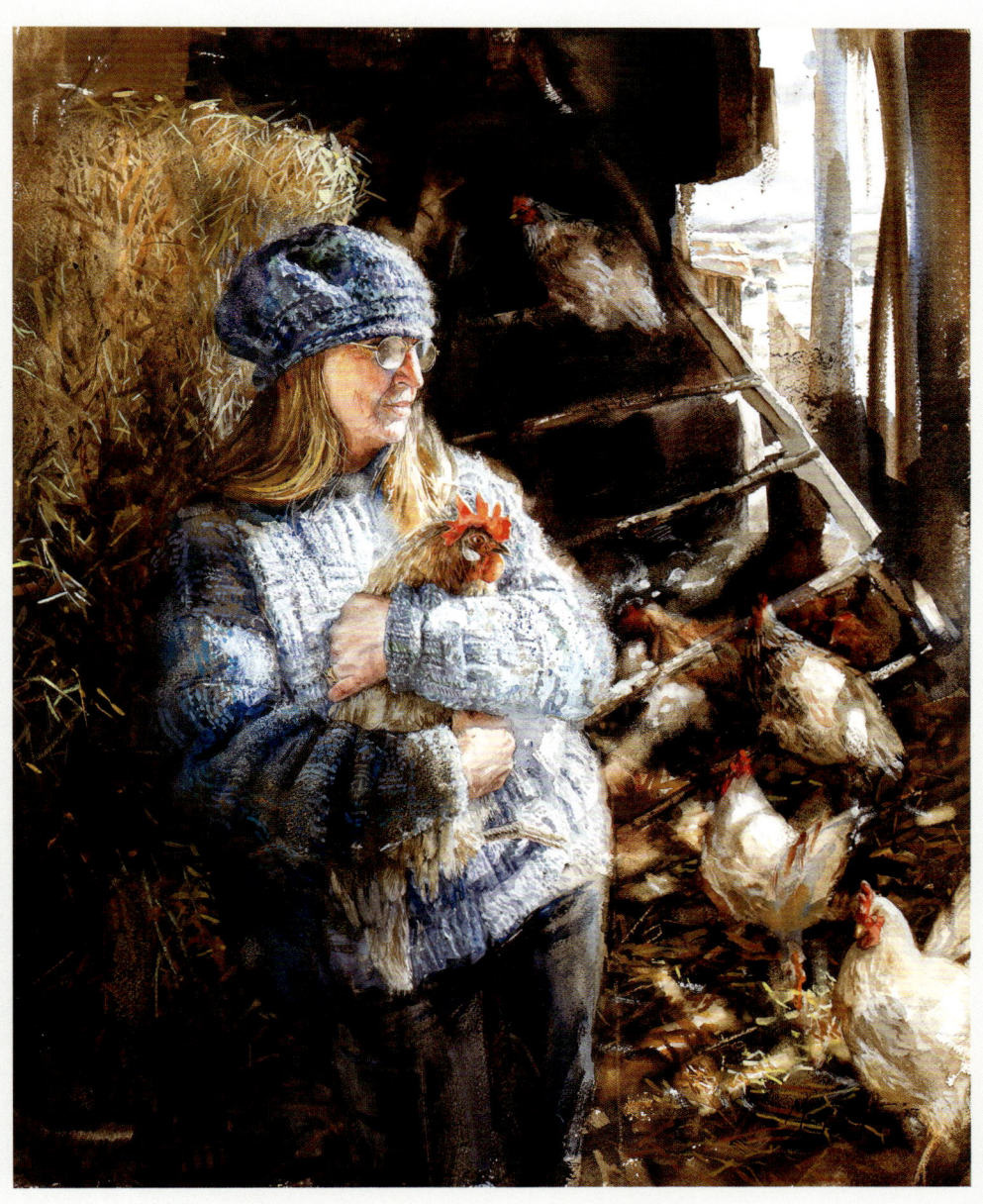

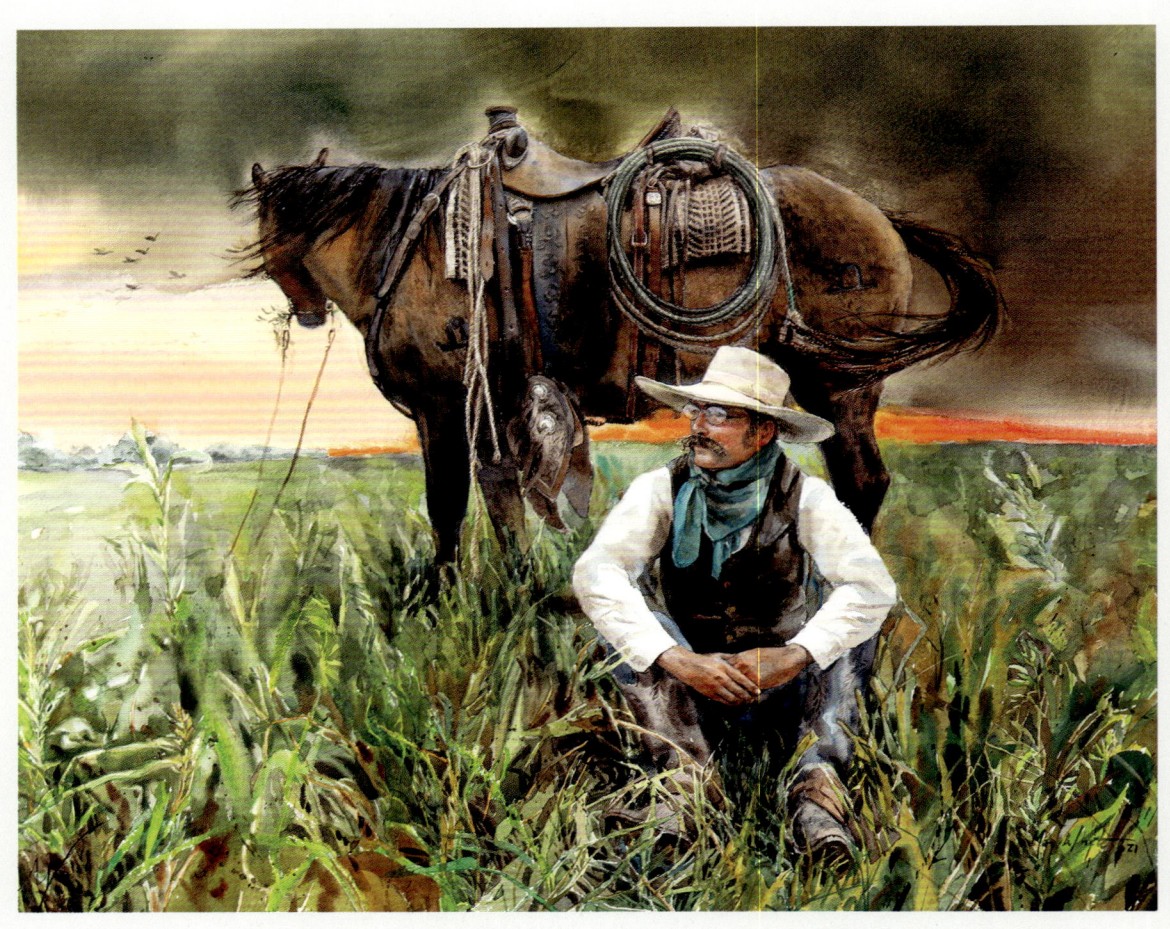

Don't wait for inspiration.
It comes while working.

—HENRI MATISSE

Students sometimes ask what they should do when they don't feel like painting. What if they just aren't inspired?

One of the biggest killers of creativity is procrastination. With enough passing time and distance from our original inspiration, even the most exciting ideas lose altitude. There never seems to be a lack of excuses for why we put off making art. "I don't have time." "I don't know what to paint." "My studio is a mess." "I just don't feel like it."

I admit there have been times I have procrastinated using each of those excuses, only to later regret a lost opportunity. When I was painting a series of southern blue-collar workers, I delayed the one watercolor I most wanted to do, of a local milliner who made beautiful hats. A year later when I finally called her shop, I was told she had passed away. Since then, I've learned to immediately go after the paintings that feel most urgent and interest me the most. It is a system that has worked for me; I never seem to run out of subject matter that ignites my imagination. Put off procrastinating, not painting.

Sometimes inspiration just needs a little nudge. Activities such as doodling, journal writing, visiting museums, and looking at art books can help fire up one's creative juices. Most important, don't put it off. As Mother Theresa said, "Yesterday is gone. Tomorrow is not here. All we have is today. Let us begin." ∎

ROPER *2022, watercolor on paper, 21 × 27 inches*

On my coffee table I have a book titled *Picasso at 90*. It is a perpetual reminder that no matter how old we are, creativity is something we can either ignore or forfeit but never lose. Every day we have the opportunity to leave our mark. We can plant our flag at the center of our experience and say *this is what gives my heart gladness*—this garden, this song, this way of painting, this recipe, this poem, this belief.

To be an artist is to give proof of God and of the beauty that surrounds us. As artists we are the conduits of awe, scribes of this very moment. We shouldn't worry if our ideas have the approval of others. What matters is that we seized upon our moment of greatest joy and brought it forth in our work.

The women at the Hebron St. Francis Senior Center on Johns Island showed me that one is never too old to dream a new dream. Well into their seventies, eighties, and nineties, each could tell a tale of setbacks, debilitating health challenges, and sorrowful personal losses. And yet, on walkers and canes and in wheelchairs, the power of their soaring spirituals can raise them to their feet.

For many years Margaret held the position at the center as the Super Senior—the eldest member of the group who greeted everyone at the door with a gentle hug and kiss on the cheek. Each Wednesday when I asked her how she was doing, the answer was always the same. "I'm blessed," Margaret would say, smiling up at me and patting my arm. Week after week it was the same response. *"I'm blessed."* According to Margaret, she was giving it all over to God each day, trusting for a dream and a blessing.

ADVENT   *2018, watercolor on paper, 24 × 22 inches*

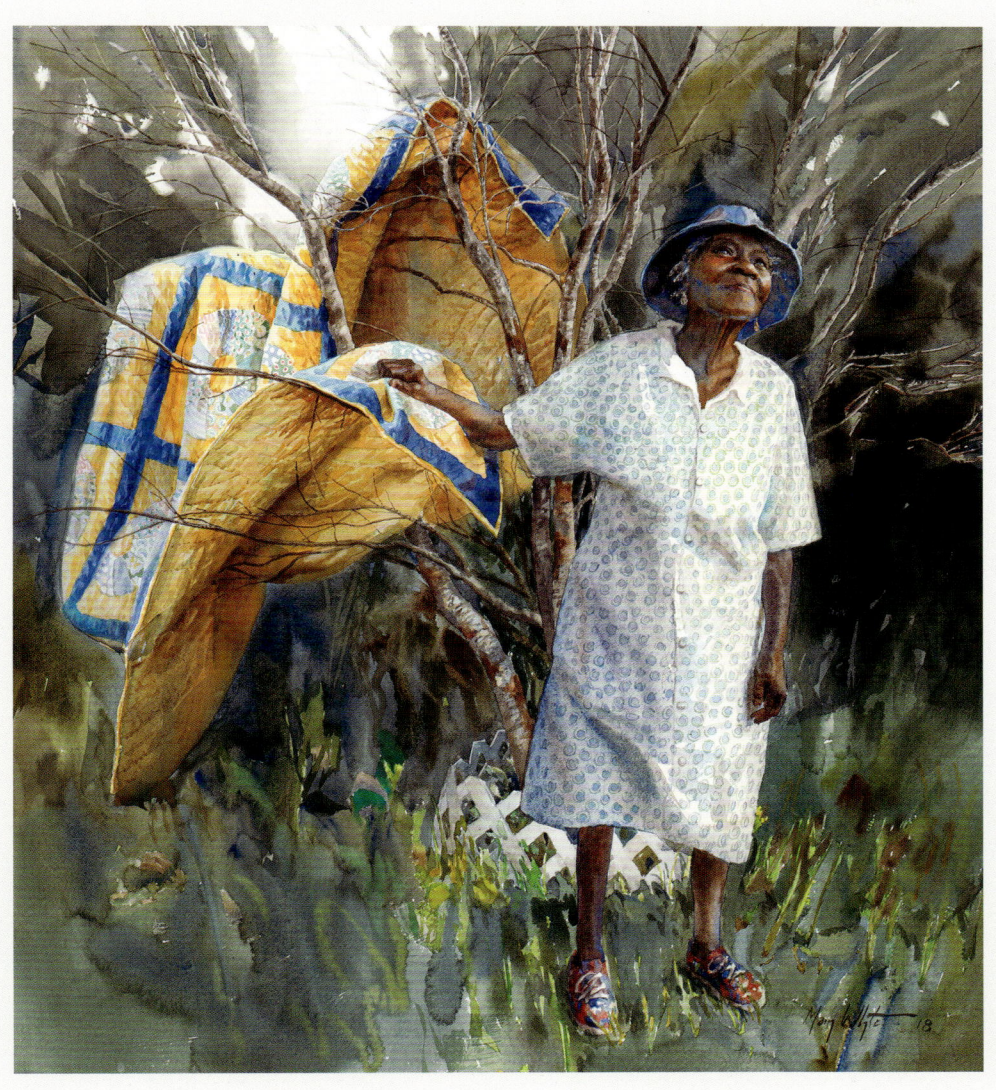

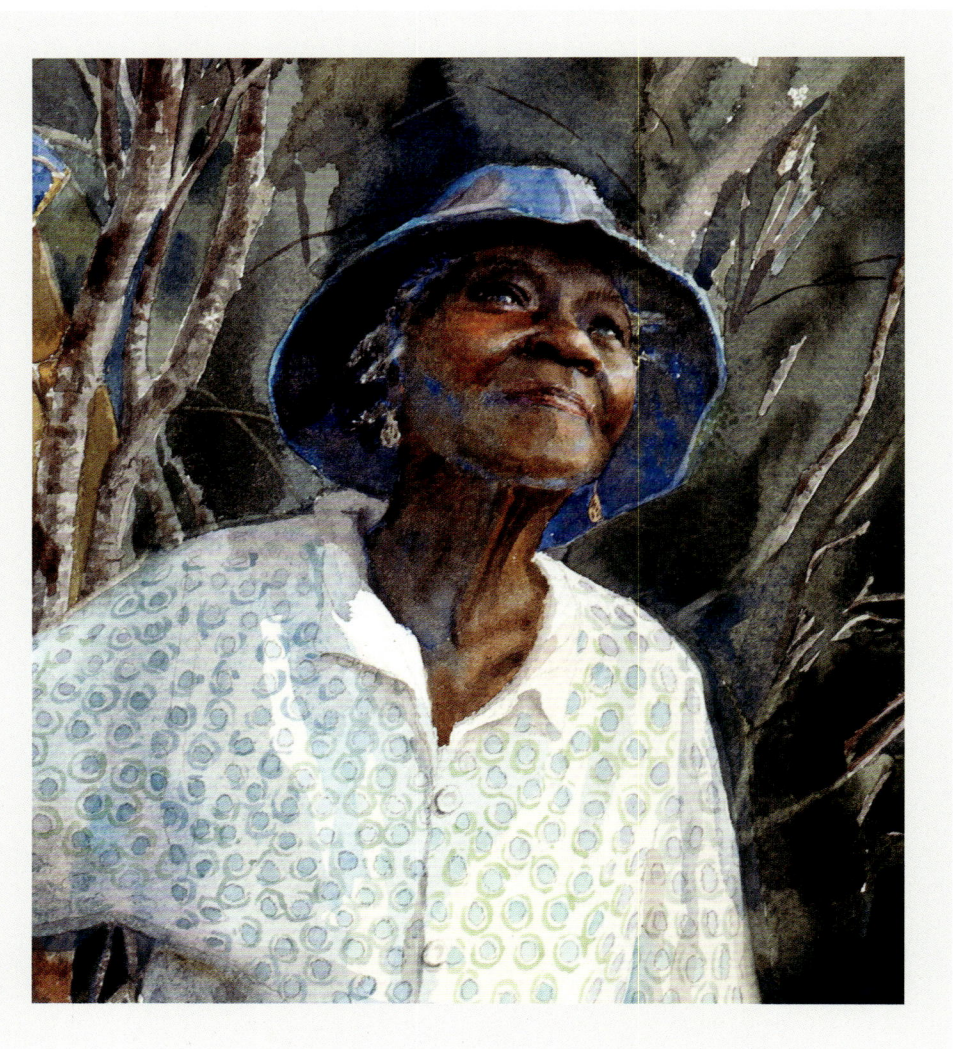

I often painted Margaret in her home, a small, red frame house on Johns Island that she shared with several members of her family. The walls in her paneled living room were covered to the ceiling with photos of grandchildren in caps and gowns, formally dressed wedding parties, and great-grandchildren cradled in hand-crocheted blankets. Squeezed in here and there, and down the hallway, were framed prints of pictures I had painted of her.

Outside Margaret's kitchen window was a small shed containing gardening equipment and lawn furniture. Scattered about the yard and up her front steps were pots festooned with plastic flowers and pinwheels. A dozen or more feral cats and kittens would scurry under the shed each time my car turned into the driveway, reappearing only when they heard the screen door open, and Margaret tapping her wooden spoon on a pan piled high with Sunday scraps. Swirling in circles, soft tails brushing her legs, the cats would yowl up at her while Margaret said a prayer over them before setting the food on the ground. Each cat, kitten, pork scrap, chicken bone, tree, and cloud was worthy of a blessing. For Margaret, there was plenty of grace to go around.

In the old days, Margaret did the wash on weekdays and then hung it to dry outside on a rope tied between two wooden posts. Dozens of blue work shirts, pants, colorful tiny socks, and bed linens would dry in the still, humid air, occasionally lifted heavenward by a warm breeze coming off the ocean.

When the posts supporting the clotheslines finally fell down, she draped the wet laundry on the bushes. Margaret said she never worried about having modern conveniences, things such as washers and dryers, as God would provide when He was ready. The next year for Mother's Day, her children put their money together and bought a brand-new clothes dryer.

For several Christmases, the seniors at the center held a Secret Santa gift exchange. A month before their holiday party, each member drew the name of another out of a basket. To whom you would be giving a gift was to be kept secret, with a maximum expenditure of five dollars. Two Wednesdays before Christmas, the women decorated the room with red and green paper ornaments, and each unwrapped their present at the same time, holding it up for the others to see and admire. I held up my gift, a small handmade pillow, with a stitched quote in the center that read, "God Never Closes a Door Without Opening Another." When I saw Margaret smile and nod, I knew the gift was from her.

We are never too old to dream a new dream or to discover a more vibrant path. As artists, with each passing year we bring more substance to the easel, both in technique and experience, drawing from a seasoned, wiser, and more expansive view of the world. I know many artists older than I who are still in their studio every day experimenting with different materials, trying new techniques, and setting challenging goals. They are the artists who will not be sidelined by time. ∎

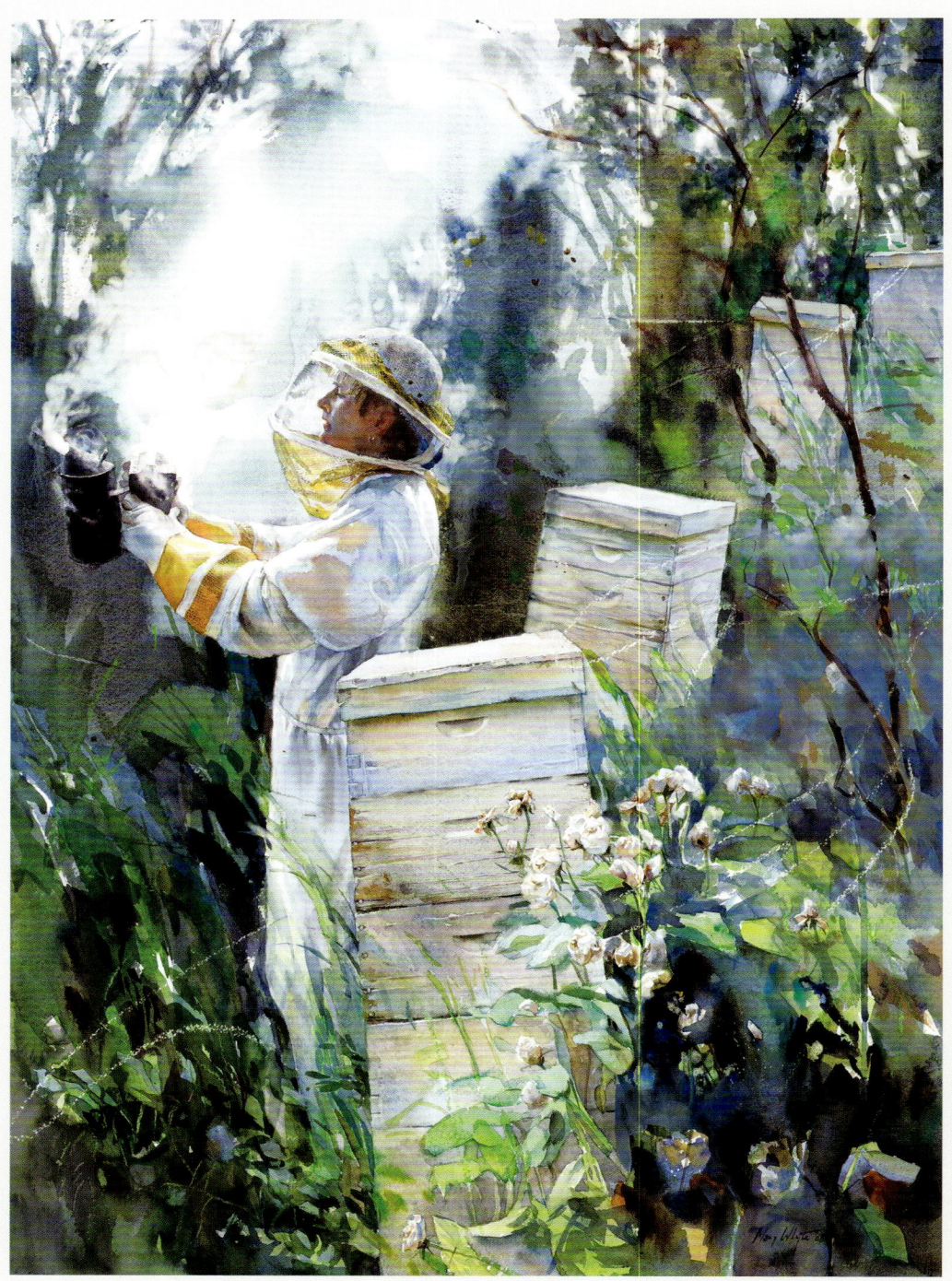

Creativity is imagination with wings. It solves dilemmas, sees around obstacles, fosters hope, and dreams what, to some, may be the impossible. Unfettered creativity is the equivalent of being given a lifetime pass to travel anywhere in the world with your dog and guitar. It is an all-expense-paid, never-ending adventure of discovery and wonder.

In traditional art academies, students are trained to duplicate the appearance of reality by copying. With practice, our eye for proportion, perspective, light, shape, value, edge, and color is honed and sharpened, enabling us to accurately render what is before us. We learn how to draw a foot and make it look like a convincing foot. Where many artists tend to fall short is thinking that being able to copy something and make it look real is the end game.

The object of painting isn't just to duplicate something. Many of the world's finest and most admired paintings are abstract. As creators, we are to go beyond the visual manifestation of an object, attaining a momentary state of being both in ourselves and in the spirit of our subject. Our aim as artists is to forgo logic, precision, and reality and press toward our senses. We are to be poets, not journalists.

Never let reality ruin a good painting. Look beyond what is really there, allowing accuracy in only when it helps to propel the feeling being strived for. Instead of copying what already exists, aim for your highest imagining. ■

BEE KEEPER'S DAUGHTER   *2008, watercolor on paper, 28.75 × 21.75 inches*

Frequently, art students assume that somewhere in the art cosmos there is a carefully curated list of subject matter that is deemed paint-worthy. Anything not included on the list is to be avoided.

In truth, *everything* is more-or-less paintable depending on our response to it. This became abundantly clear to me in a week-long class I attended when I was in my early twenties. Our teacher was the accomplished portrait painter Everett Raymond Kinstler (1926–2019). On that particular day the students were arguing that only certain subject matter has the potential for good paintings: bucolic landscapes, toddlers playing at the beach, fall sunsets, or a cat sitting by the window.

Listening, Kinstler reached into his pocket and tossed a set of keys onto the table, saying, "OK, paint *that.*" We all stood there, mouths open, staring at the keys. *That?* Certainly, such ordinary and mundane subject matter couldn't possibly translate into an appealing painting.

Kinstler set up his easel, squeezed the colors onto his wooden palette, and proceeded to create the most weepingly beautiful and intimate oil painting imaginable. The artist's depiction of the late afternoon light glinting off the keys with their soft shadows against the table's worn patina managed to project the feeling of a weary man coming home at the end of a long workday. The painting was exquisite.

It was a lesson I will never forget. ∎

HIS   *2023, watercolor on paper, 5 × 7 inches*

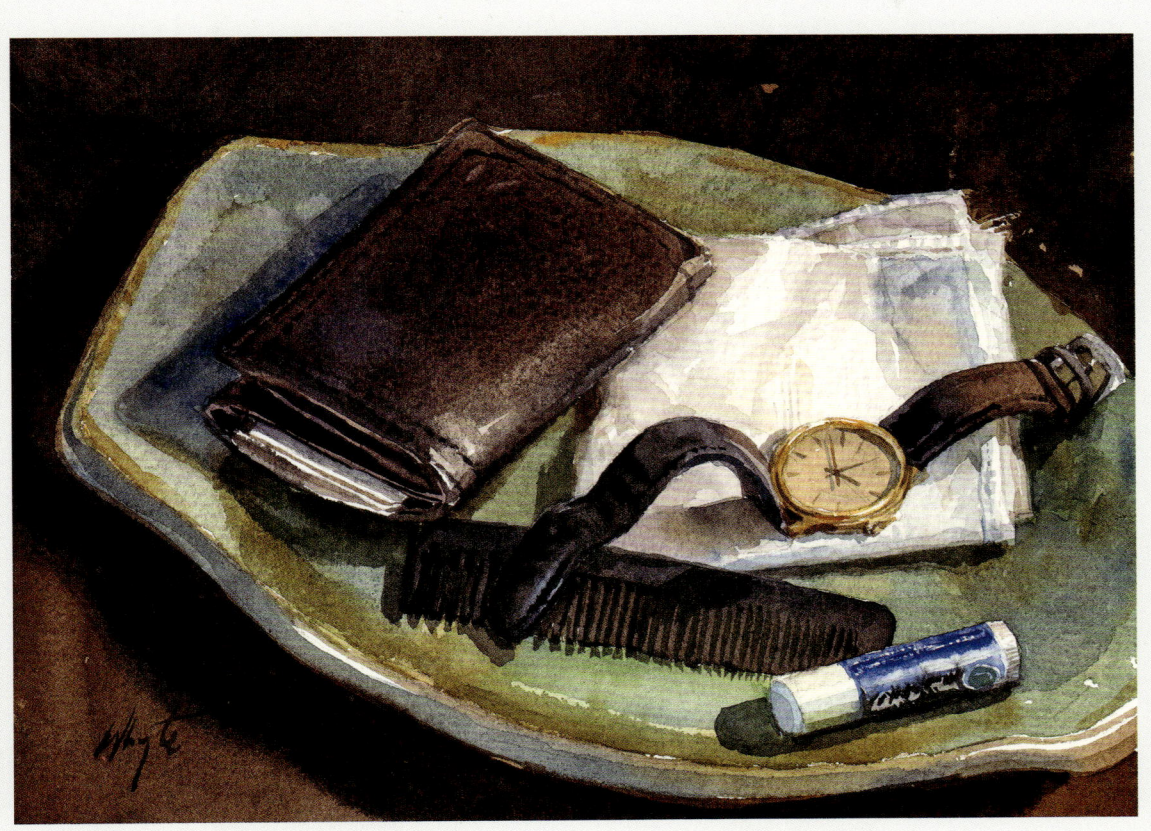

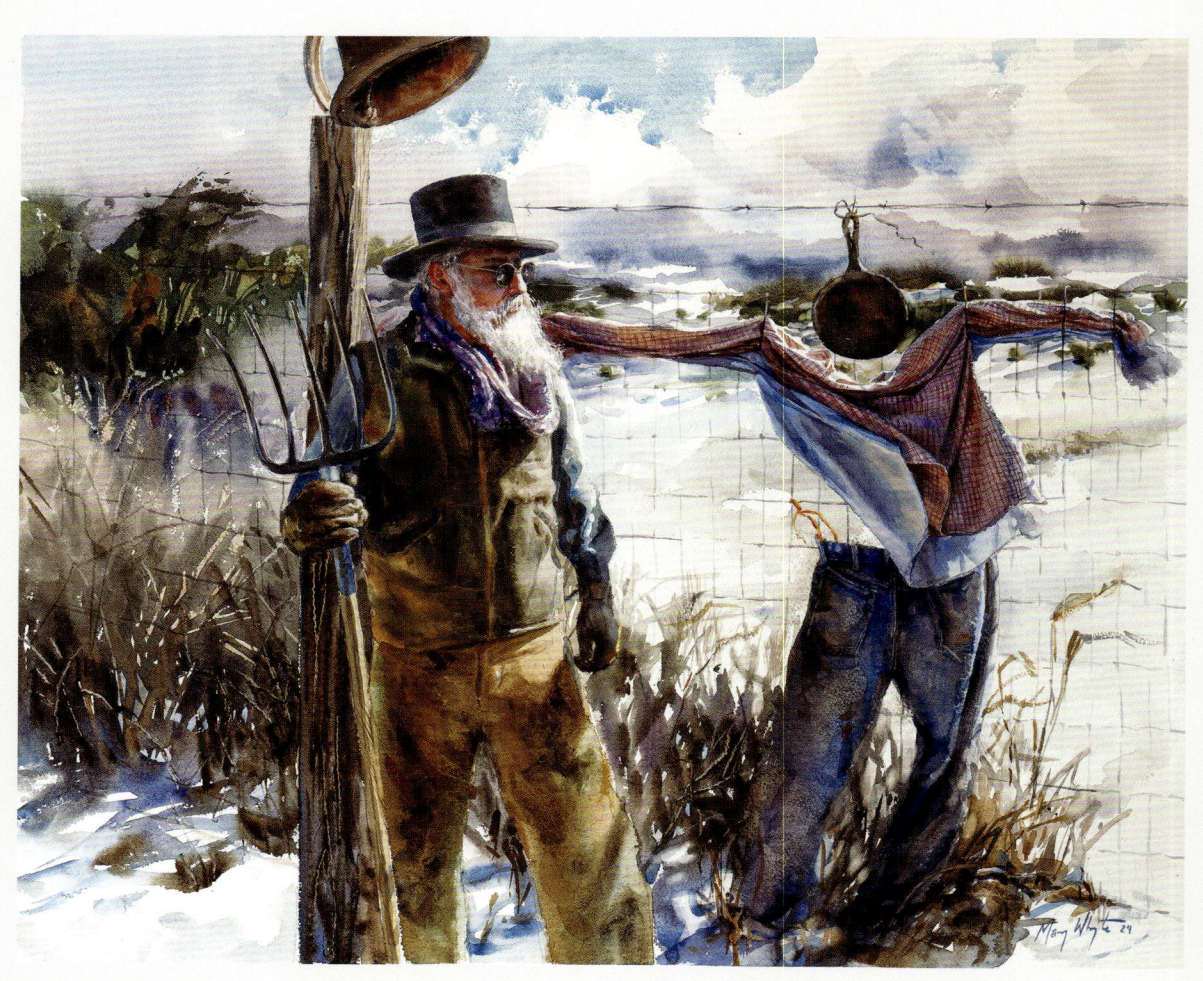

Chance is always powerful.
Let your hook be always cast:
in the pool where you least
expect it, there will be a fish.

—OVID

M any times, I have ventured out to paint not knowing whether I would find who or what I was looking for. I might have a vague destination circled on a map or sometimes the name of someone I wanted to meet, but often I've gone on instinct alone, confident that what I would find would be far better than anything I could have imagined or planned for.

In Nambe Pueblo, eighteen miles north of Santa Fe, New Mexico, I met, by chance, Anne and Eli. Set atop a bluff in the foot-hills of the Sangre de Cristo Mountains, the couple's farm is a string of wooden and metal structures cobbled together to house their chickens, geese, and goats. Two white dogs welcomed me at the gate.

Although my goal had been to paint a woman holding a chicken (*Solstice*), when Eli came around the corner of the barn, I almost dropped my sketchbook. With his white beard, colorful kerchief, round wire-rimmed glasses, and black top hat, Eli was too won-derful a subject to pass up, especially when he paused in front of the makeshift scarecrow he had made and named Pan Head. The scenario was far more surprising and unscripted than anything I could have conceived on my own.

I love painting everyday people who live their lives without the purpose or expectation of receiving accolades or recognition. Although it may be an honor to be asked to paint a celebrity or politician, I would much rather paint the person who cleans their office. ∎

PAN HEAD   *2024, watercolor on paper, 20 × 26 inches*

There are rarely, if ever, perfect working conditions for painting outdoors. It might be hot, cold, windy, humid, or buggy. Just when we get our easel set up, ominous clouds might gather on the horizon and a storm approaches. Inside the studio, conditions can sometimes be just as daunting, such as not having a workable space to create or having too many distractions. Older students often lament there is not enough time to get up the learning curve in order to gain the skills needed to paint even reasonably well. So why bother?

You are never too old or too late to pursue a dream. History is awash with seniors who made their greatest accomplishments late in life. At age eighty-seven Pablo Picasso (1881–1973) produced 347 engravings. At seventy-six, after arthritis made it too difficult to hold a sewing needle, Grandma Moses (1860–1961) took up painting and painted every day for twenty-five years. At seventy-five, Barbara Hillary (1931–2019) became the first Black woman to reach the North Pole. Diagnosed with cancer at 71 and limited to working from a wheelchair, Henri Matisse (1869–1954) called the last fourteen years of his life "une seconde vie" (second life) and created some of his most groundbreaking work.

What if you were convinced the world would end in five years? Then five years fly by and the world and you are still here. Do you want to look back thinking about what you could have done in those five years, or would you rather have spent the time pursuing your wildest dreams? Whether you ever achieve your ultimate ambitions or not, a life filled with curiosity, daring, and full-on engagement is a life you wouldn't want to miss.■

CREATION   *2017, watercolor on paper, 33 × 29.5 inches*

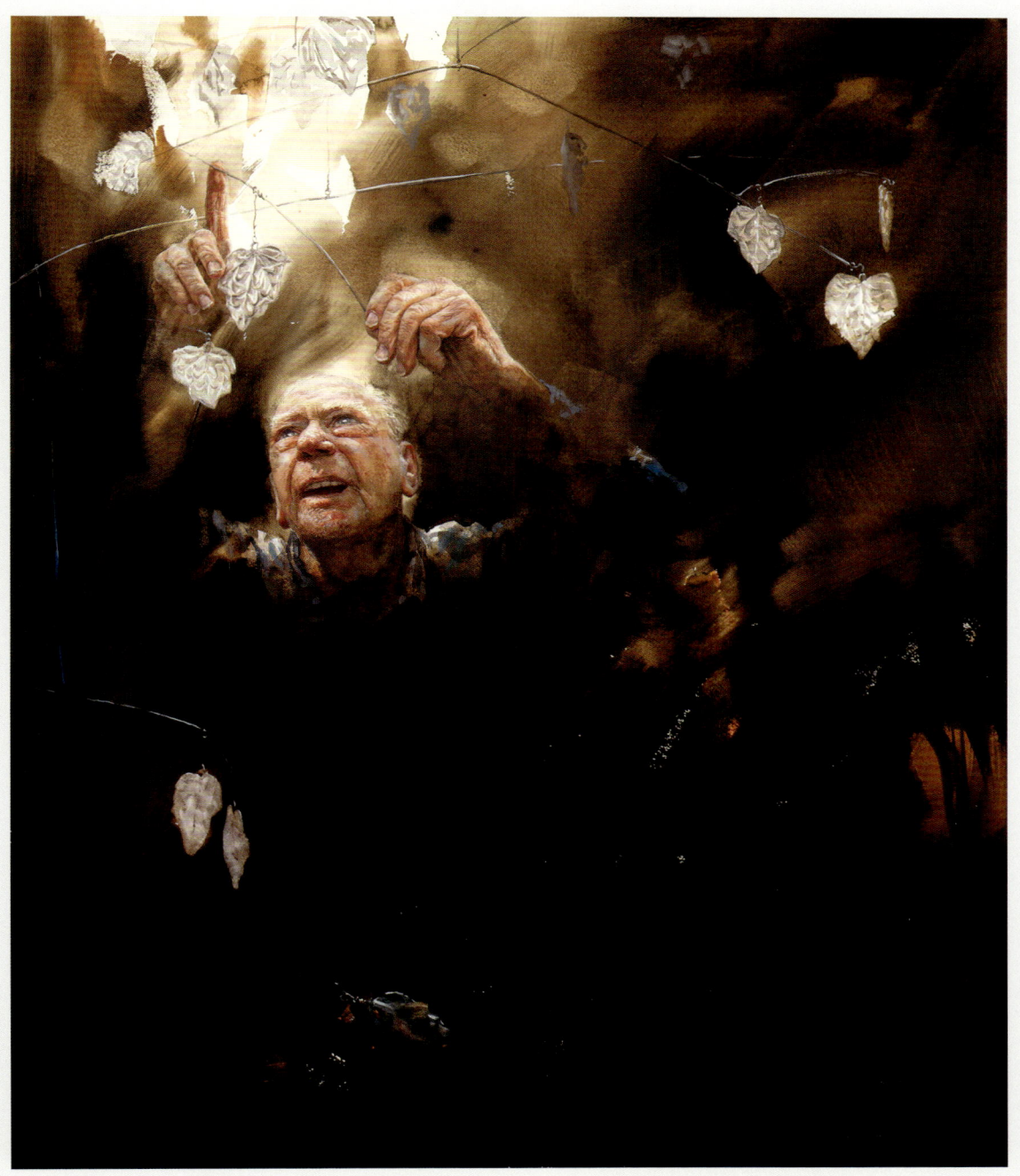

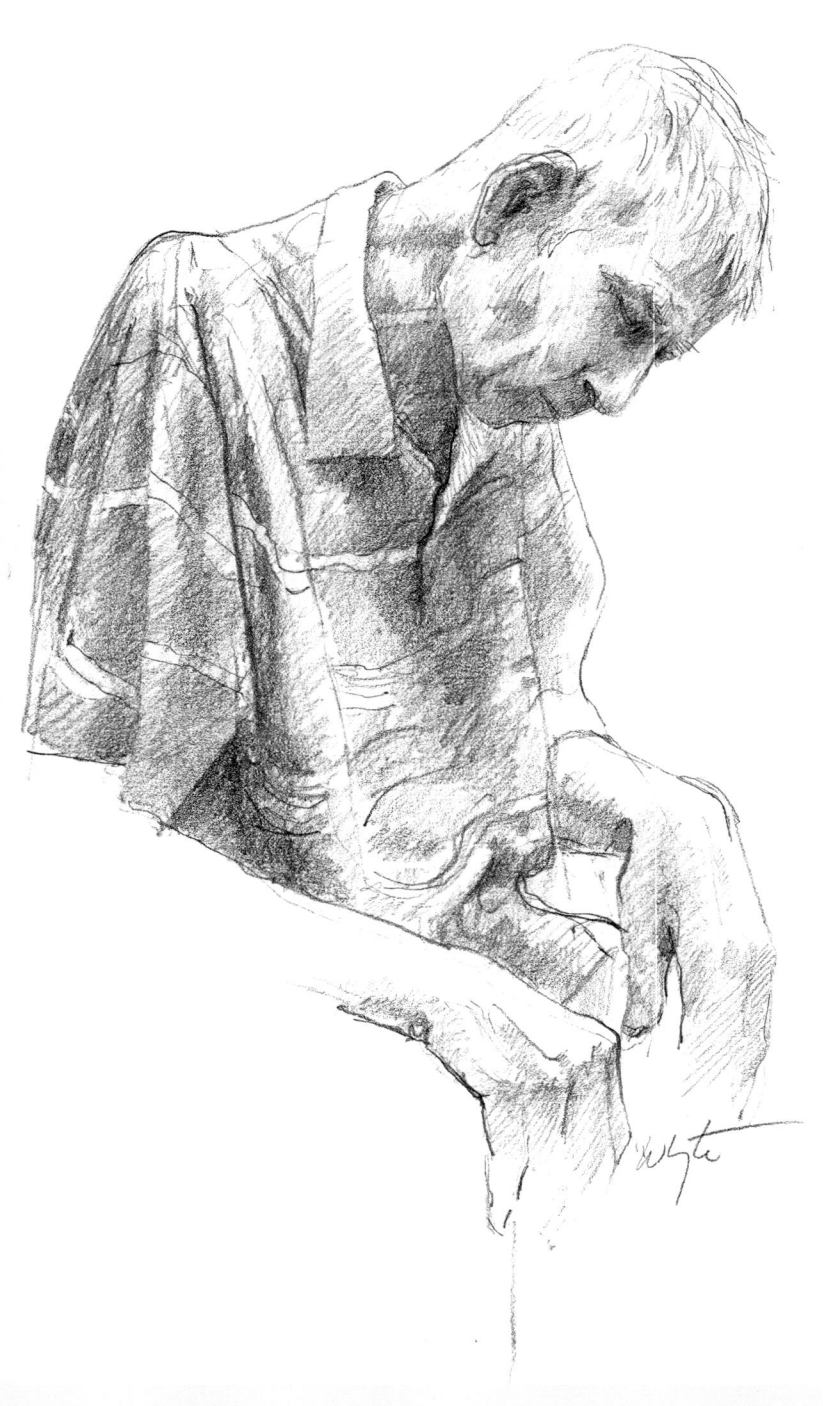

> There are only two ways to live your life. One is as though nothing is a miracle. The other is as though everything is a miracle.

> —ALBERT EINSTEIN

When I was little, I greatly admired my two older brothers, especially Bob. Seven years older than I, he was the bright, athletic, high school star with his own car and on his way to Purdue University. To me, he was the epitome of cool.

Sixty years later I would find myself visiting him at a memory care center in Sarasota, Florida. He was a resident in a home where he wasn't able to find his own room. The first time I went to visit him there, I found him in the dining room area, sitting alone on a bench, while a hired musician was doing a lively rendition of Willie Nelson's "On the Road Again." Other residents were seated at tables scattered around the room napping or doing puzzles. Bob didn't know I was coming. It had been a few months since I had last visited, and I was excited to see him. I jumped in front of him just a few feet away, my arms opened wide into an exuberant "tada!"

Staring blankly back at me was the motionless shell of someone who used to take me tobogganing at night, careening wildly down a steep, wooded ravine. He showed no recognition or response to my presence. Then a twitch in his expression registered alarm and his eyes widened. I saw his fists clench. I knew that my brother sometimes had violent episodes, so I stepped back. "Bob," I said softly, dropping my arms to my side. "It's me, Mare. Your dweeby little sister."

His white brows furrowed, and he pressed his lips tightly together. Then his face began to smooth over, his mouth sliding open into a limp smile. I did a sidestep and goofy bounce to the music, and he stood up, doing his own little boogie. We hugged, and for the first time since his wedding many years before, my brother and I danced. His steps were small and shuffled, but they heard the beat of the music as he gave me a slow twirl. When the song was over, we both grinned and bowed. I expected applause from the other residents, but there was no reaction. Apparently, busting a move in this place is nothing unusual.

MY BROTHER   *2024, graphite on paper, 11 × 8.5 inches*

Later we walked arm in arm down the hall of the facility. We stopped in front of a large, colorful oil painting of a landscape that was hanging near his room. I knew he walked past it several times a day. "Bob, look at that painting." I said, pointing to it. "What do you think?"

My brother stepped closer to take a look, his tall thin frame stooped into a languid question mark. His glasses slid down his nose.

"Do you like the colors?" I asked. "It's beautiful, don't you think?"

Bob said nothing and leaned in closer to the image. The stubble that covered his cheeks and jaw gave his face a silver cast. A remnant of something such as spaghetti sauce was on his chin. He exhaled and his mouth dropped open. "Wow," he whispered, turning to me. "That's *awesome*."

We moved down the hall and stopped in front of another painting, this time of white birds in flight. His wife, Sandy, had told me they looked at it every day when she came to visit and that it was his favorite. "Do you like this one?" I asked.

Bob shuffled closer to the painting and stood motionless, staring at it. His hands dropped to his side. I wondered what he must be seeing. His jaw fell open and he wheezed out, "Wow." He turned his face to me, his eyes wide with amazement, mouth wide, and then back to the painting. "That's *awesome*," he said, pointing a bony finger at the picture.

In all my life I had never heard my brother say "awesome." It was a word that he said had been pilfered by the younger generation as the standard day-to-day response for everything, such as ordering a side of fries, or spelling one's last name for the salesperson. *Awesome.* As if being able to spell one's name correctly is an amazing achievement.

That day, when looking at the art, my brother used the word again and again. For each painting we stopped to view, his response was as enthusiastic and as earnest as for the first one. I was hopeful that perhaps my engineer brother was exhibiting a previously unknown deep appreciation for art, until a few minutes later when he stopped in front of a bright red fire extinguisher and he proclaimed that it, too, was *awesome*.

I came to realize from my brother Bob that of all the seemingly insidious ways a body and brain might be highjacked, dementia might not be so bad after all. To live in a constant kaleidoscope of revolving wonder, where one's diminishing ability is made perfect by beauty, might be the highest achievement to which an artist can aspire. And that even to a mind stopping short, each of us might witness grace and the astonishing miracle of the everyday. ▪

"Staring blankly back at me was the motionless shell of someone who used to take me tobogganing at night, careening wildly down a steep, wooded ravine."

Art can have a higher purpose, even if it is unknown to its maker. When my exhibition depicting blue collar workers, called *Working South,* was on view, the head of a major corporation told me that when he saw the paintings he was stunned to recognize in the faces a profound humanity. These portraits were of *real people.* Because of that revelation the executive made the decision to give his employees better compensation. When the exhibition *We the People: Portraits of Veterans in America* began touring museums, many visitors reported gaining a much greater respect and appreciation for our military.

The portraits sometimes had an unexpected and positive effect on the models as well, giving them a sense of validation and increased standing within their family, workplace, and community. Christian, an Army veteran and window washer from Detroit, was one of many service men and women who wrote me a letter of appreciation, saying that although the military had taught him leadership, teamwork, and adaptive skills, being part of *We the People* had changed his life. Another model told me he hadn't felt this popular since he played football in high school. For Algie, a crabber from Savannah, being selected for a portrait was all the proof he needed that "God sees us all."

Art is so much more than making stuff. Art can challenge us to do better and *be* better. Do not settle for mediocrity when you have been called to a life of excellence. Whether we are artists or not, art can open our eyes and ask us to step up, giving us a glimpse of our best possible self. ∎

WINDOW   *2016, watercolor on paper, 38.5 × 28.25 inches*

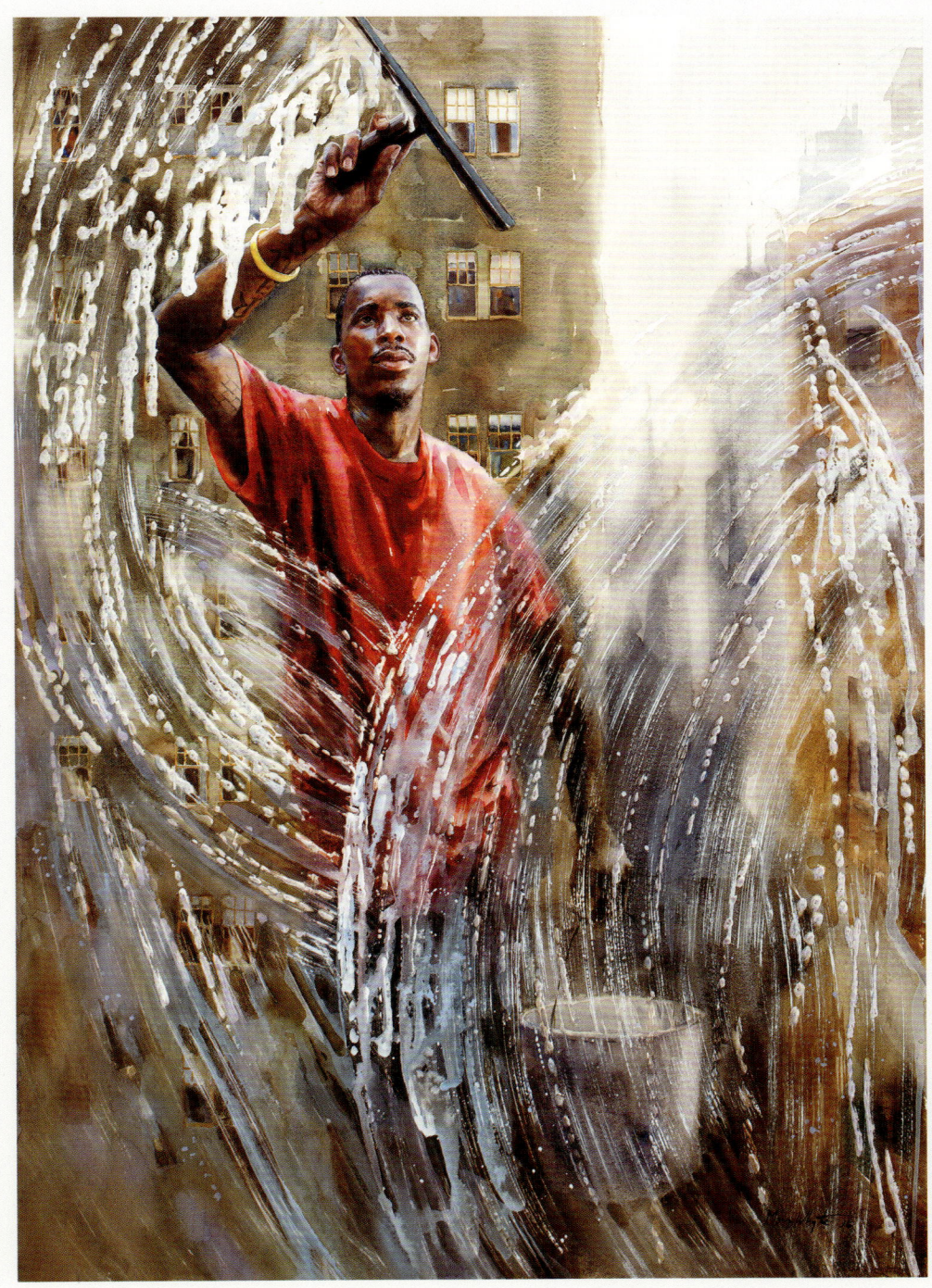

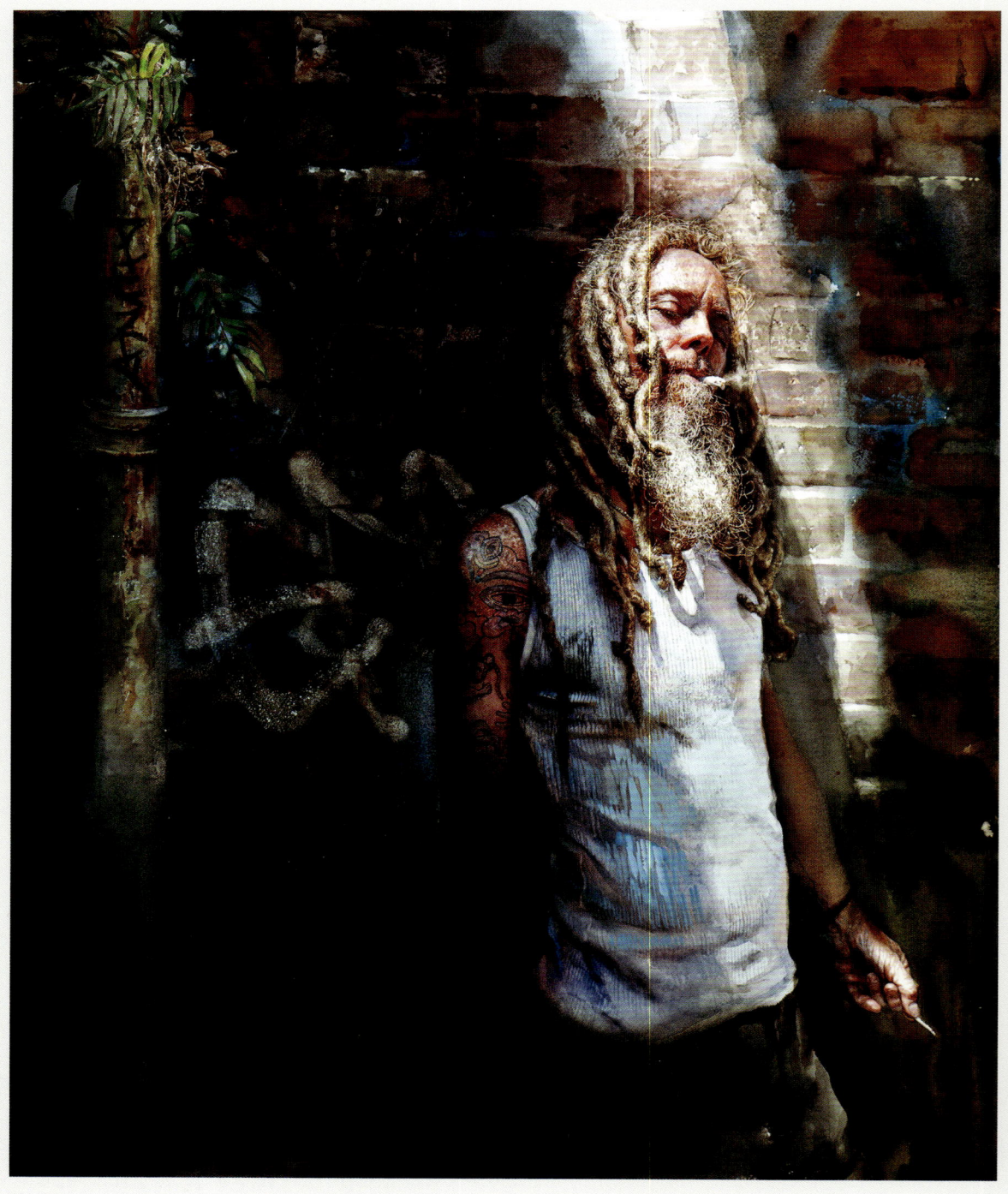

> If I create from the
> heart nearly everything
> works; if from the
> head, almost nothing.
>
> —MARC CHAGALL

Students often ask what they should paint to win a blue ribbon. They want to know whether they should paint like the exhibition juror or what is trending in the galleries?

Jurors as well as gallery owners look for much of the same qualities when selecting art. Instead of choosing paintings that are mannerist, old-fashioned, or contrived, gallerists and judges mine for brilliance, originality, and authenticity. Although the objective of most commercial galleries is to make a profit, they, like jurors, are searching for work that is the cream of the crop. When I asked one gallery owner what that might be or what the next trend in the art world would be, his response was, "None of us have any idea, but we are all hoping we find it first."

The first blue ribbon I ever received for a watercolor was from a small art league outside of Philadelphia when I was in my early twenties. While many of the other entries in the show were images of windmills, Venetian canals, or the prerequisite still life with a wine bottle and candle, mine was created just a few blocks from where I lived and depicted the back of a blue house with laundry

ABSOLUTION *2010, watercolor on paper, 22.5 × 28.5 inches*

hanging on the clothesline. At the opening, an older artist who also had work in the exhibition said to me, "What? You got first prize for painting someone's *laundry*?"

What I had submitted for the show was the only thing I really knew at the time. Within that small watercolor painting of the laundry hanging on a clothesline was my neighborhood and the entire world as I knew it.

Your unique perspective is your creative gold. Already within you is all the originality you will ever need to produce work that rises above the crowd. No one else on the planet has your one-of-a-kind history, preferences, or experiences. You are your own creative masterpiece, a ready-made, pre-ordained portfolio of original, award-winning material the world has yet to see.

Originality is born from knowing what is essential to you—in other words, knowing what specifically moves you and gives you joy. We each hold within us a self-curated list of what makes our heart sing, the absence of which would cause a significant void in our lives. As artists we are to refine, nurture, and protect our list, no matter what the outside world may think or prefer.

Achieving raw and earnest originality takes time. Glimmers of genuineness can only come slowly, step by step, painting by painting. Obtaining a much hoped for "creative breakthrough" can only happen

when the groundwork has already been laid, in preparation for the right moment and readiness of the artist.

When we are fortunate to experience a breakthrough in our work, we must be careful not to camp there too long. When we've finally found something that works and is praiseworthy, the temptation is to do more of the same. A lot more. While this may benefit some artists, especially when the objective is to make money, it can be a hindrance for others. In art, adhering to a formula can have diminishing returns. The more we repeat what we've already done, the more our art becomes watered down, putting out some of the creative fire.

It can be helpful to continuously challenge your own process and vision. If you manage to create a winning body of work, don't assume it is the best way or the only way. Keep looking for the possible. It should be of little concern to you whether others approve of your work or your subject matter. What matters is that you seized upon your idea and brought it forth.

Every time you begin a new work you must stand at the starting line, showing no reliance on proven methods, motifs, or formulas that succeeded before. Instead of demonstrating your talent, technical ability, and how you finished the painting, show what it was that made you want to begin. ▪

"Already within you is all the originality you will ever need to produce work that rises above the crowd."

Art enables us to find
ourselves and lose our-
selves at the same time.

—THOMAS MERTON

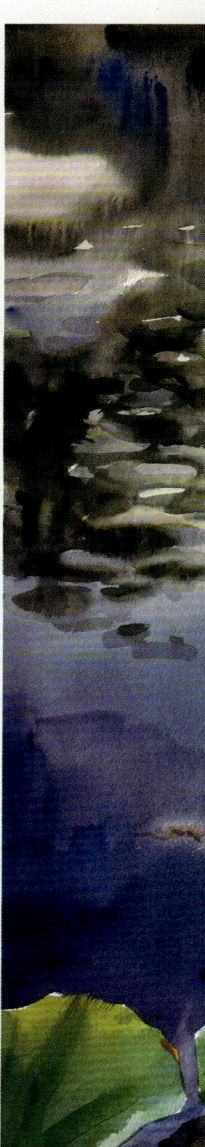

When I was in fourth grade, I remember tracing a photograph of a woman's face. I especially loved the sensuous contour of the brow bone, where it gently curves in and then out again to meet the softness of the cheek. Half a century later I find myself returning again and again to that exquisite line.

Art transports us back to our deepest familiar, while at the same time brings us closer to our most raw, honest, and yet-to-be discovered self. The experience of making art places us squarely on the universal stage of humankind where we become both performer and audience. It is in this shared community where we encounter the heart's daily journey of love, loss, hope, and joy, and recognize it to be our own. Through art we join most deeply with others.

As artists we don't choose our personal style or proclivity for a certain subject matter any more than we choose our preference for a particular flavor of ice cream. This remarkable gift of art is something I'll never be able to fully explain any more than I can say how I ended up on a barrier island in South Carolina painting a community of Gullah women, by a quiet pond in Pennsylvania watching the lotus blossoms open, along the Moon River in Georgia painting a crabber, or at NASA sketching an astronaut. Our paintings choose us. ∎

RETURN TO THE POND   *2018, watercolor on paper, 22 × 29.5 inches*

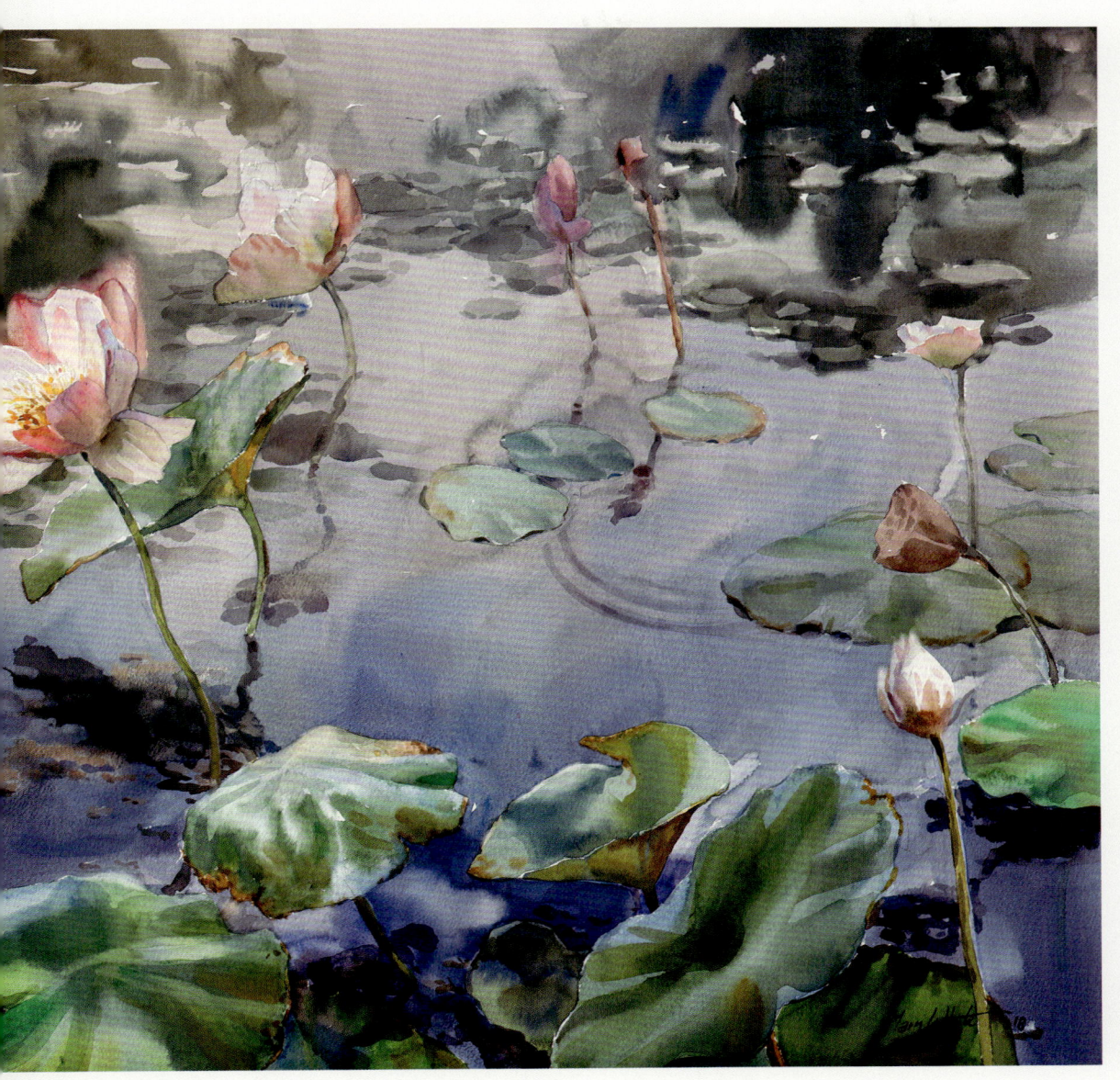

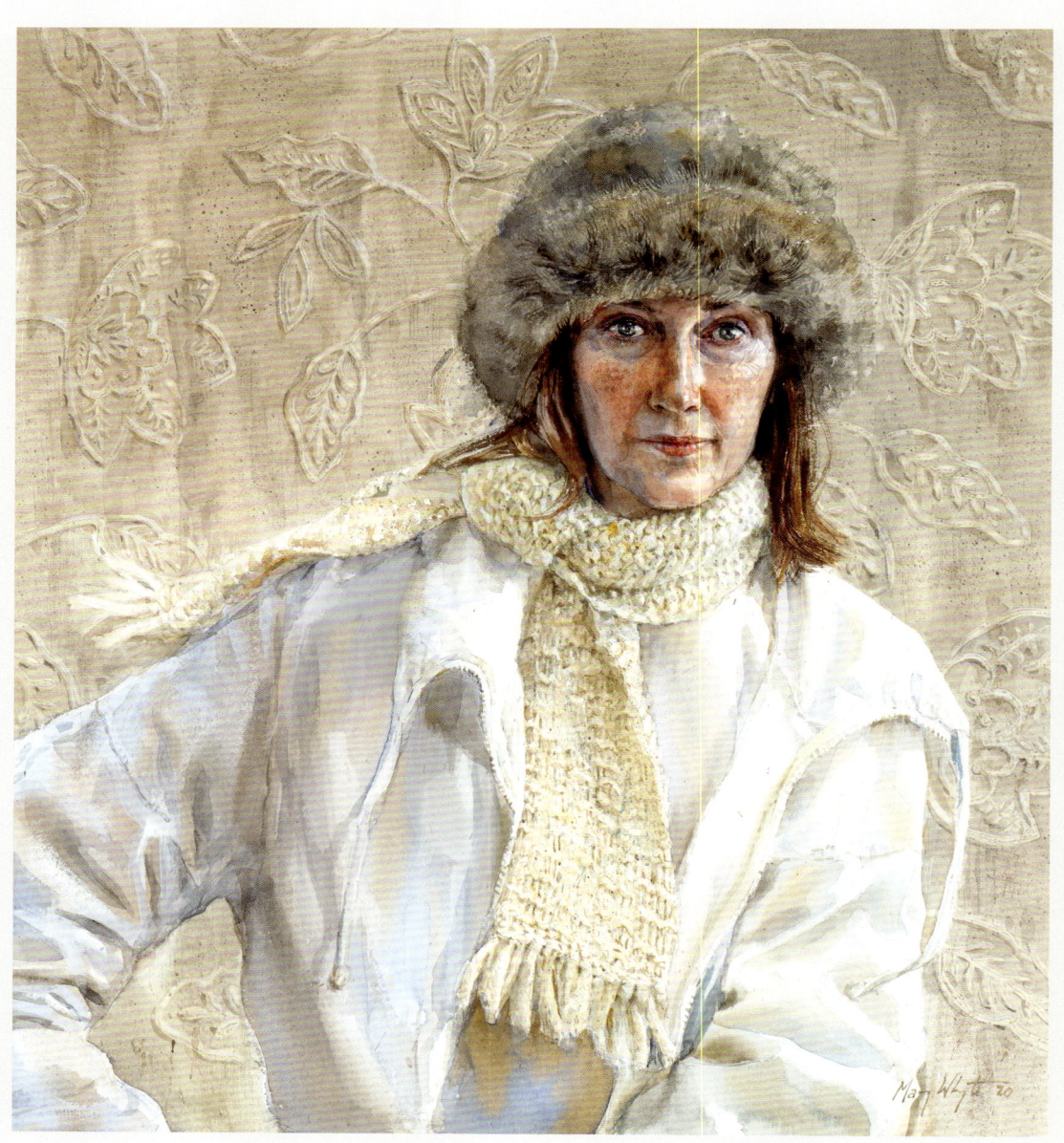

Art is, after all, only a trace—
like a footprint which shows
that one has walked bravely
and in great happiness.

—ROBERT HENRI

I paint because it fills my heart in a way nothing else can. I hope that what I paint can fill someone else's heart, too. Art can do that. No matter what your creative medium is, your moments of greatest happiness will occur when you follow the leanings of your heart. What you paint, how you decorate your home, the way you plant a garden, what you collect, the causes you support, and who you love are all made richer when they are of your own choosing, untainted by the preference or bias of others. The heart leads. Creative expression follows.

Embrace what is at this very moment your perfect place in the world.

Find beauty and creativity in the everyday.

Be the purveyor of wonder.

Have the audacity to dream.

Thus begins the grand adventure of a life well lived. ▪

WINTER WHYTE   *self-portrait, 2020, watercolor on paper, 23.5 × 22 inches*

FURTHER READING AND EXERCISES

Using the QR code and URL below, you can access a series of
exercises developed to help you discover and rekindle your
creativity. Designed for anyone who has a desire to make art,
the twenty-four assignments can be paced two per month,
over a year's time, or at whatever pace is manageable for you.
No matter what your age or life direction, and whether art is
a full-time endeavor or a hobby, it is never too late to let your
creativity blossom. Regardless of your personal goals, the simple act of engaging in art can create pathways to a life that is
transformative and filled with joy. Your creativity awaits.

If you are willing to share your work and the results of these
exercises with others, please use the hashtag #AALwithmary to see
what others in the *An Artist's Life* art community are creating. ∎

 https://www.marywhyte.com/
assets/artists-life-exercises

ABOUT THE AUTHOR

MARY WHYTE has achieved international recognition for her watercolors depicting blue-collar workers and veterans from all across the country, as well as members of South Carolina's Gullah community. She is the author of several books, including *We the People: Portraits of Veterans in America; Painting Portraits and Figures in Watercolor; Working South: Paintings and Sketches by Mary Whyte; Down Bohicket Road: An Artist's Journey; Alfreda's World;* and *An Artist's Way of Seeing.* Whyte has exhibited her work in China, Taiwan, Italy, England, and in numerous museums throughout the United States. She is the recipient of the Portrait Society of America's Gold Medal, the National Daughters of the American Revolution Medal of Honor, and the South Carolina Governor's Award for the Arts. In 2021, the artist received an honorary doctorate from Converse University. Mary Whyte and her husband, Arnold Nemirow, live near Charleston, South Carolina.

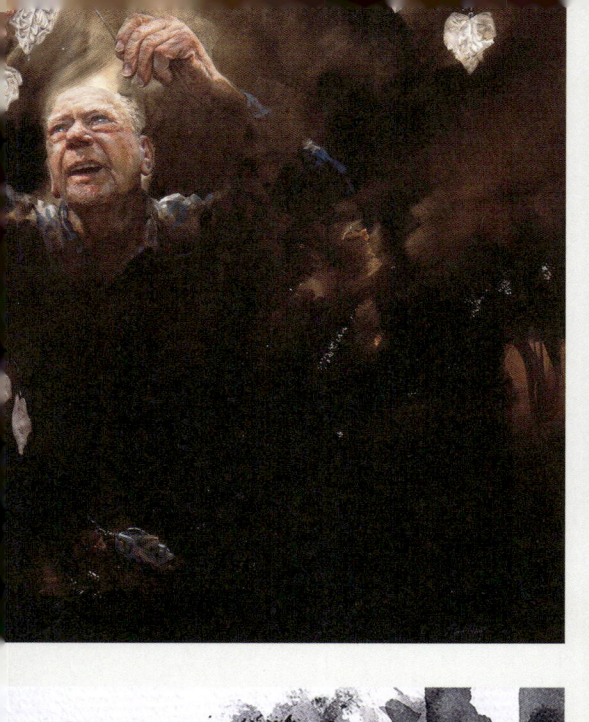
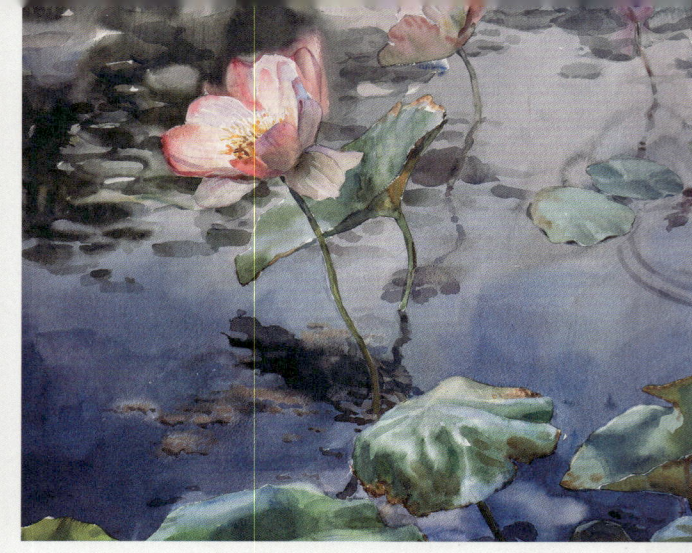
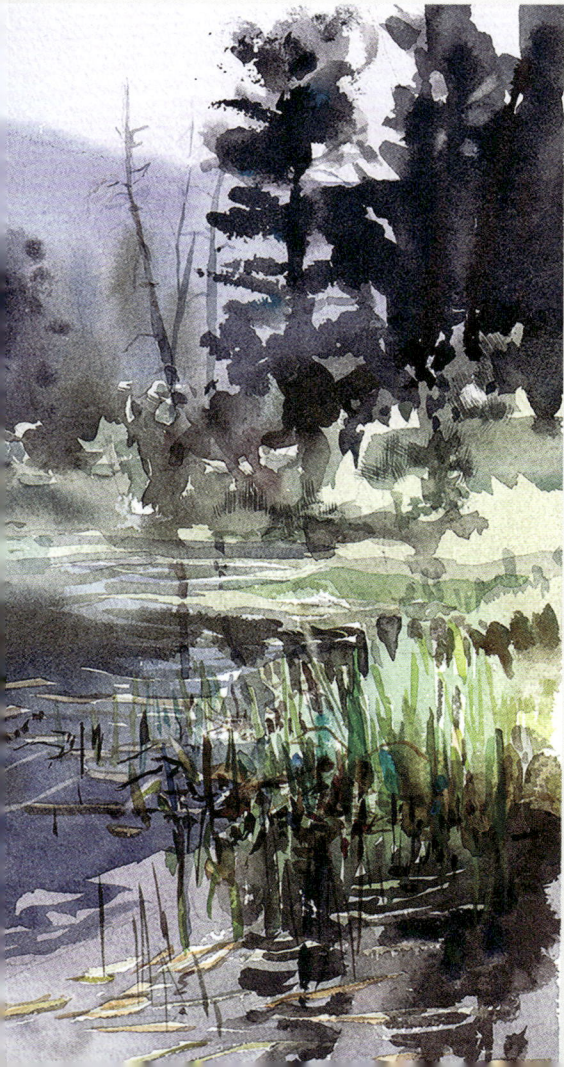
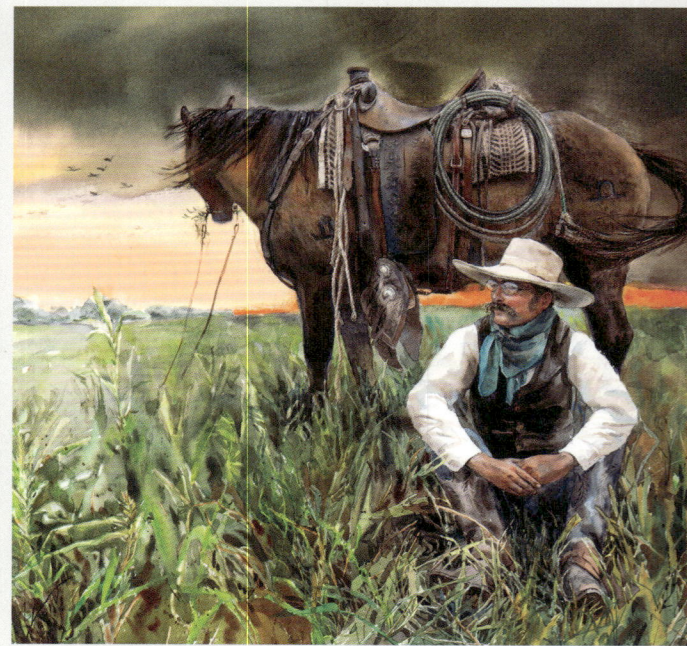
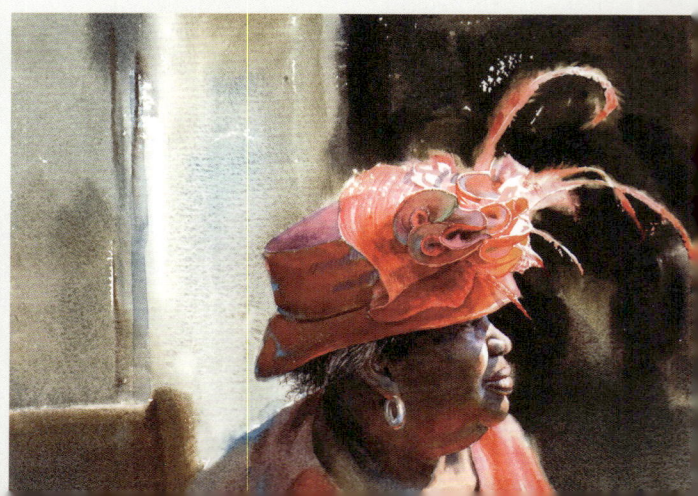